1999

LIBERALISM, EQUALITY, AND CULTURAL OPPRESSION

Liberal political philosophy emphasizes the benefits of membership in a cultural group and, in the opinion of this challenging new book, neglects its harmful, oppressive aspects. Andrew Kernohan argues that an oppressive culture perpetuates inegalitarian social meanings and false assumptions about who is entitled to what. Cultural pollution causes harm to fundamental interests in self-respect and knowledge of the good, harm that is diffuse, insidious, and unnoticed. This harm is analogous to environmental pollution, and though difficult to detect, it is nonetheless just as real. The book's conclusion is that a liberal state committed to the moral equality of persons must accept a strong role in reforming our cultural environment.

"Kernohan makes out a strong and daring case that the liberal state should not be neutral regarding people's conceptions of the good but should favor an egalitarian ethic and actively promote it within popular political culture. Socialists with this view of the role of the state have usually also been critics of liberalism per se. In this respect they have been like conservative counterparts who agree that the state should avoid value neutrality, but differ about what values it should favor. By contrast, Kernohan's challenge is internal to liberalism. It thus cannot be dismissed by liberal theorists. The book will surely spark a lively and important debate."

Frank Cunningham
Professor of Philosophy
University of Toronto

Andrew Kernohan is an independent scholar, writing and teaching philosophy in Nova Scotia.

Liberalism, Equality, and Cultural Oppression

ANDREW KERNOHAN

CAMBRIDGE
UNIVERSITY PRESS

PUBLISHED BY THE PRESS SYNDICATE OF THE UNIVERSITY OF CAMBRIDGE
The Pitt Building, Trumpington Street, Cambridge CB2 1RP, United Kingdom

CAMBRIDGE UNIVERSITY PRESS
The Edinburgh Building, Cambridge CB2 2RU, UK   http://www.cup.cam.ac.uk
40 West 20th Street, New York, NY 10011-4211, USA   http://www.cup.org
10 Stamford Road, Oakleigh, Melbourne 3166, Australia

First published 1998

Printed in the United States of America

Typeset in Meridien 10/13 pt, in Quark XPress™ [AG]

A catalog record for this book is available from the British Library.

Library of Congress Cataloging-in-Publication Data
Kernohan, Andrew William, 1952–
Liberalism, equality, and cultural oppression / Andrew Kernohan.
p.   cm.
Includes bibliographical references and index.
ISBN 0-521-62164-X. – ISBN 0-521-62753-2 (pbk.)
1. Liberalism. 2. Equality. 3. Social change. 4. Political
culture. I. Title.
JC574.K47   1998
320.51′3 – dc 21   97-47477
                                                              CIP

ISBN 0 521 62164 X hardback
ISBN 0 521 62753 2 paperback

CONTENTS

PREFACE

IN *On Liberty,* John Stuart Mill saw clearly a problem whose importance contemporary liberals have forgotten. The following quotation from *On Liberty* will serve as a motto for this book.

> . . . when society itself is the tyrant – society collectively, over the separate individuals who compose it – its means of tyrannizing are not restricted to the acts which it may do by the hands of its political functionaries. Society can and does execute its own mandates: and if it issues wrong mandates instead of right, or any mandates at all in things with which it ought not to meddle, it practises a social tyranny more formidable than many kinds of political oppression, since, though not usually upheld by such extreme penalties, it leaves fewer means of escape, penetrating more deeply into the details of life, and enslaving the soul itself. Protection, therefore against the tyranny of the magistrate is not enough. . . .[1]

Mill saw that the social and cultural environment of a society can prevent its members from leading the best life possible just as surely as can repression by the state. To Mill, writing in the middle of the nineteenth century, it seemed that stringent protection for freedom of expression would produce the necessary reforms to the cultural environment. To us, living at the end of the twentieth century, there is now much less reason to be optimistic about the efficacy of Mill's laissez-faire attitude toward the cultural environment. Expression in its various forms produces and sustains our cultural environment, and that environment is still, more than a century after Mill wrote, polluted with racist, sexist, classist, ableist, and heterosexist attitudes. Mill's solution to the problem of our oppressive cultural environment has misled contemporary liberalism.

The aim of *Liberalism, Equality, and Cultural Oppression* is to show that the egalitarian liberal state, the state consistent with the views of contemporary egalitarian liberals like John Rawls and Ronald Dworkin, ought to participate actively in the reform of the cultural environment. To do this, egalitarian liberalism must drastically modify its understanding of state neutrality. State neutrality is the doctrine that any actions – coercive, economic, or ideological – that the liberal state takes in society should not be based on the grounds that some conception of the good life is true or false. State neutrality, as liberals understand it, is implemented through unrestricted freedom of expression and a laissez-faire approach to the cultural marketplace. By contrast, I argue that the egalitarian liberal state ought, on the grounds of its own internal principles as properly understood, to adopt an advocacy strategy toward cultural reform. The advocacy strategy involves putting the non-coercive power of the state, its economic and ideological powers, actively behind cultural reform. The state should take an activist role on behalf of equality, both directly through participation in public forums and indirectly through support of groups working for social change. The advocacy strategy offers a new alternative to the familiar choice between coercive censorship and unrestricted freedom of expression, an alternative that the current debate has ignored.

The advocacy strategy retrieves from liberalism's most basic principles a more effective means for combatting cultural oppression. Again following Mill's *On Liberty*, liberalism allows that, just as the state should curtail the liberties of individuals to prevent harm to others, so also the state should modify its neutrality to prevent harm. I shall argue that the advocacy strategy is justified within liberalism by showing that certain aspects of a cultural environment can be harmful. A cultural environment is created and sustained by the expressive activities of its members. Now, there is already some awareness among liberals of the harmful consequences of free expression and the ways in which widespread cultural images and representations can legitimate and perpetuate unjust practices. For example, because people identify with their racial and ethnic groups, hate speech directed at a given group can be offensive and destructive of self-respect. For this reason, some liberals think that speech codes or legislation against hate speech can be justified. Without detracting from the importance of such harms, I wish to emphasize another harm caused by the cultural environment that is equally important, more pervasive, and even more difficult to detect. This is the harm of interfering with one of an individual's most important interests: her interest in forming a conception of what is meaningful and valuable in her life.

Liberals, such as Will Kymlicka, who have recognized the importance of the cultural environment in the formation of a person's conception of the good have seen cultural membership as beneficial to learning about the good. On this view, cultural membership provides a range of options from which people can choose their conceptions of the good life, and it shows them the content, meaning, and value of these options. In this book, however, I shall emphasize the harmful side of cultural membership. As Michael Walzer has pointed out, cultural membership also attaches social meanings to options that implicitly show people what their legitimate expectations are. Social meanings show not only what value options have but also how options should be distributed. Within the shared social meanings of a culture, people see themselves as entitled, or not entitled, to the options that make a good life possible. This is most blatant in a caste society, where someone's caste is understood to determine how his life should go. Though less obvious, it is still prevalent in non-caste societies, where people come to understand the appropriateness of roles, occupations, and lot in life to be determined by race, gender, and natural ability. If people form their conceptions of the good on the basis of false distributional assumptions, then their interest in knowing the good is harmed. They are harmed even if their self-respect is not undermined. People who are socialized into accepting subordinate roles will not be offended by expression that reinforces those roles.

In general liberals do not take a stand on the truth or falsity of a person's beliefs about what constitutes the good life. That is the point of the liberal commitment to tolerance and the neutrality of the state. They believe that it is better for a person to work out her own mistakes. However, there is one ethical belief on which egalitarian liberals must make a stand: egalitarian liberals are committed to the equal moral worth of persons. Furthermore, they are committed to a strong version of moral equality. On the one hand, they think that people should be responsible for the choices they make. So it is fair that how well a person's life goes should reflect the decisions he has made. On the other hand, they think it is unfair that how a person's life goes should reflect factors for which he is not responsible. So he does not deserve any less chance of a good life because of factors which are arbitrary from a moral point of view, factors such as his race, gender, natural abilities, or sexual orientation. For egalitarian liberals this commitment to the moral equality of persons is conceptually prior to their commitment to tolerance and state neutrality. Tolerance and neutrality are an interpretation of moral equality. Consequently, someone's belief that she deserves less out of life because of her gender is a false belief within egalitarian liberalism's own framework. If she forms a conception of her good on the basis of this false belief, her knowledge of the good is undermined. If her false belief arises because of the distributional social meanings attached to goods by her culture, then she has been harmed by her cultural environment.

Egalitarian liberals can make sense of a harm to someone's interest in knowing her good only if they are cognitivists in metaethics. Cognitivism is the view that ethical knowledge is possible, that value judgements are beliefs about value that can be true, justified, and not dependent on other false beliefs. It contrasts with noncognitivism, the view that value judgements are no more than expressions of emotion, subjective preferences for one thing or another. In the past, liberals typically have been noncognitivists about the good and have seen judgements of value as expressions of preference. This has fitted well with a defence of economic markets as mechanisms of distribution; intensity of preference is revealed by willingness to pay in a free market. The view that judgements of value are expressions of preference gives a plausible account of very simple choices that people make, like choosing a drink at a bar, but it cannot account for more sophisticated reasoning about ultimate ends. Deliberation about ends, about the projects, relationships, and ethical or religious convictions that give meaning to a life, is not like choosing a drink. Recently, I argue, egalitarian liberals like Rawls and Dworkin have tended toward views that are implicitly cognitivist in outlook. The attempt to give an adequate account of deliberation about ends has pushed egalitarian liberals to the view that value is something about which people form and test beliefs, and seek knowledge.

This incipient cognitivism has important implications for understanding cultural oppression. Once a person's interest in knowing the good is recognized, it becomes possible to see the harm that cultural membership can bring about. Typically someone is thought to be harmed when she is prevented from getting what she wants, or is made to take what she does not want. Harm is overt; people realize that they are being harmed. An oppressive cultural environment does not harm overtly; rather, it "enslaves the soul itself." People are not discontented or unhappy, for they accept inequalities as natural. On the cognitivist view, a person's wants – not her tastes in ice cream, but her ultimate ends in life – are based on beliefs about what is valuable and gives meaning to life. Her beliefs about what is good for her will depend on her beliefs about what she may legitimately expect. If the content of her beliefs about her legitimate expectations is infected with false, inegalitarian social meanings, then her knowledge of her good will be undermined. She can be harmed by her cultural environment even if she does not realize it.

There is a second reason why the harm done by an oppressive cultural environment is difficult to recognize. Such a harm is cumulative in nature; it cannot be traced back to any single expressive act or cultural representation. Inegalitarian social meanings are created and sustained by a multitude of expressive acts – "society collectively" – not by any individual act of expression. The harm done by an oppressive cultural environment is analogous to the harm done by certain types of environmental pollution. Sometimes harm is caused by point-source pollution, as, for instance, by a particular factory smokestack or farm manure pile. At other times, however, harm is brought about by non–point-source pollution, as, for instance, by the millions of cars in a large city. Pollution of the cultural environment is non–point-source pollution; the harm of cultural oppression cannot be blamed on any particular person's conduct. Analogously, Marilyn Frye has likened oppression to a cage; one bar of the cage will not hold the prisoner, but all the bars together will. The liberal harm principle has often been interpreted as applying only to individual conduct, not to the prevention of a more general harmed condition. This weak interpretation of the harm principle would not permit state action to prevent non–point-source environmental pollution. However, the strong interpretation of the harm principle would permit state action against both non–point-source pollution and an oppressive cultural environment, though it should be the smallest intervention possible that could still prevent the harm. The coercive power of the state is too blunt an instrument for dealing with the subtleties of cultural reform. Consequently, the advocacy strategy, not the censorship strategy, is the best response to cultural oppression.

This introduction has presented the argument of the book in reverse, starting with its conclusion that the egalitarian liberal state should play an activist role in cultural reform, and sketching the arguments that lead to it. The body of the book gives the argument in the other direction. It begins with a characterization of cultural oppression as an accumulative harm to someone's interest in knowing the good, describes how egalitarian liberals have become implicit cognitivists about the good, sets out what egalitarian liberalism should mean by "the moral equality of persons," sketches how people can take up inegalitarian social meanings from their culture, interprets state neutrality as requiring state action to prevent or mitigate such cultural harms, and finally defends the advocacy strategy for cultural reform against the standard liberal concerns about freedom of expression.

ACKNOWLEDGEMENTS

OVER the half dozen or so winters during which I developed the ideas in this book I have received help from many institutions and individuals. Several research grants from the Social Science and Humanities Research Council of Canada have supported me financially. The University of Toronto Department of Philosophy has given me offices, library privileges, and a philosophical community which have sustained my interest in the project.

Will Kymlicka and Jerry Gaus read two drafts of the manuscript for Cambridge University Press. They have each given me comprehensive, detailed comments which have enormously improved the rigour, organization, and readability of the final version. Many of its arguments, including most of the chapters on moral equality and on cultural reform, are my attempts to respond to their criticisms. Additionally, Will read a very early draft of the manuscript and gave me valuable advice at that stage. Michael Milde read a draft of the manuscript for the University of Toronto Press, and his suggestions helped me organize the opening chapter.

Over the years, I have discussed with many friends the ideas contained in this book. I would like to thank Anne Bastedo, Nathan Brett, Frank Cunningham, Jenny Horsman, Randall Keen, Pauline O'Connor, Lois Pineau, Arthur Ripstein, Sue Sherwin, Wayne Sumner, and Michelle Switzer for their support and advice. Jim Allison, Ann Decter, Heather Oke, and Ghada Sharkawy helped research or edit various parts of the manuscript. Chris McKinnon and Bill Seager have given me a philosophical community, along with their friendship, during summer months in Nova Scotia.

Two friends in particular, David Dyzenhaus and Cheryl Misak, extended support that included not only philosophical advice but also the use of their office and, at one point, even the loan of their house in Toronto. David has read and commented on the whole manuscript at least twice. While he should not be held responsible for any of the book's mistakes, David may fairly be held responsible for its existence. Without his encouragement, I would never have finished the project.

My family – my partner Anne MacLellan, my sister Ann Kernohan, and my parents David and Mollie Kernohan – have given me support of a different but no less important kind. My parents cheerfully took over my chores and responsibilities on the farm so that I could have the winters free to work on this project. The book is dedicated to them with my love.

1

EQUALITY, TOLERANCE, AND CULTURAL OPPRESSION

L IBERALISM is the dominant political ideology in North America and Western Europe. Liberalism is not a unified doctrine; its proponents range from Scandinavian social democrats to American libertarian capitalists. All varieties of liberalism, however, share a commitment both to the equal moral worth of persons and to the tolerance of diverse points of view on how lives should be lived. Liberalism originated in seventeenth- and eighteenth-century struggles against the aristocratic state and its established church. So one of its original tasks was to defend equality by arguing for the equal moral worth of the members of all social groups, both aristocrats and commoners. Its other important task was to defend tolerance by giving a theoretical account of how diverse religious views, both established and nonconformist, could coexist in one state. By failing to contest cultural oppression, I shall argue, contemporary liberalism has overemphasized tolerance at the expense of equality.

LIBERALISM, EQUALITY, AND TOLERANCE

Tolerance has remained a major feature of twentieth-century liberalism in both its libertarian and egalitarian variants. Tolerance for competing versions of the good life distinguishes libertarians from Christian fundamentalists, however much they may agree on government economic policy. And a commitment to tolerance distinguishes liberal egalitarians from the socialist egalitarians of the old USSR. Recent liberal writing incorporates tolerance through the principle of state neutrality. Dworkin defines neutrality like this:

> Liberalism commands tolerance; it commands, for example, that political decisions about what citizens should be forced to do or prevented from doing must be made on grounds that are neutral among the competing convictions about good and bad lives that different members of the community might hold.[1]

The liberal state is to remain agnostic about the truth or falsity of different substantive conceptions of how to lead a good life. That a life should be lived as a hermit in the desert is a disputable conception of the good. However, it is not for the state to resolve the debate. But what are the limits to tolerance? That a life should be lived promoting the subordination of women to men is also a disputable conception of the good life. Should the liberal state be neutral in this regard? If not, what is the relevant difference? Does liberalism require the "general tolerance of illiberal bigots"?[2]

Liberalism does distinguish between the foregoing two substantive views of the good life. Reasonable people might disagree about the value of a life lived as a hermit, but the view that women should be subordinated to men is not just disputable, it is inconsistent with fundamental liberal premises. Liberalism is committed to *the equal moral worth of persons,* the ethical principle that no person intrinsically matters more than any other. At the most abstract level, every person has a highest-order interest in leading as meaningful, valuable, and worthwhile a life as possible. To the liberal, then, the interests of all individuals in leading as good a life as possible matter equally, contrary to the view that women's interests should be subordinated to those of men. Reasonable, liberal people should not disagree about the wrongness of the subordination of women. Let us examine how this conclusion follows from Rawls's argument for tolerance.

Though all persons are alike in possessing an abstract interest in a good life, each person's concrete interests, his or her conception of the good, will be unique. Rawls gives an account of why reasonable people, people who are willing to propose and abide by fair terms of cooperation with other free and equal persons, will differ in their substantive conceptions of the good.[3] The most conscientious attempts to reach agreement on how to live a good life can founder on what he calls the "burdens of judgement." The burdens of judgement are cognitive factors that unavoidably hamper the pursuit of ethical knowledge. People can quite reasonably make different judgements about the good because, among other reasons, the empirical evidence either way is conflicting, the appropriate weights to be given to various considerations are not determinable, the concepts employed are vague, and the people involved differ in terms of cultural background. Different people can quite reasonably come to believe in the truth of different comprehensive doctrines about the good. Because of the indeterminacy of ethical

2

knowledge, a democratic society will come to contain a plurality of reasonable comprehensive ethical doctrines.

Reasonable people, Rawls thinks, will accept the consequences of these epistemic impediments to agreement when using the coercive power of the state. This claim leads to the following argument for tolerance:

> . . . reasonable persons will think it unreasonable to use political power, should they possess it, to repress comprehensive views that are not unreasonable, though different from their own. This is because, given the fact of reasonable pluralism, a public and shared basis of justification that applies to comprehensive doctrines is lacking in the public culture of a democratic society. But such a basis is needed to mark the difference, in ways acceptable to a reasonable public, between comprehensive beliefs as such and true comprehensive beliefs.[4]

Because of the burdens of judgement, no procedure exists by which reasonable people could agree to declare false the belief that life is best lived as a hermit. A democratic society of reasonable people cannot repress this conception of the good on the grounds that it is false, for no reasonable agreement to this effect will exist. The liberal state must be neutral between reasonable doctrines of the good life.

Now consider the moral belief that women do not matter as much as men and therefore should play subordinate roles. This belief is inconsistent with a fundamental assumption behind the project of Rawls's political liberalism. One fundamental idea implicit in the public culture of a democratic society is the view that all persons are equal who, to the requisite minimum degree, have the capacity for a sense of justice, a conception of their own good, and the powers of reason.[5] Political liberalism aims to specify "the fair terms of social cooperation between citizens regarded as free and *equal*"[6] (emphasis added). The equal moral worth of persons is not a postulate with which reasonable people in a democratic society are asked to agree or disagree; agreement to this principle is a precondition of being a reasonable person in a democratic society. Reasonable people are required to regard a belief in the equal moral worth of persons as an antecedent condition of the justification of principles of justice.[7] So a reasonable public, despite the burdens of judgement, does have a basis for judging that a belief in the subordination of women is false. Rawls's argument for tolerance does not apply to a belief that persons in one group matter less than persons in another. Rawls's liberalism is committed to both tolerance and equality; the difference is that tolerance emerges as the conclusion of an argument from epistemic constraints, while equality is an underlying presupposition. The liberal state should be agnostic about the value of being a hermit, but it should not be agnostic about the equal value of people.[8]

Similarly, Dworkin's ethical liberalism begins from the "abstract egalitarian thesis" that "from the standpoint of politics, the interests of the members of the community matter and matter equally."[9] He develops his position on equality of resources, tolerance, and state neutrality from an interpretation of what people's highest-order interests are and from an interpretation of what it means to treat these interests equally. His strategy of argument "hopes to arrive at neutrality in the course of rather than at the beginning of the argument, as a theorem rather than as a methodological axiom."[10] For Dworkin, tolerance is the conclusion of an argument whose premise is equality.

So liberalism must distinguish between (1) conceptions of the good whose truth or falsity is a matter on which reasonable people might disagree and (2) conceptions of the good that are inconsistent with the fundamental ideas implicit in a democratic society. Of beliefs about the good that reject the equal moral worth of persons, Rawls says the following:

> Political liberalism also supposes that a reasonable comprehensive doctrine does not reject the essentials of a democratic regime. Of course, a society may also contain unreasonable and irrational, and even mad, comprehensive doctrines. In their case the problem is to contain them so that they do not undermine the unity and justice of society.[11]

Dworkin's liberalism is also committed to tolerance and state neutrality, though for different reasons, reasons that I shall later discuss at length. Nevertheless, he does impose a similar qualification on liberal tolerance:

> Nor is liberal equality's tolerance global. Any political theory must disapprove other theories that dispute its principles; liberal equality cannot be neutral toward ethical ideals that directly challenge its theory of justice. So its version of ethical tolerance is not compromised when a thief is punished who claims to believe that theft is central to a good life. Or when a racist is thwarted who claims that his life's mission is to promote white superiority.[12]

Liberalism requires tolerance of all manner of views on how to lead a worthwhile life, but not of views that deny the fundamental assumption of moral equality. Liberal neutrality requires that the liberal state neither promote beliefs about the good on the grounds that they are true nor hinder their communication on the grounds that they are false. But it does permit the state to take action against conceptions of the good which, falsely, deny the equal moral worth of persons.

However, this way of interpreting the limits to tolerance overstates the liberal position. The logical inconsistency between unjust beliefs and liberal principles is not enough to legitimize the repression of someone who holds these beliefs. For instance, we can imagine a solitary monarchist who, from her soapbox in the park, preaches the ideal of the aristocratic state to an audience of jeering school children. Her beliefs contradict liberalism's principle of equal rights, but because she has no support, her views present no danger to society and are harming nobody.[13] The limits to tolerance are set not by a theoretical challenge to liberal principles but by a practical challenge to a liberal society and its members. We can imagine, instead, that the monarchist leads a large political party running a promising election campaign on a platform that consists in replacing the liberal constitution with an aristocracy of party stalwarts. In this context, the liberal state will be justified in opposing these aristocratic views by coercive means. For example, the Weimar Republic would most certainly have been justified in outlawing the National Socialist German Workers' Party in the 1920s, as is the present German state for outlawing it now.[14]

It follows that liberalism must divide ethical doctrines into at least the following categories:

(1) Doctrines whose truth or falsity is a matter on which reasonable people can disagree.
(2) Doctrines whose falsity is a matter on which reasonable people must agree, because the doctrines make claims that are inconsistent with respecting the equal moral worth of persons, and thus with liberal principles.
(3) Doctrines of the second sort whose practice or promulgation harms, or threatens to harm, liberal society.

Also, the harm done by a monarchist political party whose demonstrations disrupt traffic and litter the city with leaflets differs from the harm done by a monarchist party which seizes the reins of government. Liberalism will need to distinguish a fourth category:

(4) Doctrines of the third sort which harm fundamental, highest-order interests.

5

When Rawls talks of setting aside tolerance for doctrines that "undermine the unity and justice of society," and Dworkin of doing the same for doctrines that "directly challenge" liberalism's theory of justice, we best interpret them as referring to doctrines of the fourth type. The liberal state must take an activist stance toward this last category of ethical doctrines.

Monarchists and fascists present both a theoretical challenge to liberal principles and, in sufficient numbers, a practical challenge to liberal society. Liberal tolerance comes to an end for views like these that are false, inconsistent with liberal principles, and threaten significant harm to society as a whole. But it should also be concerned with false, unjust views that are harmful to individual members of society. Again the same pattern emerges. In a society truly free of racism, one in which all traces of legal discrimination, economic discrimination, and culturally formed racist attitudes and behaviour patterns had disappeared, a solitary white man preaching the subordination of people of African descent would be a tolerable eccentric, though his views would be both false and inconsistent with liberal equality. It would be only when a large number of others had joined him in his attitudes and behaviour that his views would generate the network of force, threats of force, economic discrimination, and cultural attitudes that would amount to oppression.

People most often think of oppression only as something that a state does to its citizens. The use of armed force against its own citizens, as in Stalinist Russia, is both obvious and in violation of the liberal principle of state neutrality. But oppression can take a more subtle form when the actions of citizens themselves bring it about. In *On Liberty*, Mill warned against social oppression, as well as state oppression:

> . . . when society itself is the tyrant – society collectively, over the separate individuals who compose it – its means of tyrannizing are not restricted to the acts which it may do by the hands of its political functionaries. Society can and does execute its own mandates: and if it issues wrong mandates instead of right, or any mandates at all in things with which it ought not to meddle, it practises a social tyranny more formidable than many kinds of political oppression, since, though not usually upheld by such extreme penalties, it leaves fewer means of escape, penetrating more deeply into the details of life, and enslaving the soul itself. Protection, therefore against the tyranny of the magistrate is not enough: there needs protection also against the tyranny of society to impose, by other means than civil penalties, its own ideas and practices as rules of conduct on those who dissent from them; to fetter the

development, and if possible, prevent the formation, of any individuality not in harmony with its ways, and compel all characters to fashion themselves upon the model of its own.[15]

Social oppression, "the tyranny of society," arises from a diffuse source, "society collectively," and can "enslave the soul" of an individual, bringing her attitudes into conformity with the norms of the culture.

Social oppression takes many forms: violence, threats of violence, threats of ostracism, economic discrimination, and so on. I am going to be concerned, in this essay, chiefly with just one form that oppression takes: the cultural formation of attitudes and beliefs about inequality. This form of oppression underlies and sustains the others. Susan Sherwin, in her summary of feminist thinking on oppression, writes:

> The most obvious systems of oppression are those maintained by the power of the state through the use of armed force . . . But other systems of oppression, including sexism, are so well established that they have been internalized by both those who suffer under them and those who benefit from them; they remain invisible to many of the people most directly involved. Many women have learned to accept as natural the socially determined obstacles that they confront and do not perceive such obstacles as restrictive.[16]

Many members of subordinate groups find overt forms of discrimination natural, acceptable, normal, and unremarkable. One reason is that they come to believe their projects to matter less than the projects of members of the dominant group. They fail to notice overt forms of oppression as wrong because they implicitly believe in their own unequal worth as persons. This theoretical belief usually is not explicitly formulated and avowed. It is tacitly believed without ever being reflected on critically. When inequality is accepted as natural, oppression has, in Mill's words, "enslaved the soul itself."

Reasonable people must agree on the moral equality of persons. A belief in the moral equality of persons cuts two ways. It implies both that a person must regard others as her equals and that she must regard herself as the moral equal of others. Consequently, if someone comes to believe that her good matters less than the good of others because of her membership in some group, then, for the liberal, her belief is false. Liberalism must recognize encultured beliefs in moral inequality as false because they are inconsistent with its foundational assumption of the equal moral worth of persons. A regime of cultural oppression often falls selectively on different groups, systematically making members of one group undervalue the worth of their own projects. An oppressed group is labelled as being of lesser moral worth by the dominant culture, and its members frequently believe that labelling. Because of her group membership, someone may value her own projects falsely and come to believe that her good matters less than does the good of members of another group. An oppressive culture misrepresents to members of oppressed groups both the value of their projects and their entitlements to resources. Cultural oppression thus perpetrates a harm somewhat akin to a fraud.

Can liberalism, consistent with its own principles, challenge cultural oppression? Does liberalism justify the state taking up an activist stance toward pollution of the cultural environment? Liberalism is a multifarious doctrine. Its various theoretical foundations include the contractarianism of Hobbes and Gauthier, the utilitarianism of Mill, the self-ownership rights of Nozick, the political liberalism of Rawls, and the ethical liberalism of Dworkin and Kymlicka. I am going to take up these questions only with regard to egalitarian liberal theorists like Rawls, Dworkin, and Kymlicka. For one thing, focussing on egalitarian liberalism serves to keep the project within manageable limits. For another, convincing egalitarian liberals to address issues of cultural oppression is a task more likely to succeed than is convincing libertarians of the same point. A theorist who is prepared to countenance the unequal distributions of economic goods permitted by libertarian theories is unlikely to take seriously the problem of cultural oppression. Finally, I believe that egalitarian liberalism has a better theory of justice than does any of the other liberalisms, though I shall not argue this large conclusion here.[17]

Kymlicka, by way of illustration, recognizes the existence of cultural oppression but argues that the liberal state should maintain its neutral stance and not intervene:

> Liberals tend to believe that cultural oppression cannot survive under conditions of civil freedom and material equality. But there may be some false and pernicious cultural representations that are invulnerable to social criticism, that survive and even flourish in a free and fair fight with the truth. Pornography and other cultural representations of women, are an example. Liberals believe that if pornography does not harm women, then the falseness of its representations of sexuality is not grounds for restricting it, not because ideas are powerless, but because freedom of speech and association in civil society is a better testing ground for ideas than the coercive apparatus of the state.[18]

On the contrary, I shall contend that the liberal state is justified in taking an activist stance in dealing with the misrepresentation of oppressed groups. It is so justified because the false representation of the oppressed as morally unequal is a harm to them. But the nature of this harm needs spelling out.

The pattern of harm in cultural oppression is analogous to the pattern of harm generated in important cases of pollution of the natural environment. Rachel Carson described the pattern of harm brought about by pesticides in her famous book *Silent Spring:*

> We know that even single exposures to these chemicals, if the amount is large enough, can precipitate acute poisoning. But this is not the major problem. The sudden illness or death of farmers, spraymen, pilots, and others exposed to appreciable quantities of pesticides are tragic and should not occur. For the population as a whole, we must be more concerned with the delayed effects of absorbing small amounts of the pesticides that invisibly contaminate our world. Responsible public health officials have pointed out that the biological effects of chemicals are cumulative over long periods of time, and that the hazard to the individual may depend on the sum of the exposures received throughout his lifetime. For these very reasons the danger is easily ignored.[19]

Pesticides accumulate in the environment and in people from a variety of sources. In some cases there is a determinate cause of the harm; in others, there is no one source that can be pointed to as the cause of the harm. Some sources of pollution, such as large factories, can generate harmful amounts of pollution all by themselves. However, the pollution created by a single small source often does not overload the earth's natural stabilizing mechanisms. The atmosphere and the land can easily cope with the emissions of just one automobile. Nevertheless, the emissions of millions of cars can accumulate, as they do in Mexico City, to a level that causes serious harm to people. Similarly the practices of a solitary racist, in isolation, have negligible effect on the cultural environment. Yet the situation is different when a significant portion of the society either openly espouses or implicitly accepts racist ethical doctrines. In this context, cultural oppression exists, and serious harm can be done to members of the group being labelled less than equal. The widespread practice and promulgation of racist ethical doctrines contribute to the pollution of the general cultural environment.

Cultural oppression, the pollution of the cultural environment by the expression of views that deny the equal moral worth of persons, is the topic of this essay. The essay will stress the analogy between cultural oppression and pollution of the natural environment, so it is worth pointing out where the analogy breaks down. The difference is that in non–point-source pollution of the natural environment the harm is often overt. People in Mexico City are well familiar with teary, irritated eyes and breathing problems. People can dispute about what the thresholds are, but at some level of pollution they will agree on the existence of a problem. Cultural oppression is not like that. Cultural oppression is covert; it functions to make inequality of moral worth seem natural to both dominant and subordinate groups. Those afflicted by cultural pollution frequently will truly believe inequality to be appropriate. Unlike the people in Mexico City, they will not notice their affliction. However, we can draw a parallel to another type of environmental pollution where the harm is hidden, and we must appeal to theory to discover it. For instance, it often takes chemical analysis to reveal the presence of pesticides in the drinking water, and it may take further scientific research to decide what the threshold of harm is. Cultural pollution is more like the pesticide case. As in the pesticide case, we have to appeal to theory – here, the agreed-upon liberal principle of the equal moral worth of persons – to see that people's beliefs in inequality are false. Then, to justify state action, we have to seek further argument to show that leading people to have false ethical beliefs is a harm.

If it can be shown to be a harm, the damage to victims of cultural oppression will resemble the damage to victims of an undiscovered fraud. Both harms involve misrepresentation and false belief, though in one case a false ethical belief, and in the second, a false factual belief. Both harms are covert; a victim of an undiscovered fraud does not know she has been defrauded, and a victim of cultural oppression thinks her plight to be natural. But the analogy breaks down in the genesis of the harms. A fraud can be perpetrated only by a determinate individual who through a determinate action or set of actions knowingly or recklessly misrepresents important information on which he intends that his victim will rely. Cultural oppression, however, is not perpetrated by the malicious acts of a determinate individual, but by the normal practices of a group. Cultural oppression is what Joel Feinberg calls an "accumulative harm," or so I shall argue in the next section.[20] There is no determinate individual who is at fault. It is perpetrated by the practices of a group of people who often are not intending anything in particular toward the victim.

Table 1 summarizes examples of the various types of harm under discussion. Physical violence is a paradigm harm. It is perpetrated by a determinate individual and is perfectly obvious to its victim. Fraud is also a harm recognized by liberalism. It also has a determinate individual

Table 1

	Overt	Covert
Individual	physical violence	undiscovered fraud
Accumulative	automobile air pollution	cultural oppression

cause. But a fraud is, of course, not obvious to its victim; it is a covert harm. The harmed condition brought about by automobile air pollution is often overt and obvious to all, but it is unlikely that any individual driver will be perceived as doing harm. Instead, the emissions of individual automobiles accumulate in the atmosphere and collectively bring about the harmed condition. The harm done by cultural oppression is both covert and accumulative, and its very existence will thus be controversial in liberal theorizing. The harmed condition brought about by cultural practices has accumulated from the actions of individuals, and to its victims it seems to be the natural state of affairs.

This essay sets itself two tasks. One is to characterize precisely what harm is done to people when they are induced to believe that they are inferior in terms of moral worth, and then to show that liberalism must recognize this as a harmed condition. The other is to show that this harmed condition, which is an accumulative harm when it is brought about by cultural practices, should be recognized by liberalism as a harm justifying an activist role by the state. I shall begin this argument by discussing the way in which cultural oppression is an accumulative harm.

CULTURAL OPPRESSION

Oppression is not something one person can inflict, just once, on another. Suppose little Johnny steals a piece of candy from little Sally, and Sally complains to her mother that Johnny is oppressing her. We might smile at Sally's use of language, though still admonish Johnny for the very real harm he has done. Little Johnny's act was unjust, but it was not oppressive. Only if Johnny were frequently stealing sweets, and perhaps inflicting other little offences, would his behaviour become oppressive to Sally. The oppression of one person by another is an ongoing practice, a series of actions, some harmful when taken individually, some not, which add up over time to oppression. Similarly, oppression is not something one person can do to a group just once. A tyrant oppresses his subjects not by putting them down in the act of conquering them but by keeping them down afterwards.

In the context of oppression, the individual acts of one person directed toward another are not themselves oppressive, and may not even be harmful when taken individually. Consider two people, Leslie and Bobbie, in a long-term relationship. Criticizing Bobbie on occasion may be a reasonable thing for Leslie to do. Leslie's intentions may be the very best, and the effects may be to the good. People criticize one another all the time; it is not generally a harmful thing to do. However, if Leslie's criticism becomes too frequent a practice, the result may be different. Leslie's continual criticism of Bobbie might severely undermine Bobbie's self-esteem, and we might legitimately judge that Leslie oppresses Bobbie.

If a sequence of actions taken by one person can be oppressive, then surely a similar sequence of actions taken not by one person but by different persons can be just as oppressive. Suppose that instead of being criticised by Leslie, Bobbie is criticised by all their friends. If Bobbie experiences significant loss of self-esteem, Bobbie might equally be said to be oppressed by this group. It might well be that no one in the group is overly critical, but the additive effects of all the criticisms nonetheless harm Bobbie.

One person can oppress another not by a single action but by a practice, a set of actions over time. This is *personal* oppression. Sometimes the individual actions may themselves be harmful, though it would be misleading to call them each oppressive. Other times, the accumulated effects of this set of actions may be oppressive, while no one member of the set is even harmful. The members of a group or society can also engage in practices that result in oppression. Such an oppressive practice is a set of actions taken not by a single person, but instead by different people each time, which are harmful either individually or collectively or both. This is *social* oppression. Again, the actions taken by the members of the group may individually be harmful actions, or they may not. In the latter case, social oppression is an accumulative harm.

When social oppression is accumulative in structure, no determinate agent or institution is oppressive, and no individual actions are harmful. One influential interpretation of oppression is Marilyn Frye's metaphor of a cage:

> Consider a birdcage. If you look very closely at just one wire in the cage, you cannot see the other wires. . . . There is no physical property of any one wire, *nothing* that the closest scrutiny could discover, that will reveal how a bird could be inhibited or harmed by it except in the

most accidental way. It is only when you step back, stop looking at the wires one by one, microscopically, and take a macroscopic view of the whole cage, that you can see why the bird does not go anywhere; and then you will see it in a moment. It will require no great subtlety of mental powers. It is perfectly *obvious* that the bird is surrounded by a network of systematically related barriers, no one of which would be the least hindrance to its flight, but which, by their relations to each other, are as confining as the solid walls of a dungeon. It is now possible to grasp one of the reasons why oppression can be hard to recognize: one can study the elements of an oppressive structure with great care and some good will without seeing the structure as a whole, and hence without seeing or being able to understand that one is looking at a cage and that there are people there who are caged, whose motion and mobility are restricted, whose lives are shaped and reduced.[21]

No one bar of a prison cell is sufficient by itself to hold a prisoner. But many such bars, arranged in the right way, will hold her. Many types of social oppression, job discrimination, for example, have this structure. Suppose an employer will not hire anyone with red hair. This is a form of discrimination, though fairly harmless and rather stupid. However, it does not amount to the oppression of red-haired people. A red-haired person can still apply to other employers who are not so eccentric. However, if the attitudes of the eccentric employer were general, red-haired people would be oppressed, for there would then exist a universal obstacle to their employment.

One form of oppression is cultural. By "cultural oppression" I mean the social transmission of *false* beliefs, values, and ideals about how to live, and the attitudes, motivations, behaviour patterns, and institutions that depend on them. Reasonable people will disagree about which enculturated beliefs, values, and ideals are false. So I shall be concerned here with a subset of false, socially transmitted ethical beliefs, ones that reasonable people, according to liberal theory, must see as false, that is to say, with beliefs in the unequal moral worth of persons.

Cultural oppression can be personal as well as social. The enculturation of false beliefs about value can take place, for instance, within the family. A patriarchal father might instill in his daughter a belief that women were created to serve men. This belief is just as much a problem for the daughter if it is transmitted directly from her father as it would be if it had a diffuse genesis in her surrounding society. This essay is mostly concerned with the social form of cultural oppression, with beliefs about value transmitted through the language, images, stories, expectations, norms, and role models presented by our cultural heritage. One reason for this emphasis is an assumption that the underlying and sustaining cause of the father's belief is his membership in a patriarchal culture. He did not invent the false idea that women were created unequal to men, and it is doubtful that he would sustain his belief if it were not confirmed and reinforced by the culture in which he lives. Nor would the belief he enculturated in his daughter survive her participation in a society wider than the family if that wider society challenged, rather than encouraged, her belief in inequality. Cultural oppression by individuals is most commonly a symptom, not a cause, of cultural oppression generally. Another reason for my emphasis on the social form of cultural oppression is strategic. Reform of the wider culture is less intrusive in people's lives than direct interference in the family. The state might require potential parents to take an ethics test on basic liberal principles before being licensed to raise children. But this idea is an affront to the liberal ethos. A more palatable alternative is for the state to challenge the beliefs prevalent in the larger society. Cultural reform in the larger context will eventually rectify false family enculturation. So this essay will not be directly concerned with false enculturation by individuals, but will instead discuss the oppression brought about by cultural membership.

I have a reason for using the term "cultural oppression." I could instead have written merely about the harmful aspects of cultural membership. But I want to use the concept of cultural oppression to connect liberalism's theoretical discourse to the theoretical discourse of those movements for social change that are fighting for a type of equality that liberal theory has had trouble understanding. The first task is to make these concerns visible in liberal theory. Liberalism's traditional focus on fighting coercion, on freedom of conscience and freedom of speech, has blocked its ability to handle more diffuse and subtle forms of power. Cultural oppression is a form of power, and liberal theorists have generally given up on using the concept of power in their analyses. An exception is J. K. Galbraith. He classifies power into *condign* power, which includes physical force and negative sanction, *compensatory* power, which includes inducement and incentive, and *conditioned* power, which he describes as follows:

> It is a common feature of both condign and compensatory power that the individual submitting is aware of his or her submission – in the one case compelled and in the other for reward. Conditioned power, in contrast, is exercised by changing belief. Persuasion, education, or the social commitment to what seems natural, proper, or right causes the in-

dividual to submit to the will of another or of others. The submission reflects the preferred course; the fact of submission is not recognized. Conditioned power, more than condign or compensatory power, is central, as we shall see, to the functioning of the modern economy and polity, and in capitalist and socialist countries alike.[22]

By its seeming naturalness, implicit conditioning becomes immune to the type of critical reflection that might allow people to evade it.

Conditioned power is the product of a continuum from objective, visible persuasion to what the individual in the social context has been brought to believe inherently correct. As we have seen, such power can be explicit, the result of a direct and visible attempt to win the belief. . . . Or the belief can be implicit in the social or cultural condition; . . . As one moves from explicit to implicit conditioning, one passes from obtrusive, ostentatious effort to win belief to an imposed subordination that is unnoticed – taken for granted.[23]

What Galbraith calls conditioned power affects not only the outcome of a person's choices but also the process of deliberative choice itself, the site of human agency in the cognitive sense. In the importance he attaches to conditioned power, he reiterates what Rousseau has written: "The most absolute authority is that which penetrates into a man's inmost being, and concerns itself no less with his will than with his actions."[24] Galbraith illustrates the concept of implicit conditioned power through an analysis of the power of men over women:

However, it will be evident on brief thought that male power and female submission have relied much more completely on the belief since ancient times that such submission is the natural order of things. . . . But only a part of the subordination of women was achieved by explicit instruction – explicit conditioning. Much and almost certainly more was (and is) achieved by the simple acceptance of what the community and culture have long thought right and virtuous. . . . This is implicit conditioning, a powerful force. Overall, this conditioned submission proceeded from belief, belief that masculine will was preferable to undue assertion of their own and the counterpart belief by men that they were entitled by their sex or associated physical and mental qualities to dominate. . . . There is proof of this power of belief in the nature of the modern effort at emancipation – the women's movement. . . . a major part of the effort has been the challenge to belief – the belief that submission and subservience are normal, virtuous, and otherwise appropriate.[25]

Implicit conditioning enculturates a woman into false beliefs about her worth, her value, and her place in the world. In making these false beliefs seem natural, it makes it extremely difficult for her to discover their

15

falsity. In emphasizing the way implicit conditioning makes inequality natural, Galbraith is echoing writers on the oppression of women. Sherwin writes:

> Although feminism values the authority of personal experience, many feminists do not accept that woman's denial that she has experienced oppression refutes the reality of that oppression. As the background condition of women's lives, oppression is often hidden in the norms of a culture that accepts male dominance as a natural ordering.[26]

The naturalness of the beliefs, and the way they are embedded in a coherent system of equally natural background beliefs, removes a woman's motivation to examine them.

Galbraith's use of the term "power" is importantly different from its usage by writers on oppression. For Galbraith, it is not the culture itself, or aspects thereof, which exercises power over people through implicit conditioning. Instead, individuals or groups can exercise power over others through, or because of, the existence of the implicit conditioning of those others by the culture. In other words, the implicit conditioning of the victims of power by the culture functions as a resource for the power holders. A sexist culture enables men to exercise power over women, but in Galbraith's view a sexist culture does not itself have the power to harm women's interests.

Galbraith holds this view because he holds a conception of power that ties the exercise of power to human agency. He quotes, with approval, Max Weber's definition of power as "the possibility of imposing one's will upon the behaviour of other persons."[27] A definition of power in terms of an agent's will, intentions, or purposes rules out the possession or exercise of power by anything but an agent capable of intentions, purposes, or acts of willing. It limits power to human agents and organizations and denies that cultural practices, which of course do not possess agency, can possess or exercise power. To understand oppression and domination properly, we must see power differently. Iris Marion Young writes:

> I have suggested that oppression is the inhibition of a group through a vast network of everyday practices, attitudes, assumptions, behaviors, and institutional rules; it is structural or systemic. The systemic character of oppression implies that an oppressed group need not have a correlate oppressing group. While structural oppression in our society involves relations among groups, these relations do not generally fit the paradigm of one group's consciously and intentionally keeping another down. Foucault suggests that to understand the meaning and operation

16

of power in modern society we should look beyond the model of power as "sovereignty," a dyadic relation of ruler and subject, and instead analyze the exercise of power as the effect of liberal and humanized practices of education, bureaucratic administration, production and distribution of consumer goods, medical practice, and so on. The conscious actions of many individuals daily contribute to maintaining and reproducing oppression, but those people are usually simply doing their jobs or living their lives, not understanding themselves as agents of oppression.[28]

Besides the power intentionally exercised by one person over another, we must also be able to see forms of diffuse power. Diffuse power arises, without anyone intending it, out of the independent activities of many agents. We cannot impute the exercise of diffuse power to the activities of any individual agents. To understand the power of culture to harm, we must understand cultural power as an accumulative phenomenon devoid of agency.

The correct view of power is, as Young suggests, closer to the view of power articulated by Foucault. In the following passage, describing the type of oppression targeted by new movements for social change, Foucault distinguishes two ways in which people are subject to power.

> Finally, all these present struggles revolve around the question: Who are we? . . . the main objective of these struggles is to attack not so much "such and such" an institution of power, or group, or elite, or class but rather a technique, a form of power. This form of power applies itself to immediate everyday life which categorizes the individual, marks him by his own individuality, attaches him to his own identity, imposes a law of truth on him which he must recognize and which others have to recognize in him. It is a form of power which makes individuals subjects. There are two meanings of the word "subject": subject to someone else by control and dependence; and tied to his own identity by a conscience or self-knowledge. Both meanings suggest a form of power which subjugates and makes subject to.[29]

Galbraith sees people as subject to implicit conditioning in the first sense; implicit conditioning makes people subject to the power of others. We must acknowledge the truth of this form of subjection. Nevertheless, we must also acknowledge that by tying them to the conceptions of the good which form their own identities, implicit conditioning subjects people to their culture.

Foucault's view of power presupposes that important forms of power can be exerted without intention. While admitting that the intentional acts of persons produce power, he does not think this to be a defining

17

feature of power: "There is no power that is exerted without a series of aims and objectives. But this does not mean that it results from the choice of an individual subject."[30] Thus, as a methodological constraint, he urges that an analysis of power "should not concern itself with power at the level of conscious intention or decision; that it should not attempt to consider power from its internal point of view and that it should refrain from posing the labyrinthine and unanswerable question: 'Who then has power and what has he in mind? What is the aim of someone who possesses power?'"[31] On Foucault's analysis of power, what an agent intends or wills is not an essential feature of power.[32]

One dangerous example of cultural oppression is the power of the commercial culture in which the developed world is immersed. The pervasive theory of value in a commercial culture holds that the value of an item is determined by the intensity of your preference for it, and the intensity of your preference for it is measured by your willingness to pay. I happen to think this is a false theory of value, but I also recognize that reasonable people might disagree with my view. Because I do not have any new arguments to share on this point, I shall confine my discussion of cultural oppression to socially transmitted beliefs in the inequality of persons, which liberals will recognize as false.

There is a sense in which the power of an inegalitarian culture is exercised equally over all members of society, over both those whom we would think of as oppressed and those whom we would not. In a sexist culture, for example, both men and women might believe, openly or tacitly, the general proposition that a woman's interests are less important than a man's. To the liberal, this socially transmitted, general belief is false. So on my account of cultural oppression, both men and women are oppressed by a sexist culture. However, it is still important to point out that men and women are not oppressed in the same way. There is an important difference of perspective. Only a woman in this culture will have the indexical belief that *her* interests are less important than a man's. Conversely, only a man will believe the sentence, "*My* interests are more important that a woman's." So an oppressive, inegalitarian culture will have different consequences for members of the different groups whose equality is in question. The inegalitarian belief, shared by rich and poor alike, that the rich deserve their wealth by virtue of their superior natural abilities is an important part of what enables the ruling class to rule. Though in a meritocratic culture both rich and poor share the dominant belief, the consequence of this ideology is continued inequality in the distribution of resources.

The seemingly odd claim that a patriarchal culture oppresses both men and women, or that a meritocratic culture oppresses both rich and poor, can be explained by contrasting Foucault's conception of power with Galbraith's. According to Foucault's conception, power requires no determinate agent. Cultural oppression arises from the non–point-source, cumulative pollution of the cultural environment. However, cultural oppression in this diffuse sense of power can make one group vulnerable to the power of another according to Galbraith's conception. The social transmission of beliefs in inequality is a form of implicit conditioning that allows members of one group to exercise power over members of another. In Galbraith's conception of conditioned power, a woman's belief that putting her interests second to those of a man is normal, virtuous, and appropriate is what brings about her submission to his will. Making women vulnerable to the power of men is one type of harm that an oppressive, patriarchal culture does.

To view cultural oppression as the social transmission of false beliefs about value requires viewing the process of belief acquisition as a process that is largely outside the control of those who acquire the beliefs. Liberals might deny this claim, and instead hold that people are in control of what they believe, that people can avoid adopting the prevailing norms. Of course, it is true that for any particular person and any particular belief about value, the person can reflect on that belief and adopt it or not. The question, however, is how universal this process can be.

THE LIBERAL THEORY OF CULTURAL MEMBERSHIP

We arrive at our beliefs about value through deliberation on our background beliefs about principles, the natural world, our selves, and the social world in which we live. This deliberation takes place within the shared social meanings of a culture. As Elster says, a political psychology "cannot limit itself to tracing the effects of beliefs and desires on individual actions and thereby on social processes. It also has to concentrate on the mechanisms by which desires and beliefs are formed."[33] In particular, we have to be concerned with the role that our culture plays in the formation of our beliefs about value. Being a member of a culture is not like being a member of a set. As a member of a culture, a person lives immersed in a system of representations, meanings, symbols, and expectations that impinge on him unasked. To what degree does he have control over the beliefs he acquires?

19

Sometimes, liberal political psychology appears to be attempting to preserve a role for voluntary choice in the formation of our beliefs about value. Kymlicka gives the following account of the role of culture in the formation of our conception of the good.

> . . . we need to look more closely at these beliefs about value which are said to give meaning and purpose to our lives. Where do they come from? Liberals say that we should be free to accept or reject particular options presented to us, so that, ultimately, the beliefs we continue to hold are the ones that we've chosen to accept. But the range of options can't be chosen. . . . The decision about how to lead our lives must ultimately be ours alone, but this decision is always a matter of selecting what we believe to be most valuable from the various options available, selecting from a context of choice which provides us with different ways of life. This is important because the range of options is determined by our cultural heritage.[34]

One interpretation of this passage is that we choose, select, or decide on our beliefs about value from the range of options presented by our cultural context much as we choose, select, or decide on a particular flavour from the range of options at an ice-cream parlour. This interpretation is not simply an inadequate account of the relationship between one's beliefs about value and one's cultural context, an impoverished political psychology. It is an impossible account, for a strong argument can be made that we can never choose or decide to believe anything at all. To believe something is to believe it to be true. So if you know that you believe something because you have decided to do so, and not because it is true, then you are not really believing it, but doing something else instead. As Bernard Williams argues, it is not a contingent fact that one cannot believe at will in the way that it is a contingent fact that one cannot blush at will.

> Why is this? One reason is connected with the characteristic of beliefs that they aim at truth. If I could acquire a belief at will, I could acquire it whether it was true or not; moreover I would know that I could acquire it whether it was true or not. If in full consciousness I could will to acquire a 'belief' irrespective of its truth, it is unclear that before the event I could seriously think of it as a belief, i.e., as something purporting to represent reality.[35]

If the components of our conceptions of the good are beliefs about value, then people cannot choose their ends as a matter of will. The ice-cream-parlour model of belief and culture is a conceptual impossibility.

A second interpretation of Kymlicka's view would utilize a more sophisticated model of the relationship between belief and culture. "Choice" has two meanings of interest to us here. *Voluntary* choice is an act of the will, as in when we choose between chocolate and vanilla ice cream without trying to present reasons on either side. *Deliberative* choice is an act of reason and reflection. Dworkin denies that people choose their beliefs in the first sense. He writes that "it is not part of any argument I have used so far that some or any or all convictions and other preferences are voluntarily chosen. Liberal equality does not assume that people choose their beliefs about ethics any more than their beliefs about geography. It does suppose that they *reflect* on their ethical beliefs and that they choose how to behave on the basis of those reflections."[36] We reflect on our beliefs from the basis of our background beliefs and the evidence before us. In the deliberative sense, it is not conceptually impossible to speak of choosing our beliefs. The choosing involved, however, is not done in the faculty of volition, but in the faculty of reason and cognition. Kymlicka seems to have agency in the cognitive sense in mind when he says that liberals should be interested in the fate of cultural structures because "it's only through having a rich and secure cultural structure that people can become aware, in a vivid way, of the options available to them, and intelligently examine their value."[37] Here the role of culture is to make people aware of options, to see what might be significant to them, so that they can use their deliberative powers to arrive at their beliefs about value.

In Kymlicka's picture, the role of culture in the formation of beliefs about value is analogous to some sort of collective imagination. In our culture we see what our options are. It might seem, then, that the role of culture is tentatively to suggest ends. If we had infinite imaginations, we would not need culture to suggest ends; we could perform that task ourselves. But culture has a far less tentative role than that, for we deliberate about our ends on the basis of other beliefs that we hold, other beliefs about value and other beliefs about the social world in which we live. The sort of deliberation that goes into forming ends does not go on forever. We are finite creatures, and the amount of critical reflection we can carry out puts boundaries on our reflection. Many, if not most, of the beliefs that enter into our deliberations have simply been uncritically adopted from our culture. Our culture not only suggests beliefs to us for consideration but also provides us the background beliefs on which our deliberation depends.

The relationship between beliefs and culture in practical knowledge is much more like the relationship between empirical beliefs and the natural world in perceptual knowledge. If I see a cat sitting on a mat over there by the fireplace, I do not choose to believe that there is a cat on the mat. My belief is quite involuntary. My belief might also be wrong. It might be a small dog, or a toy, or some sort of optical illusion. Of course, I may, depending on the context, have to take some responsibility for verifying my belief. But verification of perceptual beliefs takes time and effort, and it is impossible that I could test all my beliefs. Generally I take my perceptual beliefs as they are given to me.

I do not choose the beliefs about facts that I acquire from the natural world. Similarly, it is misleading to say that I choose the beliefs about value that I acquire from the cultural world. I do not choose the beliefs and meanings embedded in my language; I learn them. I do not choose the values I learn at my mother's knee; I identify with them. I do not choose my socialization; I undergo it. I perceive the social world just as I perceive the natural world. I see how men treat women. I see how people of my status defer to authority. I see what professions and what institutions are valued. I see what is appropriate for me to expect, and what is not, and when. I see what the rest of my society thinks I deserve. Like natural beliefs, like the belief that snow is white, these social beliefs come to seem natural to me.

Herein lies the power that culture exercises over us. The beliefs we acquire from our culture exercise this power precisely because they are not chosen. First, because they are background beliefs, because they seem natural to us, we rarely have reason to call them into question. We have no motivation to test them. Sometimes, in our privileged philosophical leisure, we examine particular background beliefs for intellectual reasons. More commonly, we examine our background beliefs only when they are called into question by social movements which contest them. We have greater motivation to examine the beliefs about value that form our explicit ends in life, but these beliefs about what is valuable in life depend upon a background of pedestrian beliefs which attract no examination.

Second, though it likely is true for each of our background beliefs that we could evaluate it and take responsibility for it if we were motivated to do so, it does not follow that we could evaluate all of our background beliefs. Of course, it is logically possible, but that is not of interest. We are finite intellects. It takes time to evaluate beliefs, and we have only so much time. For any given belief, we may be able to take that time, and it will be psychologically possible for us to evaluate it. But it does not follow that it is psychologically possible to evaluate all our beliefs. There simply is not enough time for that. In other words the following argument is invalid:

(1) For each belief we have, it is psychologically possible for us to evaluate that belief.
(2) Therefore, it is psychologically possible for us to evaluate every belief we have.

The lengthy process involved in evaluating social beliefs is particularly evident in the example of how much time, collectively, feminists have had to put into examining traditional beliefs about the so-called natural roles of men and women. Then, even with this collective effort as a support, consider how long it takes for individual women and men to evaluate these background beliefs. It is impossible to take epistemic responsibility for all the beliefs one receives from one's culture.

Third, the very content of our background ethical beliefs is determined by the shared social meanings of our culture. Our culture not only gives meanings to the various options it permits but also provides us with tacit background assumptions about who deserves what. In Chapter 3, I shall discuss inegalitarian social meanings in detail.

The model of the relationship between belief and culture that I have been sketching is an overly simple political psychology. For one thing, it needs development to be able to account for the effects of enculturation on our emotions and desires. Many of the emotions we have we experience only because of the implicit ideology of our culture, but they are still real emotions that we have and feel. The model may also be too simple in its foundationalism. It suggests that we receive certain beliefs from our culture and, from these, construct higher-level beliefs about how to lead our lives. I suspect the truth may be more complicated; the processes of perception and evaluation likely go on together, with the two cohering in some sort of equilibrium rather than one forming a foundation for the other. But this admission should not belittle the importance of cultural perception in the deliberative process.

Kymlicka's model of culture as a range of options from which persons can select their beliefs about value contrasts strongly with models to be found in cultural anthropology. Clifford Geertz, for example, sees culture as "a set of control mechanisms – plans, recipes, rules, instructions (what computer engineers call 'programs') – for the governing of behavior."[38] Human thought is, unavoidably, a traffic in significant symbols: "From the point of view of any particular individual, such symbols are largely given. He finds them already current in the community when he is born, and they remain, with some additions, subtractions, and partial alterations he may or may not have had a hand in, in circulation after he dies."[39] Even the physical evolution of the human brain has been a response not just to the natural environment but to the cultural environment on which early humans became increasingly dependent. As a consequence, "our ideas, our values, our acts, even our emotions, are, like our nervous system itself, cultural products – products manufactured, indeed out of tendencies, capacities and dispositions with which we were born, but manufactured nonetheless."[40] If something even close to Geertz's view of cultural membership is correct, liberalism must abandon the view that we choose our background beliefs about value from a culture which does no more than propose options.

The truly pernicious aspect of the liberal, voluntarist, ice-cream-parlour model of belief and culture is not its mistakenness, but its complicity in hiding the power that culture exercises over us. The voluntarist model paints the process of belief enculturation as something that is always within the control of the individual and for which the individual must take responsibility. Thus the voluntarist model makes it seem as though we are free of any power that our social enculturation might have. But cultures also transmit beliefs about value in ways that individuals find unavoidable. If these beliefs are inconsistent with the equal moral worth of persons, then we have a type of cultural oppression that liberals must acknowledge.

I wish to argue that the liberal state must take an active role in challenging cultural oppression. The following is a summary of the argument that I shall offer:

(1) Liberalism must regard beliefs in the unequal moral worth of persons as false.

(2) If the transmission of false beliefs in moral inequality by individuals causes harm to significant interests, then the liberal state must abandon universal tolerance and combat this individual harm.

(3) The transmission of false beliefs in moral inequality does cause significant harm.

(4) Therefore the state must combat the transmission of false beliefs by individuals.

(5) If the social transmission of false beliefs in inequality (i.e., the cultural oppression of groups) is a harm, then it is an accumulative harm.

(6) It is just as important for the state to combat accumulative harms as it is for the state to combat individual harms.

24

(7) Therefore the liberal state must take an active role in reforming culture and combatting the cultural oppression of groups.

I take it that I have now established premises (1), (2), and (5). To make the argument sound, the rest of the essay will seek first to establish (3), the harmfulness of false ethical beliefs, and second to establish (6), the importance of accumulative harms.

Establishing that the having of false beliefs about value is a harmed condition is not straightforward. Earlier I suggested that the transmission of false beliefs about value was a harm akin to a fraud. But fraud and cultural oppression are different in the following way: If you buy a pig in a poke, and then when you get home you open the poke and let a cat out of the bag, you have been defrauded. You are defrauded because, through the vendor's misrepresentation, you did not get what you wanted. You wanted a pig, and instead you got a cat. But cultural oppression makes inequality seem natural and thus makes groups of people want less than their fair share. Many of a person's most important wants are based on her beliefs about value. If she systematically undervalues her own worth, she will believe that she deserves less and will come to want less. Feinberg says that a harm is a setback to someone's interests, and someone's interests are deep-rooted and stable wants that have some hope of fulfilment.[41] How, then, is she harmed if she receives less than her fair share? She has, after all, received what she wanted. In the next chapter, I shall argue that one answer to this question, an answer which liberals must accept, is that people have an abstract, highest-order interest in knowing their good and that the transmission of false ethical beliefs harms that interest.

2

LIBERALISM AND THE
EPISTEMOLOGY OF VALUE

THE culture we live in is the totality of socially transmitted beliefs, meanings, values, ideas, norms, and institutions that form the background to our lives. I have stipulated that cultural oppression is the social transmission of false ethical beliefs. I am using "ethics" here in its broad sense to include both claims about an individual's moral obligations to others and claims about an individual's good or well-being. Considerable indeterminacy exists concerning the truth or falsity of ethical beliefs, and reasonable people can disagree about many ethical claims, especially those having to do with what constitutes someone's well-being. For egalitarian liberalism, however, there can be no indeterminacy about a belief in the unequal moral worth of all persons. Such beliefs must be regarded as false. It follows that cultural practices which transmit such beliefs are oppressive. But it does not yet follow that transmitting them is harmful. Harms are setbacks to interests; someone's interests consist in getting what he wants, and what he wants is still what he wants whether those wants are based on true beliefs about value or on false beliefs.

CULTURAL OPPRESSION AND SELF-RESPECT

One harm that egalitarian liberalism should see in the social transmission of false beliefs about moral inequality is a harm to people's self-respect. For Rawls, self-respect is perhaps the most important primary good. It is a primary good because someone needs to have self-respect in order to pursue her conception of the good, no matter what she believes to be valuable in life, and no matter what it is she wants to achieve. Without self-respect, "nothing may seem worth doing, or if some things have value for us, we lack the will to strive for them. . . . Therefore the parties in the original position would wish to avoid at almost any cost the social conditions that undermine self-respect." For Rawls, self-respect or self-esteem "includes a person's sense of his own value, his secure conviction that his conception of his good, his plan of life, is worth carrying out." The circumstances which sustain this aspect of self-respect include "finding our person and deeds appreciated and confirmed by others who are likewise esteemed and their association enjoyed."[1]

In an inegalitarian culture, one containing a widespread belief that some persons are of less inherent moral worth than others, it is likely that members of the group labelled inferior will not find their persons and deeds appreciated and confirmed by others. They will receive confirmation neither from members of the group labelled superior nor from their own group, since members of both groups share a view of moral inequality. "Now," Rawls writes, "our self-respect normally depends upon the respect of others. Unless we feel that our endeavors are honored by them, it is difficult if not impossible for us to maintain the conviction that our ends are worth advancing."[2] Under these circumstances, members of the group labelled inferior will suffer injury to their self-respect and will be harmed in their ability to implement their various conceptions of the good. So, for example, a woman living in a sexist culture will not find many of her endeavours, particularly those outside the realm of what is thought appropriate to a woman, honoured and respected by either men or other women. Under these conditions, she will find it difficult to maintain the conviction that her ends are worth advancing.[3] Charles Taylor makes a similar point about recognition by a society:

> . . . our identity is partly shaped by recognition or its absence, often by the *mis*recognition of others, and so a person or group of people can suffer real damage, real distortion, if the people or society around them mirror back to them a confining or demeaning or contemptible picture of themselves. Nonrecognition or misrecognition can inflict harm, can be a form of oppression, imprisoning someone in a false, distorted, and reduced mode of being. Thus some feminists have argued that women in patriarchal societies have been induced to adopt a depreciatory image of themselves. They have internalized a picture of their own inferiority, so that even when some of the objective obstacles to their advancement fall away, they may be incapable of taking advantage of the new opportunities. And beyond this, they are condemned to suffer the pain of low self-esteem.[4]

The misrecognition or nonrecognition that does the harm may, sometimes, be the doing of a determinate individual, someone like a parent who is important enough in a person's life. More important, though, is misrecognition by society at large, by the prevailing patriarchal attitudes of the whole culture.

So cultural oppression can result in harm to self-respect and thus harm someone's interest in implementing her conception of the good. One reason that this injury to self-respect may be difficult to see as a harm is that it is an accumulative harm. A failure by just one man, in an otherwise non-sexist culture, to respect and honour equal opportunities for women would not harm anyone's self-respect. It is only when such attitudes are widespread in society that it is difficult for a woman to maintain her confidence in a nontraditional endeavour. The harm to self-respect brought about by a socially transmitted belief in inequality is not generally caused by any one determinate individual, but by the attitudes and actions of many, many people. No one failure to recognize and confirm the person and deeds of another is, by itself, a harm to her self-respect. Only if such failures are widespread enough, only if more than some threshold percentage of the society holds these attitudes, will her self-respect be undermined.

Harm to self-respect, however, captures only one aspect of the harm done by cultural oppression, for someone's self-respect is relative to a particular conception of the good. Given a particular conception of the good, self-respect gives someone the self-confidence required to implement it. But the fact that a person has self-respect is independent of the content of his conception of the good. He may well have formed a conception of the good that is based on a belief in his own lesser inherent moral worth. A serf in a manorial society is a paradigmatic example of the moral inequality that liberalism has fought against. Yet a self-respecting serf, someone who is confirmed by his social world in the pursuit of his attenuated ends, is perfectly possible. In pointing out that his principles of justice would not necessarily be chosen in societies that "have other ways of affirming self-respect," Rawls writes:

> Thus in a feudal or in a caste system each person is believed to have his allotted station in the natural order of things. His comparisons are presumably confined to within his own estate or caste, these ranks becoming in effect so many noncomparing groups established independently of human control and sanctioned by religion and theology. Men resign themselves to their position should it ever occur to them to question it; and since all may view themselves as assigned their vocation, everyone is held to be equally fated and equally noble in the eyes of providence. This conception of society solves the problem of social justice by eliminating in thought the circumstances that give rise to it.[5]

The problem is that a serf in the manorial system will base his conception of the good on beliefs about his own inequality that the liberal must see as false, while nevertheless he is confirmed in the implementation of his reduced conception of the good by the cultural milieu in which he lives. The self-respecting serf is culturally oppressed, yet not harmed in his self-esteem.

Closer to home, we can imagine a contemporary housewife and mother who has come to believe in women's inequality and has based her life plans on that assumption. Her endeavours enjoy much respect, support, and encouragement from her husband, her social group, and society generally. Her self-confidence in pursuing her ends is very high. In one of the paradoxes of liberation, she may well experience feminists, who argue against her assumption that women should take a secondary role in society, as trying to undermine her self-confidence in her plans. Claims of equality are a threat to her self-respect. If the self-confident housewife has been harmed by a sexist culture transmitting false beliefs in women's inequality, it is apparently not a harm to self-respect.

A harm to someone's self-respect is a harm to his interest in implementing his conception of the good, whatever that may be. Frequently the social transmission of false beliefs in inequality will bring about such harms. Most often such harms will be accumulative in nature. But there is more to it than this. Cultural oppression can also bring about a harm to the very process of forming a conception of the good. I shall argue that this is a harm to our interest in knowing our good, and that egalitarian liberals must take this harm seriously.

COERCION, ENDORSEMENT, AND KNOWLEDGE

My strategy will be to examine how liberalism might answer this question: Why is it wrong to coerce people? Liberalism's answer will, I believe, provide a reason for also seeing the inculcation of false beliefs about value as a harm. In a liberal culture we take the wrongness of coercion for granted. Historically, the mission of liberalism was to liberate individuals from the coercive power of the aristocratic state and its established church. People living in liberal democratic states see the absence of state coercion as natural, and its presence as requiring strong and precise justification. The wrongness of coercion seems too obvious to require a reason. Asking for such a reason is not to condone coercion in any way, but is a means to clarify what the underlying principles of liberalism are.

It follows from the equal moral worth of persons that their highest-order, most abstract interests are equally worthy of consideration and respect. At the most abstract level, a person's highest interest is in leading the most valuable and worthwhile life possible. If the state coerces someone into leading a life that is less good than he could have led without the intervention, then state coercion will have harmed his highest-order interest. So, in the case of malevolent despotism, we have a reason for the wrongness of coercion: It harms a person's highest-order interest in leading as good a life as possible. But people are frequently mistaken in the good they pursue; their lives would go better if they pursued some other good. If the state coerced them into living their lives in a better way, what would be wrong with that? There is some cost associated with the discomfort of being coerced, but this might well be balanced out by the benefits of pursuing the right sort of ends. On the face of it, benevolent despotism need not harm people's highest interests, but instead may be beneficial. What, then, is wrong with coercive state paternalism?

We can object to coercive state paternalism on the grounds that coercing someone into embracing some conception of the good cannot make it a conception of the good for that person. This line of argument has its origin in Locke's *A Letter Concerning Toleration:*

> . . . the magistrate has no power to enforce by law, . . . the use of any rites or ceremonies whatsoever in the worship of God. And this . . . because whatsoever is practised in the worship of God is only so far justifiable as it is believed by those that practise it to be acceptable unto him. – Whatsoever is not done with that assurance of faith, is neither well in itself, nor can it be acceptable to God.[6]

Even if a life of prayer is the best life to lead, forcing someone to pray against her will cannot make prayer a component of the best life for her.

Following Dworkin, I shall call Locke's claim the "endorsement constraint." A person's endorsement of a conception of the good is necessary for it to be a good for her. Dworkin has given arguments for the endorsement constraint grounded in his theory that the value of someone's life comes from her life being a skilful response to the challenges facing her, rather than from the impact her life has on the world. Dworkin points out two options with respect to the relationship of endorsement to the components of a good life. On what Dworkin calls the *additive* view, someone's endorsement is a sufficient condition for increasing the value to him of the components of his conception of the good: "If he endorses those components, then this increases the goodness of his life; it is frosting on the cake. But if he does not, the ethical value of the components remains."[7] On what Dworkin calls the *constitutive* view, someone's endorsement of a component of the good life is a necessary condition for that component to increase the good in his life: "no component may even so much as contribute to the value of a person's life without his endorsement."[8] The constitutive view is Dworkin's view, and it embodies the endorsement constraint. Dworkin's constitutive view of endorsement avoids the danger of incorrigibility implicit in making endorsement both necessary and sufficient for value.

Dworkin argues for the constitutive view by example, through two-way comparisons between endorsed and repudiated lives. So we have the misanthrope who is left alone and the misanthrope who has unwanted friendship thrust upon him. We have the practising atheist and the atheist who is forced to pray in the shadow of the rack. We have the active homosexual and the homosexual who abstains out of fear. We have someone who takes religious orders and someone who leaves them to enter politics because of pressure from others.[9] In each case we compare an endorsed component of the good life with a repudiated alternative. The atheist endorses a life free of the church and repudiates wasting her time in prayer. By forcing her to do what she repudiates, the magistrate cannot be thought to be making her life go better for her. So her endorsement of prayer seems necessary if prayer is to make her life go better.

Dworkin believes that someone's endorsement is an essential prerequisite to the formation of her conception of the good. As Kymlicka puts it, "my life only goes better if I am leading it from the inside, according to my beliefs about value."[10]The endorsement constraint is supposed to achieve this, to make assent necessary without making decisions incorrigible. But it is fairly easy to see why the endorsement constraint is too weak and why we must be prepared to add a stronger constraint, for endorsement can be manufactured in perverse ways. Consider the following example suggested by Richard Taylor as a possible solution to the meaninglessness of the labours of Sisyphus:

> Let us suppose that the gods, while condemning Sisyphus to the fate just described, at the same time, as an afterthought, waxed perversely merciful by implanting in him a strange and irrational impulse; namely, a compulsive impulse to roll stones. We may if we like, to make this more graphic, suppose they accomplish this by implanting in him some substance that has this effect on his character and drives. . . . Now it can be seen why this little afterthought of the gods, which I call perverse,

was also in fact merciful. For they have by this device managed to give Sisyphus precisely what he wants – by making him want precisely what they inflict on him. . . . Whereas otherwise he might profoundly have wished surcease, . . . his life is now filled with mission and meaning.[11]

Dworkin anticipates this sort of objection. He writes: "In any case, endorsement must be genuine, and it is not genuine when someone is hypnotized or brainwashed or frightened into conversion. Endorsement is genuine only when it is itself the agent's performance, not the result of another person's thoughts being piped into his brain."[12] So the endorsement constraint is not the only condition on people forming a conception of the good. We must also have one or more constraints on endorsement itself which will ensure that the endorsement is genuine. Already the liberal defence of liberty is not as simple as it seemed. Since coercion overrides endorsement, the endorsement constraint gives us an argument against coercion. But the genuineness or authenticity constraint must be satisfied as well. We might be able to satisfy authenticity by adding to the absence-of-coercion constraint something like the absence-of-deception constraint. Preventing deception, however, may sometimes conflict with preventing coercion. We would then have to weigh the two constraints against one another, and perhaps abandon a blanket prohibition against coercion.

The core task of the endorsement constraint is to make the individual's opinion authoritative over her conception of the good. By making first-person endorsement necessary to any potential end being valuable to its possessor, the constraint is supposed to rule out the possibility of coercive state paternalism. The state cannot impose a contrary but more valuable end on the individual. But we have no good reason to believe that a person's judgement need be authoritative over the genuineness of her endorsement. When people are hypnotized, or brainwashed, or have thoughts piped into their heads, they are not aware of these impediments. If people could be aware of them, they would not be efficacious. Only second parties may be able to judge whether an individual's endorsement is genuine.

Dworkin has said the following about the distinction between genuine and nongenuine endorsement. Suppose the state does obtain someone's sincere conversion and endorsement of a conception of the good through various constraints and inducements.

> Has his life then been improved? The answer turns on an issue I have so far neglected: the conditions and circumstances of genuine endorsement. There must be some constraints on endorsement; otherwise any

critical paternalism could justify itself by adding chemical or electrical brainwashing to its regime. We must distinguish acceptable from unacceptable circumstances of endorsement. The distinction, as we know from the history of liberal theories of education, is a difficult one to draw, but any adequate account of acceptable circumstances would, I believe, include the following proposition. We would not improve someone's life, even though he endorsed the change we brought about, if the mechanisms we used to secure the change lessened his ability to consider the critical merits of the change in a reflective way.[13]

So now the argument depends on the assumption that the "ability to consider the critical merits of the change in a reflective way" is morally important. Dworkin has to assume that we have a significant interest in critical reflection which is harmed by endorsement induced through brainwashing. But what is this interest in critical reflection, and why is it so important? We do not engage in critical reflection solely for its own sake.

One answer might be that we have an interest in having true beliefs about the good, and that critical reflection is important because it allows us to get our beliefs right. This would solve the brainwashing problem if brainwashing were always malevolent, if it always induced false beliefs about the good. But we can also imagine benevolent brainwashing, whose effect is to induce in people true beliefs about what is valuable in their lives. We can imagine that, run by the right experts in the art of living, benevolent brainwashing is actually better than regular critical reflection at getting beliefs about value right. If our interest is merely in having true beliefs about value, then benevolent brainwashing might be the best route to the truth. We need another answer to the question of why critical reflection is important.

A better answer is that we have an interest not only in having true beliefs about the good but also in having knowledge of the good. Critical reflection is important because it allows us to come to know our good. To protect our interest in having the best life possible, I contend that what we need is not the endorsement constraint but what I shall call, by analogy, the "knowledge constraint." In the best life, forming a conception of the good is simply coming to know what is best for us. Our highest-order interest is in coming to know what is best for us and then being able to implement it. Factors which prevent us from achieving the required knowledge can harm our most fundamental interests. The components of our conception of the good, our ends, are value judgements. These judgements are beliefs about value. The desires which lead us to action, our choices, depend on these beliefs. At a minimum, knowledge is justified true belief.[14]We can be said to know a proposition only if the proposition is true, if we believe, assent to, or affirm that proposition, and if we have good reasons for affirming that proposition, that is, if it coheres with our other judgements and is justified by them.

From even this minimal understanding of knowledge, we can see that the knowledge constraint not only implies the endorsement constraint but also solves some of its problems. For someone to know her ends, she has to believe or affirm them, or, in other words, she has to endorse them. Someone can fail to know her good if her ends are false. But forcing someone to adopt even true ends against her own beliefs cannot help her achieve knowledge of the good. The reason is that knowledge of a proposition requires belief in the proposition, and a person can believe a proposition only if she thinks it to be true. She will believe it to be true only if she thinks that she believes it because it is true. But if someone is openly forced to assent to a proposition (even a true one), she will realize that she is assenting because she is forced to, not because she believes the proposition to be true. Someone cannot be made to believe a proposition by overt force, though she may be made to verbally assent to it, adopt it, or even act on it. So the attempt to coerce someone into believing a proposition is a harm to her interest in coming to know her good.

From her interest in knowing the good, it also follows that a person has an interest in having her ends justified by other beliefs that she affirms, or, in other words, that her ends cohere. Because of this, someone's ends must be revisable in the sense that they have to respond to the reasons that justify them. If one had an end that was fixed in some way and was resistant to change even when the reasons which justified it changed and required it to change, then it would not be the product of reasons, but would be the product of causes. Benevolent brainwashing which inserts true ends into a person's conception of the good still harms the person's interest in knowing her good. It has the effect of making a person endorse ends which do not cohere with her other ends. Even though her induced ends are true ones, they are not justified on the basis of the other beliefs she has. She must, at least implicitly, have reasons for her beliefs.[15]Critical reflection must aim not simply at true beliefs but at justified true beliefs.

The structure of the preceding argument can be summarized in the following way. Our interest in leading as good a life as possible explains what is wrong with the coercion of a malevolent despot who forces people to lead bad lives. It does not explain, however, what is wrong with the coercive paternalism of a benevolent despot who forces people to lead good lives. If we add that people have an interest in leading a life that not only is a good life but also is a life they believe to be good, and we note, with Dworkin, that people cannot be forced to assent to beliefs about value, then we can say what is wrong with coercive paternalism. But now we have to explain what is wrong with malevolent brainwashing, which induces fake assent to false beliefs about value. We can explain this by saying that people have an interest not only in leading a life they believe to be good but also in having that belief be true. Still we have to explain what is wrong with benevolent brainwashing, which induces fake assent to true beliefs about value. We can explain this by positing that people have a significant interest in knowing the good, an interest not just in having true beliefs about value but also in having these beliefs be justified by other true beliefs that they hold. So our interest in knowing the good can be undermined in two different ways: first, if we come to have beliefs about value that are false, and, second, if we come to have beliefs about value that are true but which depend on, or are justified by, other beliefs that are false.

Something like the knowledge constraint was first, as far as I know, put forward by John Stuart Mill. His argument for freedom of conscience and freedom of expression in *On Liberty* has two divisions. First, he argues that our views of the good might be mistaken, so we require freedom of expression as a means to correct these mistakes. Second, he argues that even if our views are true, we still need freedom of expression as a means of knowing that our views are true. Freedom of expression is required to combat prejudice, for

> ... assuming that the true opinion abides in the mind, but abides as a prejudice, a belief independent of, and proof against argument – this is not the way in which truth ought to be held by a rational being. This is not *knowing* the truth. Truth, thus held, is but one superstition the more, accidentally clinging to the words which enunciate a truth.[16][emphasis added]

Freedom of expression enables people to hear opposing views on the right way to live a life. "He who knows only his own side of the case, knows little of that" (p. 55). In the absence of discussion, people may forget the grounds of their opinion, which will become mere rote and not "a vivid conception and a living belief" (p. 57). I plan to challenge Mill's view that untrammelled freedom of expression is the best way of satisfying the knowledge constraint, but I think his principle, the knowledge constraint, is right. To protect people from harm to their highest interest in leading the best life possible, we have to protect from harm a central component of this interest, that is, their highest-order interest in knowing what is best for themselves.

Recently, it has been the communitarians who have emphasized that we form our conception of the good not by choosing it but by coming to know it. Sandel writes that there are two ways we can envision a person coming by her ends: "one is by choice, the other by discovery, by 'finding them out'."[17]We form our conception of the good by coming to know what is good for us, and in so doing we create our identity as persons. "For a subject to play a role in shaping the contours of its identity requires a certain faculty of reflection. Will alone is not enough. What is required is a certain capacity for self-knowledge, a capacity for what we have called agency in the cognitive sense" (p. 152). Our cognitive agency will reveal that our conception of the good is held in common with the rest of our community, the product of a process of moral socialization: "we can know a good in common that we cannot know alone" (p. 183). If communitarians see the forming of a conception of the good as identical with coming to know the good, then communitarians should also be bound by the knowledge constraint. Social or cultural conditions which undermine our capacity to know the good should not be permitted in a communitarian society.

The discussion of brainwashing has been a philosopher's fantasy employed to sharpen our view of the issues involved. Our cultural environment, however, is not a fantasy. Our knowledge of the good comes from our social and cultural context. As individuals, we do not acquire all of our beliefs by the application of scientific method. Our background beliefs are simply accepted from (or thrust upon us by) our surrounding culture. We have neither the time nor the intellectual capacity nor the resources to critically evaluate each and every one of them. Our justifications for our ends often depend on these enculturated beliefs. If the enculturated beliefs upon which our justifications depend are false, our knowledge of our ends will be undermined. Liberalism is agnostic about the truth or falsity of most beliefs about value, but not about beliefs in the moral inequality of persons. Such beliefs it will regard as false. An inegalitarian culture pollutes the cultural environment with behaviours, representations, and speech acts that lead to false beliefs about the worth of persons. This form of cultural oppression will be a harm to a person's interest in knowing her good, for if a person forms a conception of the good that depends on a false assessment of her own worth, or of the worth of other people, she will fail to know her good.

An inegalitarian culture oppresses and harms people in several ways. It harms people indirectly by making other forms of oppression, such as intimidation, violence, and discrimination, seem natural and justified. It harms people directly by harming their highest-order interest in forming and implementing their conception of the good. First, it harms their ability to implement their conception of the good by undermining their self-respect. Second, it harms their interest in coming to know what their good is. If egalitarian liberalism is to recognize the second, subtler form of harm, then it must assume that it is possible for someone to *know* her good. This assumption is controversial, for it might be that egalitarian liberals do not think that the good is something knowable. They might be noncognitivists about conceptions of the good and hold that a judgement of prudential value is just an expression of preference for something. They might hold that a conception of the good is just a bundle of preferences, not a coherent set of beliefs about what is valuable in life. I shall argue that egalitarian liberals like Dworkin and Rawls have implicitly become cognitivists about much of what is valuable in a person's life. They should therefore see the pollution of the cultural environment with behaviours, representations, and speech that transmit beliefs in inequality as a harm to people's interest in knowing the good.

Cognitivism in ethics is the view that we do, or at least could, possess ethical knowledge. Minimally, it requires that we could be justified in believing ethical judgements and that ethical judgements express propositions which can be true or false.[18] It contrasts with noncognitivism, which is the view that ethical judgements do not express propositions that have truth values, but something else instead: prescriptions, or emotional attitudes of approval/disapproval, or preferences, or endorsements. In political philosophy, utilitarian and contractarian liberals have mostly been noncognitivists about people's ends in life, taking people's judgements about their good to be expressions of personal preference. Such liberals are *metaethical subjectivists* in that they believe that the sources of prudential value are in people's subjective psychological states such as their actual or considered preferences. They are not, however, necessarily *value subjectivists*. They may not hold that the objects of value,

Table 2

	Metaethical subjectivism (Noncognitivism)	Metaethical objectivism (Cognitivism)
Value subjectivism	Value judgement expresses a preference for some psychological state	Value judgement states a belief that some psychological state is valuable
Value objectivism	Value judgement expresses a preference for some nonpsychological state of affairs	Value judgement states a belief that some nonpsychological state of affairs is valuable

the things valued, are subjective psychological states like pleasure or satisfied wants. The objects of value may well be objective states of affairs that obtain independently of the valuer's or anyone else's subjective assessment of their desirability. Similarly, a cognitivist position in metaethics is not committed, without further argument, to the claim that people have only objective ends. Cognitivists as well as noncognitivists can hold that subjective states are valuable. An objectivist cognitivism is certainly possible – the truth conditions of someone's value judgement might refer to what is written in a religious text rather than to her preferences – but, by itself, a cognitivist position in the metaethics of ends leaves unanswered the question of the objectivity of ends. The terms "subjective" and "objective" are ambiguous between their ethical and metaethical uses. Table 2 summarizes these uses.

Gauthier is an example of a contractarian liberal theorist who holds a noncognitivist, metaethical subjectivist, view of the good. He identifies value with a measure of considered preference and claims that, though people can know value in the sense of empirical knowledge of the strength of preferences, they cannot have any ethical knowledge. He writes:

> Subjectivism is not to be confused with the view that values are unknowable. Evaluation, as an activity of measurement, is cognitive. Preference, what is measured, is knowable. What the subjectivist denies is that there is a knowledge of value that is not ordinary empirical knowledge, a knowledge of a special realm of the valuable. . . . Knowledge of value concerns only the realm of the affects; evaluation is cognitive but there is no unique 'value-oriented' cognition.[19]

On Gauthier's view, ethical knowledge is not possible. So it does not make sense to say that someone has an interest in having it. The no-

38

tion of a harm to someone's highest-order interest in knowing her good is a non-starter.

I contend that egalitarian liberals like Dworkin and Rawls have moved away from the economist's notion of value espoused by Gauthier and have accepted a partly cognitivist account of what is valuable in a person's life. The issue is one of moral psychology. What is the nature of the fundamental components of someone's conception of the good? On the one side is the pure noncognitivist account espoused by Gauthier: The components of a conception of the good are purely motivational, noncognitive psychological attitudes like wants and preferences. On the other side is a pure cognitivist account: The components of a conception of the good are purely cognitive, nonmotivational attitudes like beliefs about what is valuable in life. Dworkin and Rawls both give mixed accounts, where the components of a person's conception of the good are both preferences and beliefs about value. For both, the most important components are the beliefs about what is valuable in life. For both, then, cultural oppression harms a person if it undermines his knowledge of his good.

The pure noncognitive account most resembles Hume's motivational psychology.[20] On a Humean account, beliefs cannot motivate people's actions. Even if you believe that something awful will happen to you unless you move out of the way, you will not do so unless you have a desire to avoid harm to yourself. If a conception of the good guides or motivates a person's action, then its components must be motivational psychological attitudes like preferences. On a Kantian account, however, motivational attitudes are not necessarily independent of beliefs about value. The "good will" is guided by principles that can be known by reason. The Kantian account is a cognitivist one because ethical belief guides preference. We can also imagine an account in which people act directly on their beliefs or convictions.[21] However, the pure Humean account is the one frequently attributed to liberals generally.

I am not going to defend the cognitivist view about value against the problems that it raises. Rather, I shall propose a test by which to tell whether or not an author's moral psychology is cognitivist. The test cannot be as easy as simply looking to see if an author talks of preferences or of beliefs about value, for any plausible moral psychology must contain both preferences and beliefs. Cognitivists must give an account of the motivational force of value. Beliefs are not usually thought to motivate people to action. So cognitivists about value must give an account

39

of desires or preferences to do what is believed valuable. And noncognitivists, like Gauthier, are perfectly prepared to admit that people form beliefs about value, but only in the sense of forming beliefs about how much they prefer something. Noncognitivists must also admit what Raz has called the "reason-dependent character of desires."

> . . . agents do not wish to have their desires satisfied if their belief in the existence of a reason for their desires is unfounded. One does not wish to have the medicine one desires if it does not have the medicinal properties that one believes to be the only reason for having it.[22]

Noncognitivists about ends seldom claim that a person's ends are brute passions. Instead, they postulate that ends are the actual preferences a person has after consideration of what she believes to be the facts. Or else they postulate that ends are the counterfactual preferences a person would have if she had all the relevant information.[23] So the noncognitivist must admit that motivational attitudes can depend on beliefs about the natural world. A person will modify her preferences and desires in response to changing beliefs about the world. If someone's beliefs about the world were different, then her motivations would be different. We may not know the details of the mechanism that accounts for the belief dependence of desires, but the noncognitivist must allow that it exists.

The cognitivist about ends will borrow this mechanism to give an account of the motivational force of evaluations, for whatever mechanism accounts for the dependence of desires on beliefs about the natural world can also account for the dependence of desires on beliefs about value. The noncognitivist about ends is perfectly willing to admit that someone's beliefs about what is valuable will depend on what she finds herself desiring. This direction of dependence makes desire and preference primary, and evaluations mere expressions of preference. However, the other direction of dependence, the dependence of desires on beliefs about value, makes cognitive states primary, and evaluation a cognitive activity. Brink gives the following account of motivation in his sustained argument for moral cognitivism:

> We all begin with certain ends and desires; we are attached to, and have desires for, particular people, activities, and states of affairs more than others. Now these ends and desires reflect *evaluative judgments*. In the case of most things we desire, we desire them *because we think these things valuable*. This is true of our preferences for many activities and relationships as well as for states of the world. This sort of value-laden explanation may not be required for all desires. For instance, gustatory

preferences do not seem to presuppose the greater value of the preferred smell or taste. But even if there is no need for value-laden explanations of gustatory preferences, this is not the case with many desires;
they require value-laden explanations. At least part of the explanation
of the fact that I want to be a professional philosopher involves my belief that philosophy is a valuable activity; I would not have this desire if
I did not think that philosophy was a valuable activity. Part of the explanation of my wanting to relieve my neighbor's suffering is that I
think pain and suffering are bad; if I were somehow to come to think
that there was nothing objectionable about pain and suffering, I would
probably have very little concern about my neighbor's situation.[24]

Some of our desires, like a preference for chocolate ice cream, are just
brute preferences, and a simple noncognitivism makes sense of these.
But more complex desires, like a choice of profession, are dependent
on our beliefs about what is valuable. And it is these complex desires,
not our brute preferences, which deserve to be called our ends in life.

It is the direction of explanatory dependence that shows whether an
author thinks that preferences or beliefs about value are primary. This
is our test. An author is a pure cognitivist about the good if he or she
thinks that all preferences must be explained by a prior belief in what
is valuable. An author has a mixed theory if he or she thinks that some
preferences depend on beliefs about value. Rawls and Dworkin both
have mixed theories. Dworkin explicitly concedes that our most important ends are fundamentally beliefs about value. For Dworkin, ethics
"has two departments: morality and well-being. The question of morality is how we should treat others; the question of well-being is how we
should live to make good lives for ourselves."[25] So someone's conception of the good is his sense of well-being:

> Someone's sense of well-being includes preferences that define his self-
> interest in what they often call the narrow sense: his preferences for
> money, pleasure and security, for example. It also includes, and more
> fundamentally, his more general beliefs about what kinds of life it is
> good or desirable for him to lead: what kinds of experiences he should
> aim to have, what kind of associations he should try to develop, what
> character he should hope to have.[26]

Dworkin gives a mixed cognitivist/noncognitivist account of the nature
of a conception of the good, with the cognitive components more central
and fundamental. Dworkin distinguishes between volitional and critical
interests. Someone satisfies his volitional interests when he "has or
achieves what in fact he wants." Someone satisfies his critical interests by
"having or achieving what he *should* want"[27] (emphasis in original). For

himself he gives avoiding dental work as an example of a volitional interest, and having a close relationship with his children as an example of a critical interest. A critical interest is clearly an ethical interest and is best seen as embodied in ethical beliefs or convictions. Of his children, he writes that

> I do not think that having a close relationship with my children is important just because I happen to want it; on the contrary, I want it because I believe a life without such relationships is a worse one.[28]

Here the direction of the explanatory dependence is clear. For a critical interest, the motivating desire depends on beliefs about what is valuable. This dependence is again clear when he discusses the cultivation of tastes:

> We can, it is true, cultivate tastes at some level. We can try to be the kind of person who likes classical music or skiing. But if we decide to try to acquire these tastes, we do so only in virtue of a conviction we have that it is desirable to be a person with the tastes in question, and we do not choose that conviction, or any of the other convictions that make up our personality, any more than we decide to acquire other beliefs we have.[29]

Dworkin believes that this dependence of motivation on beliefs about value is contingent, not conceptual:

> . . . people generally want what they think it is in their critical interests to have. If they think it is in their critical interests to have close relationships with their children, they will want to do so. But that is not inevitably the case. At least part of the complex problem philosophers call *akrasia* arises because people do not actually want what they believe it in their critical interest to have. So I may think that my life would be a better life, in the critical sense, if I worked less and spent more time with my family, and yet I find that I actually don't want to, or don't want to enough.[30]

For Dworkin, the dependence of wants on beliefs about what is valuable is an empirical one that breaks down when people's convictions are not strong enough to determine the wants and preferences that move them to action.

Rawls appears to have started with an account of the good as something akin to the economist's view of preference satisfaction, but he has modified and amplified this account in such a way as to cross the line from noncognitivism to cognitivism about many of our more complex and central ends. Rawls never said that someone's conception of the good is a bundle of actual preferences. Instead, he says in *A Theory of Justice* that someone's conception of the good is "expressed by a rational plan of life." Someone's plan of life is "what he intends to do in his life" and is what characterizes "the coherent, systematic purposes of the individual, what makes him a conscious, unified moral person."[31]The rational plan of life for a person is the one "which he would choose with deliberative rationality," where it is assumed that

> . . . there are no errors of calculation or reasoning, and that the facts are correctly assessed. I suppose also that the agent is under no misconceptions as to what he really wants. In most cases anyway, when he achieves his aim, he does not find that he no longer wants it and wishes that he had done something else instead. Moreover, the agent's knowledge of his situation and the consequences of carrying out each plan is presumed to be accurate and complete. No relevant circumstances are left out of account. Thus the best plan for an individual is the one which he would adopt if he possessed full information.[32]

This hypothetical plan is the "objectively rational plan for him and determines his real good."

> But if the agent does the best that a rational person can do with the information available to him, then the plan he follows is a subjectively rational plan. His choice may be an unhappy one, but if so it is because his beliefs are understandably mistaken or his knowledge insufficient.[33]

The good life for a person is then "the successful execution of a rational plan of life."[34]Now the point I want to emphasize is that, for Rawls, the noncognitive, motivational intentions, purposes, and desires that compose someone's conception of the good are rational in that they depend on cognitive beliefs about himself and about the world. Our good is something we can be mistaken about, and we are mistaken when our conception of the good depends on false beliefs. Insofar as we have an interest in getting our conception of the good right, we have an interest in both self-knowledge and knowledge about the world. For Rawls, "the value of knowing the facts is derived from their relation to the successful execution of rational plans . . . there are no grounds for attributing intrinsic value to having true beliefs."[35]

So for Rawls, purposes and preferences are dependent on beliefs about the world and about the self. This is perfectly compatible with a Humean moral psychology. But his moral psychology becomes non-Humean when he argues that conceptions of the good are further constrained by people's capacity for a sense of justice. In this, Rawls differs from the utilitarians. For utilitarians, the satisfaction of any informed preference has value, despite the preference being a selfish one, requiring more than a fair share of resources, or an unjust one, requiring the violation of the rights and liberties of others. Utilitarians count all such preferences equally in their decision procedures and then rely on their aggregation and maximizing procedures to permit only states of affairs in which fair and just preferences happen to get satisfied. By contrast, Rawls writes:

> The principles of right, and so of justice, put limits on which satisfactions have value; they impose restrictions on what are reasonable conceptions of one's good. In drawing up plans and in deciding on aspirations men are to take these constraints into account.[36]

So people's conceptions of the good are dependent not only on their beliefs about the world, but also on their beliefs about the principles of right and justice. In his claim that people are ethically responsible for their ends, Rawls crosses the line into a cognitivist moral psychology:

> In general, it is a necessary feature of moral feelings, and part of what distinguishes them from the natural attitudes, that the person's explanation of his experience invokes a moral concept and its associated principles. His account of his feeling makes reference to an acknowledged right or wrong.[37]

In the case of moral beliefs about how to treat others, Rawls is explicit in thinking that motivations depend on and are explained by moral convictions. People's motivations depend on their beliefs about moral obligation.

Rawls reiterates and reinforces these factual and moral constraints on conceptions of the good in his most recent work. In *Political Liberalism* he lists three kinds of desires that may enter into a person's conception of the good: object-dependent, principle-dependent, and conception-dependent desires. Object-dependent desires, firstly, are desires where "the object of desire, or the state of affairs that fulfils it, can be described without the use of any moral conceptions, or reasonable or rational principles."[38]These include desires for food and drink, social status, and attachments to others. Principle-dependent desires, secondly, are desires that depend on rational principles, like beliefs about the best means to our ends, and on reasonable principles, like beliefs about justice and fairness. Conception-dependent desires, finally, are desires that depend on conceptions or ideals of ourselves. I want to stress here Rawls's acknowledgement that at least some of the desires that are the components of someone's conception of the good depend on her beliefs about principles and ideals. Rawls notes

> . . . the obvious non-Humean character of this account of motivation and how it runs counter to attempts to limit the kinds of motives people may have. Once we grant – what seems plainly true – that there exist principle-dependent and conception-dependent desires, along with desires to realize various political and moral ideals, then the class of possible motives is wide open. Capable of reason and judgment, we can understand complex religious and philosophical, moral and political doctrines of right and justice, as well as doctrines of the good. We may find ourselves drawn to the conceptions and ideals that both the right and the good express. How is one to fix limits on what people might be moved by in thought and deliberation and hence may act from?[39]

I take it, then, that Rawls is a cognitivist regarding at least some components of people's conceptions of the good. True, some of our simpler ends in life may be simple preferences, and our judgement that something is valuable may be simply an expression of our object-dependent desire for it. But our more complex and more central ends are ideals about ourselves, beliefs about the best way to lead our lives. In Rawls's moral psychology, motivations to action depend not only on what people want but also on what they believe to be valuable.

A moral psychology in which desire depends on beliefs about what is valuable gives a better account of people's ultimate ends than does a noncognitivist account. Liberals have traditionally been concerned with tolerance regarding religious matters. In such matters, it seems false, if not insulting, to say that a religious person's belief that a religious life is valuable depends on her preference for such a life. Rather, she believes her religious life is valuable because she thinks her belief to be true, and her motivating desire, or choice, of such a life depends on her belief that a religious life is the most valuable one.

Rawls suggests the Aristotelian position that a person's highest-order interest is in exercising her capacities for a conception of the good and a sense of justice.[40]Dworkin disagrees with Rawls's view on our highest-order interests:

> Our highest-order interest is not an interest in exercising a capacity because we find that we have it . . . but rather we develop and train capacities of the sort Rawls describes because we have a certain interest. The only answer we can accept to the question of our highest-order interest is something like this. It lies in having as good a life as possible, a life that has in it as much of what a life should have. Almost everyone acts as if he or she had that interest, and it is necessary to assume it in

45

order to make sense of the kind of deliberation or judgement we exercise at important moments in our lives.[41]

According to Dworkin, a person's highest-order interests lie in leading as good a life as possible. Granting that a life led because of the threat of force cannot be the best life, then a person must lead her life on her own, according to her own conception of the good. A person must first form and then carry out her conception of the good. To carry out her conception of the good she must be supported by the social and cultural bases of self-respect. For her to lead as good a life as possible, her conception of the good must consist in true beliefs about her good. To ensure the authenticity and genuineness of her conception of the good, not only must she have true beliefs about her good, but also she must know her good. So a person has a highest-order interest in knowing her good. A person does not come to know her good in isolation. Instead, she comes to know her good against a background of values implicit in her culture. Because she is a finite being, she cannot adequately reflect on all the values she acquires from her cultural background. She will simply accept many beliefs about value without remarking on them. Reasonable people will disagree on the truth or falsity of many of these background beliefs. However, reasonable liberals will not disagree about the falsity of the belief that people are of unequal inherent moral worth. If she acquires this false background belief through her culture, then she is a victim of cultural oppression. Her cultural membership can harm her highest-order interest in knowing her good. The harm done by an oppressive culture will not be a harm done by any individual, but will instead be an accumulative harm. The nature of accumulative harms, and how liberalism can accommodate them, will be the topic of the last two chapters.

I wish to emphasize that the value of a culture is ambiguous. On the one hand it can be beneficial to our interest in knowing the good. This is the side of culture of which Kymlicka reminds us. Cultural membership is "a good in its capacity of providing meaningful options for us, and aiding our ability to judge for ourselves the value of our life plans."[42] To have a cultural structure is to have a context for making meaningful choices about how to live. On the other hand, culture can harm our interest in knowing the good. The truth of Kymlicka's claim about the benefits of cultural membership must not detract attention from the sometimes harmful character of particular cultural practices. A patriarchal culture is harmful when it engenders in women false beliefs about their self-worth. The task set by our interest in knowing the good is not to destroy culture but to reform it. Human beings cannot live their lives outside a cultural framework, but we have to make sure that this framework is liberating and not oppressive.

3

THE MORAL EQUALITY OF PERSONS

A T the deepest levels of its theory of justice, egalitarian liberalism is committed to the moral equality of persons. A person's belief that she is morally less worthy than others is thus false, as is another person's belief that he is morally more important than others. People who form conceptions of the good that either incorporate such beliefs or depend on them will fail to attain knowledge of their good. I have been arguing that a culture which leads to this situation harms its members. However, people seldom explicitly avow the moral inequality of other persons. Many, if not most, people in modern democratic states sincerely believe in the moral equality of people who differ in terms of sex, race, or degree of ability. Yet sexist, racist, and ableist attitudes flourish at another level. Classist and heterosexist attitudes are perhaps more overt; open disparagement of the poor, for example, is common in political discourse. Explicit beliefs about moral inequality seldom feature in practical deliberation. People do not often think to themselves, "Other people are entitled to have X, but I don't matter as much ethically as other people do, so, though it would be good for my life, I don't believe that having X should be one of my ends." So the question of how inegalitarian beliefs get incorporated into people's beliefs about value is an important one.

There are two ways to be inegalitarian. One is to deny the moral equality of persons openly. The other is to affirm equality, but to have the wrong interpretation of what "equality" means. The Roman Catholic church, for example, no doubt sees itself as upholding the moral equality of persons, but what it means by "equality" is weak. Men and women are equal in their hopes of salvation, but they are not considered equal in their access to the priesthood. The meaning of moral equality is contested. Nozick, a libertarian liberal, and Rawls, an egalitarian liberal, both sincerely believe in the moral equality of persons, but they have very different theories about the meaning of "equality." According to Nozick, moral equality means that persons have equal rights of self-ownership and the liberties, property rights, and contractual arrangements that follow from self-ownership.[1] In contrast, to Rawls, moral equality means respecting each person's interest in forming, revising, and pursuing a just conception of the good by distributing fair shares of all-purpose goods (importantly: income, the basic liberties, and opportunities for careers).

Egalitarian liberalism has a particular conception of the moral equality of persons. In this chapter, I shall use Rawls's work to explicate what that theory is and to show how the theory extends naturally to the issue of cultural oppression. What many people mean by "equality" often will be different from what egalitarian liberals mean; so according to the egalitarian liberal view, their beliefs are false. At the end of this chapter, I shall look at how cultural membership can lead people to form conceptions of the good that depend on false beliefs about equality.

EXTENDING RAWLS'S THEORY OF MORAL EQUALITY

A theory of moral equality is a theory of sameness and of difference. Its first task is to specify in what respect people should be treated the same. It has to answer the question, Equality of what? Various answers have been proposed for the dimensions along which people should be treated the same: welfare, resources, income, liberties, advantage, satisfaction of needs, consideration of desert, opportunities for welfare, capabilities for functioning, satisfaction of their interests in leading a good life. A theory of equality has to say what is the best *measure* of equality. The question of how people should be treated equally has received much attention, and, indeed, egalitarian theories of distributive justice are probably the most extensively developed theories of justice between human beings available in philosophy.[2] I do not propose to resolve the measurement issue here; nothing I say will assume the truth of any particular theory. Instead, I shall discuss the other task of a theory of moral equality, which is to specify what is a legitimate reason for treating people differently. Equality does not always demand sameness. Though egalitarians might wish equal medical treatment for all, as Benn and Peters quip, "we should not wish rheumatic patients to be treated like diabetics."[3] A good part of the content of a theory of equality is negative; it involves saying that such and such is not a good reason for treating people differently. A theory of moral equality must include a theory of the *grounds* of equality. This is the aspect of Rawls's theory of moral equality with which I shall be dealing.

Rawls thinks that we should treat persons as moral equals. This would contrast, for example, with a utilitarian theory of justice holding that we must treat people's preferences equally, not the people themselves. Human beings have many contingent features that might serve to characterize their moral personhood: height, weight, intelligence, hair colour, and so forth. So Rawls has to specify what he means by moral personality. He does this initially by the traditional method of looking for what differentiates humans from animals:

> I turn now to the basis of equality, the features of human beings in virtue of which they are to be treated in accordance with the principles of justice. Our conduct toward animals is not regulated by these principles, or so it is generally believed. On what grounds do we distinguish between mankind and other living beings and regard the constraints of justice as holding only in our relations to human persons?[4]

Since the advent of interest in animal rights and environmental ethics, this technique of argumentation does not have the rhetorical force that it once enjoyed. As Rawls acknowledges for his own theory, egalitarian theories of justice, which are sophisticated discussions of justice between humans, do not extend easily to cover issues concerning the just treatment of animals and of the environment.[5] Rawls answers the question of how to distinguish persons from other living things with a theory that assigns persons two moral powers:

> The natural answer seems to be that it is precisely the moral persons who are entitled to equal justice. Moral persons are distinguished by two features: first they are capable of having (and are assumed to have) a conception of their good (as expressed by a rational plan of life); and second they are capable of having (and are assumed to acquire) a sense of justice, a normally effective desire to apply and to act upon the principles of justice, at least to a certain minimum degree. . . . We see, then, that the capacity for moral personality is sufficient condition for being entitled to equal justice.[6]

In later work, he also talks of "viewing each person as a moral person moved by two highest-order interests, namely, the interest to realise and to exercise the two powers of moral personality."[7] Treating persons as moral equals implies respecting equally their two highest-order interests. Rawls's conception of moral equality operates at the highest levels of his theory, as an axiom rather than a theorem. In his most recent *Political Liberalism*, it is a fundamental idea of a democratic society that "having these powers to the requisite minimum degree to be fully cooperating members of society makes persons equal."[8] The parties to the hypothetical social contract that determines the principles of justice also assume it, for the purpose behind the conditions of the original position is "to represent equality between human beings as moral persons, as creatures having a conception of their good and capable of a sense of justice."[9]

Respecting the moral equality of persons is an extremely abstract conception of equality. We can make it more concrete in two ways. The first is by detailing the ways in which persons are to be treated the same – of what it is that they are to get equal amounts. The second is by detailing the grounds on which persons may, or may not, claim differential treatment. It is this latter aspect of equality in its negative form (i.e., identifying grounds that do not legitimate differential entitlements) which will be of interest here. Liberal equality originated in reaction to the inequalities of the aristocratic state, inequalities in rights and privileges based on blood and birthright. The liberal theory of moral equality begins with the denial that parentage is a relevant ground for differential treatment. Rawls generalizes this reaction against aristocratic class distinctions in his denial that natural ability can form grounds for differential desert. In explaining his egalitarian principle of distribution, he writes as follows:

> Perhaps some will think that the person with greater natural endowments deserves those assets and the superior character that made their development possible. Because he is more worthy in this sense, he deserves the greater advantages that he could achieve with them. This view, however, is surely incorrect. It seems to be one of the fixed points of our considered judgements that no one deserves his place in the distribution of native endowments, any more than one deserves one's initial starting place in society. The assertion that a man deserves the superior character that enables him to make the effort to cultivate his abilities is equally problematic; for his character depends in large part upon fortunate family and social circumstances for which he can claim no credit. The notion of desert seems not to apply in these cases. . . .
> But these intuitive considerations help to clarify the nature of the principle and the sense in which it is egalitarian.[10]

The possession of natural abilities is just as "arbitrary from a moral point of view"[11] as the assertion that people deserve differential entitlement based on birth in an aristocratic society. Therefore, people do not deserve more because of their natural abilities.

We can plausibly extend the egalitarian liberal interpretation of moral equality by extending Rawls's critique of aristocratic and meritocratic distributions. Much of the content of Rawls's commitment to the equal moral worth of persons is negative; it is the denial that people deserve, are entitled to, or may legitimately expect differential treatment of their highest-order interests in leading a good life simply because they are more talented. Natural talent, like birth and breeding, is not something for which a person can claim responsibility. Natural talent is thus a factor that is arbitrary from the moral point of view, and thus it cannot be a ground for differential desert or entitlement. Similarly, a lesser natural ability is not something for which a person can be held responsible or treated differently. A meritocracy, like an aristocracy, is unjust. Yet other factors, other natural characteristics of persons, such as skin colour, sex, age, disabilities, ethnic background, and sexual orientation, are similarly factors for which people cannot be held responsible.[12] So, as a natural extension of Rawls's view of the moral equality of persons, treating people's highest-order interests differently on any of these grounds would be arbitrary from a moral point of view. The egalitarian liberal interpretation of moral equality should be a strong one; any view of equality that grounds differential treatment of people's highest-order interests on arbitrary factors is a false view.[13]

It is at this point that the egalitarian liberal view of equality connects to the oppression of groups. A group can be defined in at least two ways: A group can be defined on the basis of its members sharing a common conception of the good life, or a common ethical identity. A group can also be defined on the basis of its members sharing a common natural feature, physical characteristic, or historical origin. Sometimes the two definitions can coincide, as when people of Latvian descent share a way of life, or when African-Americans develop a common identity. A liberal state is tolerant when it treats groups equally by being neutral regarding their shared conceptions of the good. A liberal state is egalitarian when it treats groups equally by not permitting shared natural features to affect entitlements to a good life.

It is the second way of thinking about groups that allows oppression. Membership in a group (women, blacks, Hispanics, Jews, Asians, aboriginals, gays, lesbians, senior citizens, working-class people, poor people, mentally or physically challenged people) is not voluntary like membership in an association. It is on the basis of historical and natural circumstances that people place themselves into groups, and they are also placed by others on the same basis. These circumstances are arbitrary from a moral point of view and are not legitimate grounds for desert and entitlement. In an analysis of oppression, Marilyn Frye, whose metaphor of the cage was quoted earlier, describes the importance of natural features as criteria for group membership:

> The image of the cage helps convey one aspect of the systematic nature of oppression. Another is the selection of occupants of the cages, and an analysis of this aspect also helps account for the invisibility of the oppression of women. . . . When you question why you are being blocked, why this barrier is in your path, the answer has not to do with individual talent or merit, handicap or failure; it has to do with your membership in some category understood as a "natural" or "physical" category. The "inhabitant" of the "cage" is not an individual but a group, all those of a certain category. If an individual is oppressed, it is in virtue of being a member of a group or category of people that is systematically reduced, molded, immobilized. Thus, to recognize a person as oppressed, one has to see that individual *as* belonging to a group of a certain sort.[14]

The various sorts of oppression that people face – racism, sexism, classism, ageism, ableism, heterosexism – presuppose assigning people to groups based on some physical characteristic. Each *ism* is based on a natural feature that is arbitrary from a moral point of view. So any belief that someone is less (or more) deserving of exercising her capacity for forming, revising, and pursuing a conception of the good because of her possession of this natural feature must be seen as *false* by the egalitarian liberal.

A culture that leads people to form such false beliefs is an oppressive one. It will contain what Karen Warren calls a "logic of domination."

> A *conceptual framework* is a set of *basic* beliefs, values, attitudes, and assumptions which shape and reflect how one views oneself and one's world. It is a socially constructed lens through which we perceive ourselves and others. It is affected by such factors as gender, race, class, age, affectional orientation, nationality, and religious background. Some conceptual frameworks are oppressive. An *oppressive conceptual framework* is one that explains, justifies, and maintains relationships of domination and subordination. When an oppressive conceptual framework is *patriarchal,* it explains, justifies, and maintains the subordination of women by men. . . . A logic of domination is not *just* a logical structure. It also involves a substantive value system, since an ethical premise is needed to permit or sanction the "just" subordination of that which is subordinate. This justification typically is given on grounds of some alleged characteristic (e.g., rationality) which the dominant (e.g., men) have and the subordinate (e.g., women) lack.[15]

The members of a culture may think of themselves as committed to the moral equality of persons, but if they harbour views of differential desert and entitlement that are based on arbitrary factors, they are not committed to moral equality as egalitarian liberalism should understand it. The social transmission of false beliefs about distributional equality contributes to the cultural oppression of groups. Cultures transmit beliefs that certain sorts of lives are appropriate only for members of certain groups, as defined by morally arbitrary features. Examples are familiar. The view that one's family status at birth should determine occupation and life prospects is constitutive of a caste society. The views that nursing is not an appropriate profession for men and that men should not stay at home to bring up children are both widespread. The view that women who participate actively in public meetings are pushy and aggressive is common.

No liberal, including Rawls, would want to say that all aspects of persons are arbitrary from a moral point of view. Liberals see individuals as having some degree of moral autonomy, and part of the idea of moral autonomy is that individuals must bear responsibility for their choices. Egalitarian liberalism must, therefore, make a distinction between those aspects of a person for which he can be held morally responsible – his choices and the risks he voluntarily assumes – and those aspects that are beyond his control – his circumstances and his brute luck – and for which he cannot be held responsible. Rawls's concept of moral personality incorporates the necessity for this distinction. In discussing what justice requires regarding people with expensive tastes, people who choose conceptions of the good which require more than a fair share of primary goods, he writes:

> . . . as moral persons citizens have some part in forming and cultivating their final ends and preferences. It is not by itself an objection to the use of primary goods that it does not accommodate those with expensive tastes. One must argue in addition that it is unreasonable, if not unjust, to hold such persons responsible for their preferences and to require them to make out as best they can. But to argue this seems to presuppose that citizens' preferences are beyond their control as propensities or cravings which simply happen. Citizens seem to be regarded as passive carriers of desires. The use of primary goods, however, relies on a capacity to assume responsibility for our ends. This capacity is part of the moral power to form, to revise, and rationally to pursue a conception of the good.[16]

What it is to be a person, in Rawls's view, includes the moral power to form, revise, and pursue ends. Just as a person can be held responsible for revising what ends she forms, she can also be held responsible for what ends she chooses to pursue. If she pursues unjust ends, this is not arbitrary from a moral point of view. This allows us to distinguish between the ethical values, and the just deserts, of a Mother Theresa who gives her life to others and a drug addict who steals more than his share of what is available to support his chosen way of life.

Rawls's discussion of the grounds of equality makes it obvious that racist, sexist, ableist, and aristocratic theories of equality are false ones, for the grounds on which they argue for differential treatment – skin colour, biological sex, genetic endowment, birth and parentage – are not characteristics for which people are responsible. Such grounds are arbitrary from a moral point of view. Meritocratic theories of equality, however, are more difficult. In a meritocratic theory the grounds for differential claims are complex. The grounds for difference include both natural talent and effort. The effort someone makes both "depends in large part upon fortunate family and social circumstances for which he can claim no credit" and depends on choices about work and leisure that are part of his conception of the good. A choice of an unfair share of leisure is an expensive taste with regard to contributing a fair share to the social product, and thus Rawls would consider it a preference for which people must be held responsible. People will vary in terms of the degree to which they choose to be lazy and the degree to which their lower levels of effort are due to depression, lack of self-esteem, or enculturated hopelessness. A given person may differ along these dimensions at various times in her life. Rawls's response is not to say that people can never be held responsible for the effort they make, but instead to note that deciding to what degree people should be held responsible for their efforts is not a workable policy.[17]

> The precept which seems intuitively to come closest to rewarding moral desert is that of distribution according to effort, or perhaps better, conscientious effort. Once again, however, it seems clear that the effort a person is willing to make is influenced by his natural abilities and skills and the alternatives open to him. The better endowed are more likely, other things equal, to strive conscientiously, and there seems to be no way to discount for their greater good fortune. The idea of rewarding desert is impracticable.[18]

Even if distinguishing the chosen and the circumstantial aspects of effort is impractical, Rawls's response – to treat all aspects as morally arbitrary circumstances – is not the only possible response. The fiscal conservative is inclined to make the opposite generalization: Some of the poor are feckless. It is impractical to distinguish who is and who is not.

Therefore, let us make all the poor responsible for not having tried hard enough. Plausibly, however, the number of people who are poor because they are feckless is very much smaller than the number of people who are poor either because they lack the preconditions of effort or because they possess less natural ability. So we shall go less wrong in treating people as moral equals by making the Rawlsian assumption than by making the fiscal-conservative assumption. A similar problem arises in the egalitarian treatment of heterosexism. For some people, a gay or lesbian life may be a matter of affectional preference, a choice they make, while for many others it will be a matter of affectional orientation, something they find out about themselves. Affectional preference is a matter of tolerance for the egalitarian liberal, but affectional orientation is a matter of equality. The intolerant social conservative is likely to argue that since distinguishing preference from orientation is impractical, discrimination is legitimate. The liberal may reply on both toleration grounds and equality grounds. Ableism presupposes a similar distinction, but one that it is more practical to make. Egalitarian liberalism may legitimately treat differently the claims of someone whose disability is a consequence of his choice to drive recklessly and the claims of someone whose disability is a consequence of her genetic luck.

Rawls's treatment of effort as a morally arbitrary characteristic of people is based on the assumption that there is no practical way of disentangling choice and circumstance. Nevertheless, consistency with egalitarian liberal ideals requires working on the disentangling problem and adopting a better solution if one is available. This concern motivates Dworkin's concern to treat people as moral equals in a way that is both insensitive to their natural endowments and sensitive to their chosen ambitions.[19] His complex theory of equality of resources involves a hypothetical insurance scheme in which people are insured against the lack of natural abilities. The level of social insurance justifies a progressive and redistributive income tax that relieves the inegalitarian effects of a market system. I shall not be concerned here with the details; the important point is that, for consistency, the egalitarian liberal should seek a practical way of disentangling ambition and endowment.

This point is relevant, for identical reasons, to a similar problem that afflicts Rawls's account of responsibility for choices. Cohen raises the problem this way:

> But it is not easy to reconcile what Rawls says about effort with what he says about tastes. . . . On my reading of it, effort is partly praiseworthy and partly not, but we cannot separate the parts, and the indicated

policy consequence is to ignore effort as a claim to reward. Now, the passage about tastes begins with the thought that "citizens have *some* part in forming and cultivating their final ends and preferences," though it ends by assigning a more wholesale responsibility for them to citizens. If we stay with the opening thought, then we can wonder why partial responsibility for effort attracts no reward at all while (merely) partial responsibility for expensive taste formation attracts a full penalty (and those who keep their tastes modest reap a welfare reward). And if we shift to the wholesale responsibility motif, we can wonder why beings who are only in a limited way responsible for the effort they put in may be held wholly responsible for how their tastes develop.[20]

Now presumably a major reason that citizens have only some, and not the whole, part in "forming and cultivating their final ends and preferences" is their membership in a particular culture. Because reflecting critically on all of their ends is psychologically impossible, they will take up some of them unreflectively from their cultural background. Some of these ends may be unjust – preferences for more than a fair share, an enjoyment of discrimination – and it is these ends that Rawls holds persons responsible for revising:

> An individual who finds that he enjoys seeing others in positions of lesser liberty understands that he has no claim whatever to this enjoyment. The pleasure he takes in others' deprivations is wrong in itself: it is a satisfaction which requires the violation of a principle to which he would agree in the original position. The principles of right, and so of justice, put limits on which satisfactions have value: they impose restrictions on what are reasonable conceptions of one's good. In drawing up plans and deciding on aspirations men are to take these constraints into account. Hence in justice as fairness one does not take men's propensities and inclinations as given, whatever they are, and then seek the best way to fulfill them. Rather, their desires and aspirations are restricted from the outset by the principles of justice which specify the boundaries that men's systems of ends must respect. We can express this by saying that in justice as fairness the concept of right is prior to that of the good. A just social system defines the scope within which individuals must develop their aims, and it provides a framework of rights and opportunities and the means of satisfaction within and by the use of which these ends may be equitably pursued. The priority of justice is accounted for, in part, by holding that the interests requiring the violation of justice have no value. Having no merit in the first place, they cannot override its claims.[21]

These considerations put the egalitarian liberal in a difficult position. People do take up inegalitarian ethical beliefs about entitlement and desert from their cultural environment. Reflecting critically on all their beliefs is psychologically impossible for them. Yet egalitarian liberalism holds people responsible for revising all their inegalitarian distributional beliefs. Even a committed egalitarian can unreflectively harbour a particular inegalitarian distributional belief: "Because of my gender, living in such and such a way is not appropriate for me." The solution, I think, is this: If the egalitarian liberal state is going to hold people responsible for revising false beliefs about unequal desert and entitlement, then it must itself take responsibility for people's cultural environment. It must ensure a cultural environment that continually exposes and challenges inegalitarian ethical beliefs, rather than encouraging or sustaining them. This project of cultural reform will also prevent or reduce cultural oppression, the social transmission of false ethical beliefs, which harms people's interest in knowing the good. Rawls's theory of equality requires making a distinction between those aspects of a person for which she can and cannot be held morally responsible. Preserving an attractive notion of choice and responsibility requires egalitarian liberalism to reform the cultural environment in which people deliberate about ends. Otherwise, holding people responsible for their choices will be impractical.

The egalitarian liberal theory of equality entails that physical features of persons, ones for which they cannot be held morally responsible, may not be used as reasons for differential treatment of their fundamental interests. Nevertheless, on the face of it, most egalitarians will have a strong intuition to the contrary for a certain range of cases. Sen and Dworkin have urged it as an objection to Rawls's egalitarian theory of distribution that in giving the same shares to persons who face larger obstacles to their pursuit of the good, it does not treat people as moral equals.[22] For example, someone who is physically disabled from birth faces, through no fault of her own, a much more difficult time in pursuing her conception of the good than does someone who has been luckier in the genetic lottery. Rawls might suggest that the disabled person be responsible for revising her conception of the good to make do with the life she can afford on the same resources as luckier persons, but this demand is unreasonable. In such a case, characteristics for which a person cannot be held morally responsible are good egalitarian grounds for differential treatment.

However, I think we have to be clear that it is not the person's physical disability by itself that is the ground for differential treatment. We are not arguing that simply because she has a certain physical characteristic she is therefore entitled to different treatment. Instead, we are arguing that (1) she is a moral person, with a highest-order interest in exercising her capacity to form, revise, and pursue a conception of the good, and (2) as a factual premise, her disability is an obstacle to her exercising this capacity, and therefore (3) the moral equality of persons requires special treatment of her interests. The premise of moral equality carries the moral weight in this argument, not the assumption that the disabled deserve more because of their disabilities. Notice that if we try to justify a meritocracy by substituting an analogous factual premise, namely, that (2') someone's natural gifts are an obstacle to his exercising the capacity to form, revise, and pursue a conception of the good, the factual premise is implausible.

So equality grounds do exist for difference as well as for sameness. Differential treatment must be justified through a positive equality premise, and not simply by the natural features of persons that are often used to characterize groups. On the liberal conception of tolerance, the state must be neutral between competing conceptions of the good. A group cannot legitimately claim differential treatment simply on the ground that the conception of the good shared by its members is expensive. The liberal state will not compensate members of a religious group, for example, whose beliefs require the construction of expensive monuments and temples. Yet groups can legitimately claim differential treatment on equality grounds. Because equality is prior to tolerance in the foundations of egalitarian liberalism, such equality considerations can override state neutrality. Suppose we have a society in which the majority of its members overtly, but superficially, avow racial equality. At a deeper level, however, the majority members make unexamined and inegalitarian distributional assumptions and harbour false beliefs about the racial minority. For example, they might have the false factual belief that members of the minority are statistically less intelligent than members of the majority and have the false ethical belief that greater intelligence is a ground for differential desert. The members of the racial majority will make choices about hiring, layoffs, and promotions based on these false beliefs. The aggregative effect of these choices will be an *economic environment* in which the racial minority will face statistically obvious discrimination. Because the racial majority avows and legislates racial equality, there will be no overt discrimination. Nonetheless, it will remain that members of the racial minority will face obstacles to the pursuit of their good that are not faced by the majority. On equality grounds there will be good reason for compensation for these obstacles, that is, for affirmative-action programmes.

59

To continue this example, another result of the aggregative choices, behaviours, and expressive acts of the majority will be a *cultural environment* that sustains false distributional assumptions. Members of the minority race will be harmed if they form conceptions of the good which incorporate or depend on applying these assumptions to themselves. The oppressive cultural environment poses an obstacle to the exercise of the moral power to form and revise a conception of the good. I am going to argue later that one of the best strategies for reforming such an inegalitarian and oppressive cultural environment is for the state to fund the activities of individuals and associations who are actively contesting and encouraging the examination of such assumptions. The members of these associations will share a conception of the good which involves agitating for equality. Funding these associations involves giving a larger share of resources to members of a group with a particular shared conception of the good. However, funding is not given to these associations as a reward for the truth of their beliefs; it is given to facilitate their role in removing obstacles to equality in the cultural environment. On neutrality grounds, as usually understood, the liberal state ought not to pursue this strategy. On equality grounds, however, this is an excellent strategy for reducing the obstacles faced by the minority. For the egalitarian liberal, equality must be prior to neutrality.

EQUALITY, SOCIAL MEANINGS, AND DELIBERATION

In the preceding section I have partially sketched the egalitarian liberal theory of moral equality. I say "partially" because I have deliberately avoided discussing how we should measure equality. Instead, I have discussed the grounds on which egalitarian liberalism should evaluate claims for differential consideration of people's fundamental interests. Rawls begins with a theory of what is morally significant about persons: their capacity to form, revise, and pursue a conception of the good and to integrate this with their sense of justice. Morally, equality then requires distinguishing between a person's choices, for which she is morally responsible, and her circumstances, which are arbitrary from a moral point of view. So we may reasonably deny a person equal treatment on the grounds that she has chosen to be a thief, but not on the grounds that her circumstances include her sex or her skin colour. The Rawlsian theory of moral equality entails that certain statements (e.g., "Because I am a woman, I should not expect to become a farmer.") are false. Unfortunately, statements like that last one may exist as unexamined ethical assumptions in a person's deliberations about how to live her life. In this section, I want to discuss how such distributional assumptions get incorporated into a person's belief structure and what effect they have on her search for knowledge about how to live.

A person can have false beliefs about moral equality in many different ways. He can believe, wrongly, that all persons are not morally equal. This form of inegalitarianism is blatant and obvious. Less obvious is the situation in which a person believes in moral equality, but what he means by "the moral equality of persons" is too weak by egalitarian liberal standards. Such a person might believe, for example, that if everyone can vote and all are equal before the law, his society has achieved moral equality. Discrimination on the grounds of sex and race is then permissible in the marketplace. Egalitarian liberalism must see this theory as wrong, and many of the person's distributional beliefs as false. Even less obvious is a case in which someone subscribes to the egalitarian liberal theory of equality, but nonetheless fails to draw the correct conclusions in particular cases. People are finite reasoners, so nothing is surprising about them being inconsistent. Reasoning about equality is difficult.

A cultural environment that both makes false distributional assumptions appear natural and provides no resources for their examination makes reasoning about equality especially difficult. A cultural environment does this by supplying its members with social meanings for "equality" that conflict with the egalitarian view. To illustrate this problem with cultural membership, I shall compare the egalitarian liberal views of Will Kymlicka with the egalitarian communitarian views of Michael Walzer. Kymlicka describes the value of cultural membership in a liberal society as follows:

> Put simply, freedom involves making choices amongst various options, and our societal culture not only provides these options, but also makes them meaningful to us. People make choices about the social practices around them, based on their beliefs about the value of these practices (beliefs which, I have noted, may be wrong). And to have a belief about the value of a practice is, in the first instance, a matter of understanding the meanings attached to it by our culture.[23]

The options that we may choose, the practices that we may engage in, and the goods that we may acquire do not confront us as mere physical entities, but as entities with meanings given by our societal culture. These social meanings are *evaluative* because they attach values to

61

merely physical goods, values that form the basis of our beliefs about value. These are the values that we use in initial deliberations about our ends and often incorporate unreflectively into our conceptions of the good.

Walzer's theory of goods makes the same point. Walzer uses the term "goods" very widely, to include at least the following: community membership, security, welfare, money, commodities, office, hard work, free time, education, kinship, love, divine grace, recognition, and political power. These are the options and practices that a person will want to incorporate into her conception of the good, and they carry social meanings with them.

> All the goods with which distributive justice is concerned are social goods. They are not and they cannot be idiosyncratically valued. . . . Goods in the world have shared meanings because conception and creation are social processes. For the same reason, goods have different meanings in different societies. . . . A solitary person could hardly understand the meanings of the goods or figure out the reasons for taking then as likable or dislikable.[24]

We see goods through the lens of culture, and they have social meanings that underlie the evaluative judgements of members of the culture. However, besides having evaluative meanings, Walzer points out that goods also carry *distributional* meanings.

> But it is the meaning of goods that determines their movement. Distributive criteria and arrangements are intrinsic not to the good-in-itself but to the social good. It we understand what it is, what it means to those for whom it is a good, we understand how, by whom, and for what reasons it ought to be distributed. All distributions are just or unjust relative to the social meanings of the goods at stake.[25]

Kymlicka is concerned to point out the beneficial aspects of cultural membership. It provides evaluative social meanings to the options about which people must deliberate in their choices of ends. People can, of course, go wrong in Kymlicka's picture, either by misunderstanding the evaluative meanings of options or by mistakenly choosing the wrong option for themselves. An oppressive culture, however, will have a harmful aspect: Goods will have inegalitarian distributional social meanings. In an oppressive culture, the social meanings of goods will incorporate distributional factors that are arbitrary from a moral point of view. The members of a sexist culture will share an understanding that certain jobs are inappropriate for women. In a racist culture, it will appear normal and unremarkable that members of a racial minority have a lower standard of living. Members of a heterosexist society will share a belief in oppressive stereotypes and will react differently to gay hairdressers and gay truck drivers. Most members of a meritocratic culture, rich and poor alike, will share a belief that natural ability should determine material ability to form, revise, and pursue a conception of the good. In a meritocratic culture, distribution according to desert is what the moral equality of persons means.

One of a person's critical interests is her choice of a career. The actual nature and meaning of a career, however, are determined by the person's culture. Suppose someone decides to become an academic philosopher because, like Brink, she believes philosophical research is a valuable activity.[26] What it means to be a professional philosopher is not something she can determine. The nature of her chosen option is governed by implicit rules and conventions that set out the stages of a career and prescribe the goals and accomplishments that define success.[27] She cannot define her own rules and still be a philosopher, as philosophy is now understood, any more than she can make up the rules of chess as she goes along and still be playing chess. These rules are not explicitly defined but are embedded in the shared meanings and common practices of her academic subculture. What it is to be a philosopher, philosophy's rules and conventions, will change over time. Socrates, once a paradigm philosopher, would now be no more than a loquacious layabout, failing to meet the educational and publication expectations of contemporary academia.

The contemporary culture of academic philosophy is highly meritocratic. It defines itself by the pursuit of excellence. Within this subculture it seems perfectly natural and just that those with greater natural abilities should be rewarded differentially. It seems perfectly appropriate that someone who has published three influential books should be rewarded more highly than an equally industrious colleague who has published one unread book and has two unpublished manuscripts in a desk drawer. It might not be unjust that the more accomplished writer receive more research leave, but it is certainly a meritocratic assumption that she receive additional merit pay. The subculture also sustains an implicit, unreflective, meritocratic assumption that academics generally deserve higher pay than the day-care workers who look after their children, even though early childhood education is undoubtedly more important than the education of undergraduates.

Implicit acceptance of the distribution of rewards based on natural ability is part of what it means to be an academic philosopher. This assumption frequently comes to the fore in controversies over affirmative-action appointments in academic departments. There are those to whom what it means to be an excellent philosophy professor is research ability on topics currently deemed interesting. And there are others who contest this meaning, people who wish to establish that what it means to be an excellent philosophy professor is defined by ability to reach out to and teach the student body of a contemporary university with all its race, gender, and ethnic diversity. This controversy is not just an argument over truth, but a contest over meanings, with one side seeking to displace the social meanings of the other and reform the academic subculture.

What a philosophical theory means by "moral equality" and what an individual means by "moral equality" are two distinct things. People do not start from a theoretical premise about moral equality and then work out its implications in particular cases. Instead, their deliberations start from a collection of often unexamined judgements about particular cases. For example, to a given individual, "moral equality" could mean, in theory, either that persons are treated as moral equals when they are treated equally before the law or that persons are treated as moral equals when they are not prevented from exercising their two moral powers by factors that are arbitrary from a moral point of view. "Moral equality" will also have a practical meaning which will be embodied in all those cases involving distributions to others and to himself that he accepts without making a protest on equality grounds. Because people are finite reasoners, the theoretical and practical aspects of an individual's concept of moral equality will not always be consistent. People are not perfectly logical, so simply persuading someone to accept the correct meaning of "moral equality" through philosophical argument will not immediately bring all his individual judgements into line with the theory. Philosophical conversion alone will not make people egalitarian in their actual lives. Becoming egalitarian involves a process of critical reflection. This will involve a person in examining what practices and options mean to him, discovering what distributional assumptions these meanings contain, and revising these assumptions to make them consistent with his concept of moral equality.

People do not speak a private language; the meanings of goods are inherently social. People do not learn how to identify cows by looking up the meaning of "cow" – "female bovine that has calved at least once" – and then applying the concept. Instead, they learn to identify cows from other speakers in their surrounding culture. Frequently they perpetuate the mistakes of their immediate society; urban people are often surprised to find out that bulls, steers, and heifers are not cows. In an analogous way, people will learn the ethical meaning of goods – what their values are and to whom they are appropriate – on a case-by-case basis from their cultural environment. Frequently they perpetuate the mistakes of their culture; people make false assumptions about the ethically appropriate distributions of these goods. Social meanings provide the propositional content for many of a person's evaluative and distributional beliefs. The sources of meaning within a cultural environment include not only speech and texts but also customary practices, habits, behaviours, images, and other cultural representations that do not have propositional content. A single pornographic picture does not say to the observer that human sexuality means erotic domination. It does not express any proposition at all, let alone define what "sex" means. Still, widespread production and consumption of images of erotic domination will affect the social meaning of human sexuality. In a pornographic culture, the meaning of sexuality will become inegalitarian. Men and women will come to view sexual practices, and who should get what from whom and how, in terms of dominance and submission. The social meaning of sexuality will come to have an inegalitarian distributional aspect. People will unreflectively take up an inegalitarian meaning for sex and incorporate it into how they think they should lead their lives.

Inegalitarian distributional social meanings transmitted by a culture will undermine its members' knowledge of the good. This can happen in three ways. People form beliefs about what is valuable based on reasoning that accepts their culture's social meanings. Most obviously, they can believe that others, defined by some morally arbitrary characteristic, are resources for their own amusement and enjoy "seeing others in positions of lesser liberty," or take pleasure in another's deprivations.[28] Some men think this of their wives. Such ethical beliefs are false, and preferences based on them have no value. This is one sense in which the right is prior to the good. Egalitarian liberal justice will render false some beliefs about how to live. Rawls wrote that "the priority of justice is accounted for, in part, by holding that the interests requiring the violation of justice have no value. Having no merit in the first place, they cannot override its claims." One interpretation of this remark is that the liberal state need not give equal consideration to unjust preferences, because the liberal state should consider them as having no value.

However, a stronger interpretation is that beliefs about how to lead a life that are inconsistent with the egalitarian liberal theory of justice are false and consequently are of no value to the person who has formed them. The weaker interpretation leaves open the question of whether or not an unjust conception of the good life is of any value to the person who forms it. The stronger interpretation entails the weaker, for if a conception of the good is valueless to the one who forms it, it is valueless to the state as well.

A second way in which inegalitarian distributional social meanings can undermine someone's knowledge of the good arises if she depends on them in her deliberations about the good and they lead her into mistaken beliefs about her good. Domestic work carries a social meaning that makes it seem obligatory to many women and optional to most men. Suppose a woman accepts this assumption and builds a vision of her life on this basis. If domestic work had carried a more egalitarian social meaning, she would have made another choice about her life. Suppose also that this life is in fact wrong for her; devoting her life to her professional career would have been a better choice for her. An inegalitarian distributional assumption has directly undermined her knowledge of the good. There is a third way in which inegalitarian distributional assumptions undermine knowledge: Even if she had been correct in her vision of her life, if her beliefs about what was valuable had been true, her knowledge of the good still would have been undermined, for, by hypothesis, her beliefs depended on a false distributional assumption and, though true, did not amount to knowledge.

False assumptions about moral equality, grounded in inegalitarian social meanings, can lead someone to misidentify her good. In a sexist culture, a woman may assume, just because she is a woman, that her interests matter less than those of a man and may believe that she should subordinate her good to that of her husband. In one scenario, a woman becomes a traditional housewife without ever seriously considering an alternative. Whether or not the life of a traditional housewife is the best one for her, she fails to attain knowledge of her good because her conception of the good is based on a false, inegalitarian assumption. If she had not assumed that her life should centre around her husband's, she would have thought about her life differently. In another scenario, a woman realizes that her life would have gone better if she had chosen to continue her career, but her belief that she should subordinate her interests to those of her husband outweighs this realization in her deliberations. She understands that she is sacrificing her interests to those of her husband. Nevertheless, in her final choice of how to live her life, the inegalitarian assumption is a more significant factor for her than is her forgone career. If she had understood her options through the lens of a different, more egalitarian set of social meanings, she would ultimately have avoided her mistake. In a third scenario, a woman reflects on her assumptions about distribution according to gender and breaks free of inegalitarian assumptions. Yet she and her partner face a choice situation in which only one of them can continue his or her career. (This has become a common circumstance for young academic couples.) She faces a difficult dilemma, but, at least, in her deliberations she is not misled by the assumption that his career is more important. She may ultimately choose to put his career first, and that decision may be correct or mistaken, but her knowledge of the good is not undermined by her cultural environment.

Someone might object that paying too much attention to moral equality might also undermine our knowledge of the good. We do take morally arbitrary factors into account in our personal relationships. Birth and breeding are grounds for caring more about your own children than the children of others. The doctrine of the moral equality of persons, with its implied strict impartiality, applies to the state, not at the personal level. Consequently people have no reason to remove inegalitarian judgements from their personal thinking and may even have good reason to keep some of them. However, the objection misinterprets the guiding intuitions. You do not believe that your children are morally more important than the children of others; what you believe is that your duties to your children are more pressing than your duties to the children of others and that your emotional bonds to your own children are stronger. In any society, someone must accept the burden, and receive the joys, of child-rearing. An inegalitarian society might distribute the obligations of child-rearing inequitably, perhaps only to the biological mother. An egalitarian society could bring up children in public nurseries, but it makes sense to respect natural affections and assign child-rearing obligations to biological parents. You should legitimately care more for your biological children not directly because of their birth and breeding but because a reasonable interpretation of their moral equality assigns you that obligation. It just so happens that grounds that are arbitrary from a moral point of view and egalitarian considerations do not conflict.

Kymlicka stresses only the evaluative aspect of the social meaning of goods. In doing so he emphasizes only the beneficial side of cultural membership. Walzer points out that the social meanings of goods have a distributional aspect. If the distributional social meanings are inegalitarian, as in an oppressive cultural environment, people will suffer a harm to their interest in knowing the good. Walzer's point allows us to see the harmful side of cultural membership. However, egalitarian liberals will part company with Walzer on how to deal with distributional social meanings. Walzer believes that justice must be relative to the shared social meanings of a culture:

> A given society is just if its substantive life is lived in a certain way –
> that is, in a way faithful to the shared understandings of the members.
> . . . In a society where social meanings are integrated and hierarchical,
> justice will come to the aid of inequality.[29]

Egalitarian liberals will disagree. They think that the moral equality of persons stands outside the shared understandings of a society and is a point of view from which to criticize the culture. Discussions of caste societies point up this disagreement. To Walzer, in an Indian village where grain is distributed according to the caste system, justice "does not rule out the inequality of the portions; it cannot require a radical redesign of the village against the shared understandings of the members. If it did, justice itself would be tyrannical."[30] This contrasts with the views of Dworkin and Rawls. In the course of arguing that unrestricted equality of preference fulfilment is not the best theory of distributive justice, Dworkin writes:

> Suppose everyone accepts a caste theory so that, though Amartya is
> somewhat poorer than others, the distribution leaves his preferences as
> a whole equally fulfilled because he believes that he, as a member of a
> lower caste, should have less, so that his preferences as a whole would
> be worse fulfilled if he had more. Bimal, from a higher caste, would
> also be less satisfied overall if Amartya had more. In this situation, un-
> restricted equality of success does recommend a distribution that no
> other conception of equality of welfare would. But it is unacceptable
> for that very reason. An inegalitarian political system does not become
> [egalitarian] just because everyone believes it to be.[31]

Rawls's views on caste societies are similar. He thinks that caste societies create distributions that are arbitrary from a moral point of view:

> The natural distribution is neither just nor unjust; nor is it unjust that
> persons are born into society at some particular position. These are sim-
> ply natural facts. What is just and unjust is the way that institutions
> deal with these facts. Aristocratic and caste societies are unjust because
> they make these contingencies the ascriptive basis for belonging to

more or less enclosed and privileged social classes. The basic structure of these societies incorporates the arbitrariness found in nature.[32]

In order to create a just society, people must give up the inegalitarian distributional assumptions of a caste society.

> Thus when the belief in a fixed natural order sanctioning a hierarchical society is abandoned, *assuming here that this belief is not true,* a tendency is set up that points in the direction of the two principles of justice in serial order.[33] [emphasis added]

For Walzer there is no standpoint outside the shared meanings of a culture from which to criticize it, whereas for egalitarian liberals, there is. This disagreement reflects different conceptions of how to do philosophy. Walzer writes:

> One way to begin the philosophical enterprise – perhaps the original way – is to walk out of the cave, leave the city, climb the mountain, fashion for oneself (what can never be fashioned for ordinary men and women) an objective and universal standpoint. . . . But I mean to stand in the cave, in the city, on the ground. Another way of doing philosophy is to interpret to one's fellow citizens the world of meanings that we share. Justice and equality can conceivably be worked out as philosophical artifacts, but a just or egalitarian society cannot be. If such a society isn't already here – hidden, as it were, in our concepts and categories – we will never know it concretely or realize it in fact.[34]

Walzer does not think that this means we have to accept the social meanings of our culture, just that we have to criticize them from the inside. The shared understanding of social goods is not monolithic; the dominant understanding must contend with other understandings that resist it. For example, in the Catholic church of the middle ages, the dominant view allowed the church to sell ecclesiastical office. Yet this dominant understanding existed alongside a view that the meaning of church office excluded its being bought and sold.[35] The existence of these resistant understandings within the culture provided the starting point for social criticism.

Though egalitarian liberalism may disagree with Walzer in theory, it should learn from him in practice. For Dworkin, equality is the foundational idea of political morality and provides an external theoretical standpoint for criticism. "An inegalitarian political system does not become [egalitarian] just because everyone believes it to be." Rawls has a hierarchical view of social meanings. Equality is one of the fundamental ideas of a democratic culture. Comprehensive doctrines that do not accept it are unreasonable and must be contained, not accepted into the overlapping consensus. Nevertheless, Walzer may be correct strategically. Not only must justice not be tyrannical, it also must avoid the appearance of tyranny. In practice, coercion may not be the best strategy for the reform of an inegalitarian cultural environment. Coercive interventions in culture lead to resentment and resistance and may undermine the legitimacy of the state in the eyes of its citizens. In the final chapter, I shall discuss other strategies that the liberal state may follow in reforming an oppressive culture. These strategies require abandoning the doctrine of state neutrality as it is usually understood, but they avoid the blunt instrument of coercion.

4

NEUTRALITY AND THE HARM PRINCIPLE

I shall now begin to argue that an egalitarian liberal state should be governed by a severely modified conception of state neutrality in its approach to an oppressive culture. An oppressive culture embeds its members in inegalitarian social meanings which support beliefs about unequal entitlements that egalitarian liberals must regard as false. The profession, practice, and promulgation of these beliefs harm important interests. Cultural oppression, construed narrowly as the social transmission of false beliefs about inequality, can undermine self-respect and harm highest-order interests in knowing the good. Most generally, these harms are accumulative harms. Accumulative harms, however, present difficulties to liberal theory. Liberalism does permit political interference with individual conduct to prevent harm to others, but it usually employs an individualistic interpretation of harm which fails to properly recognize accumulative harms.

Mill's harm principle states that "the only purpose for which power can be rightfully exercised over any member of a civilized community, against his will, is to prevent harm to others."[1] The harm principle also applies to the neutrality of the liberal state. Larmore writes:

> The state should not seek to promote any particular conception of the good life because of its presumed *intrinsic* superiority – that is, because it is supposedly a *truer* conception. (A liberal state may naturally restrict certain ideals for *extrinsic* reasons because, for example, they threaten the lives of others.)[2] [emphasis in original]

The parenthetical sentence claims that though state intervention cannot be justified on the ground that a way of life is inferior, it is justified on the ground that the way of life is harmful to others.

ACCUMULATIVE HARMS AND THE HARM PRINCIPLE

There is an ambiguity in the interpretation of the harm principle. Should the principle offer protection against harms or only against harmful conduct?[3] Harmful conduct is activity carried out either maliciously or recklessly that causes harm to others. The harmful-conduct interpretation fits most naturally with the background individualist assumption of our legal system regarding the assignment of blame and responsibility to individuals. Harms must be assigned to individuals in order for legal mechanisms of guilt and liability to work. Hence, individual harmful conduct must be identified in order to use the harm principle. Harms, though, are set-backs to people's interests,[4] whether or not brought about by harmful conduct. All harmful conduct, by definition, results in harm, and, most often, harms result from harmful conduct. But in the case of accumulative harms, a harmed condition can arise which does not result from harmful conduct.

How we determine what is to count as a harm also presents a problem of interpretation for the harm principle. On the one hand, if we count mere hurt, offence, annoyance, and mental distress as harms, the principle will countenance political interference with most every activity, and liberty will amount to nought. On the other hand, if we count only physical damage to persons as harm, most every activity will be permitted, and there will be little scope for the political protection of persons. Cultural harms and many environmental harms, however, have an interesting structure which straddles these extremes; sometimes activities which individually are merely annoying, innocuous, or even beneficial add up to, in the first case, a harm to a highest-order interest, and in the second, to physical damage. In this chapter, I shall argue that the harm principle should be interpreted as permitting the liberal state to adopt policies to prevent accumulative harms.

An accumulative harm is a harm done *by* a group, not *to* a group. It is a harm to another person brought about by the actions of a group of people where the action of no single member of that group can be seen, by itself, to cause the harm. Most often, an accumulative harm will also be a public harm, a harm which cannot be done to one individual without at the same time being done to a whole community or populace, but there is no conceptual necessity to this fact; accumulative harms may be serious individual harms. A public harm can take two forms: Either it is a harm to the interests of individual members of the group or it is a harm to the group's interests that is not a harm to the interests of any individual member. The latter, a harm *to* a collectivity, is the sort of harm that could give rise to what are often called collective rights. For example, Raz characterizes a collective right as a right whose correlative duties are justified by the interests of individual members of a group in a public good, where "the interest of no single member of that group in that public good is sufficient by itself to justify holding another person to be subject to a duty."[5] A harm *by* a collective, what I call an accumulative harm, is the converse of a harm *to* a collective. Accumulative harms can arise out of otherwise harmless activities. Feinberg describes the accumulative harm of air pollution like this:

> If there were only one automobile allowed to operate in the entire state of California, its exhaust fumes would soon be dissipated and no harm to the ambient air would even be worth mentioning. One hundred cars might begin to threaten the air quality but it is unlikely that they would bring it to the threshold of harmfulness. But somewhere between those minor exhaust emissions and those produced by millions of cars without catalytic converters the threshold of harm is reached.[6]

Sometimes one individual source of pollution may cross the threshold into harm all by itself, but often many sources are needed. The accumulative-harm cases, however, cannot be said to involve harmful conduct; no individual, maliciously or recklessly, causes the accumulative harm. Similarly, to create harmful cultural pollution, the behaviours, representations, and expressive acts of many people will be required. Substituting racists for automobiles in Feinberg's description of air pollution, we get a description of a racist culture:

> If there was only one racist promoting his viewpoint in the entire state of California, his pronouncements would soon be dissipated, and no harm to the ambient non-racist culture would even be worth mentioning. One hundred racists might begin to threaten the culture's commitment to racial equality, but it is unlikely that they would bring it to the threshold of harmfulness. But somewhere between those minor cultural acts and those produced by millions of people with racist attitudes the threshold of harm is reached.

Taken in isolation, the behaviour of a solitary racist is likely to be no more than offensive. But the cumulative effect of the behaviour of many racists will create an oppressive culture which crosses a threshold into being harmful.

I am going to argue for an accumulative interpretation of Mill's harm principle regarding state neutrality; the state should take an active role in society to prevent both individual harmful conduct and accumulative harms. Feinberg explicitly endorses only the individual interpretation and so must distort his theory in order to deal with environmental and cultural pollution. I shall focus primarily on forms of environmental pollution as examples of accumulative harms. Now, in their actual practice, liberal states have moved to prevent accumulative environmental harms. They have prohibited leaded fuel and the use of chlorofluorocarbons after the accumulation of these pollutants was shown to be harmful. In banning the production of these pollutants, liberal states have balanced the threat of harm to vital interests in security of the person with the harms to commercial interests brought about by regulating the economic marketplace. Egalitarian liberalism has tended not to have a laissez-faire attitude toward the market in any case, so the restriction on commercial freedoms has not seemed important. But the balance of harms is different when the state moves to prevent cultural pollution. In cultural pollution, the polluting acts are acts of expression broadly construed. Interfering with acts of cultural pollution will appear to interfere not only with a commercial freedom but also with a basic liberty: freedom of expression. This raises the stakes. If the acts in question are not harmful in themselves, the liberal state may be reluctant to abandon its neutral stance toward them. This reluctance is wrong. Also at stake are vital interests in knowing and acting on one's good. The fact that the harms done to these highest-order interests are accumulative should not make a difference to the role of the state.

We cannot ignore accumulative harms just because we cannot trace the harm to its causes. Epistemic over-caution may be a virtue in the sciences, but practical judgements have to be made, even without all the information that we think desirable. Accumulative harms arise because we do not know all the causal connections which we believe we should know, yet accumulative harms must still be dealt with. There is no way to apportion an environmental harm to the contributions which create it.[7] Consider the harms of secondhand tobacco smoke. A single exposure does no harm, but continual exposure may. Now there are two sorts of ways that a person might be continually exposed to secondhand smoke. In one, she might live with a heavy smoker and be exposed to many individual acts of smoking, all by the same person. In the other, she might be exposed to the smoking of many thousands of people in her workplace, in her shopping environment, and in her social and public life. Suppose that both women are harmed. In the individual-perpetrator case, we would have no trouble in recognizing that a harm was done, and who did it, despite the genesis of the harm in many different acts. In the multiple-perpetrator case, the consequences are no less harmful than in the first case. Yet, until recently, there had been a problem in seeing this harm as something more than

74

an unlucky fact of nature, and there is still ambiguity as to what should be done about it. Because no one is clearly to blame, we are unsure of what to do. Nonetheless, the harm done in the second case needs just as much fixing as does the first. Why should it be relevant to our need to prevent the harm that the first harm was the consequence of many similar acts by one individual, while the second harm was the consequence of many similar acts by different individuals?

In dealing with accumulative harms, we must, I think, give up on trying to impute them to individuals. Instead, we must attempt to prevent accumulative harms through state intervention that will be workable and fair, but will not depend on knowing who did what to whom. But giving up on imputing accumulative harms is not without implications. It means that we must adopt a particular interpretation of the harm principle; sometimes the state may need to govern conduct that is not individually harmful in order to prevent harm to others. Sometimes the state may need to intervene for reasons that have nothing to do with the consequences of individual actions. But rethinking these issues will actually put us further ahead. As a society, we are sometimes blind to accumulative harms, assuming, when we cannot find a perpetrator, that they are facts of nature not requiring, or even permitting, solution. And when we do try to fix accumulative harms by blaming people for their putative shares in producing them, our solutions have little legitimacy in the eyes of those inconvenienced, who quite rightly fail to see why they should be blamed. We must learn, first, to identify social problems despite their accumulative structure and, second, to find solutions that do not presuppose a model of praise and blame.

I take it that the harm principle puts limits on the neutrality of the liberal state. The harm principle, as applied to the doctrine of state neutrality, admits of two possible interpretations. On the one hand, we have the more usual interpretation, the individual-harm principle:

(1) The state may adopt policies that otherwise would violate neutrality only if individual activity is, by itself, causing harm to others.

The individual interpretation of the harm principle is the most natural and the most obvious. For instance, Raz writes that "it is true that an action harms a particular person only if it affects him directly and significantly by itself. It does not count as harming him if its undesirable consequences are indirect and depend on the intervention of other actions."[8] On the other hand we have an interpretation suggested by the pollution cases, the accumulative-harm principle:

(2) The state may adopt policies that otherwise would violate neutrality only if individual activity either is, by itself, causing harm to others or is part of an accumulative activity which brings about harm to others.

Each polluter can admit that pollution is harmful while arguing that his own individual activities are not causing harm. It might seem that a pollution case would require weighing the interests of polluters in their commercial freedoms against the interests of potential victims in their personal security. But not so, claims the polluter: "My little source of pollution by itself causes no harm to others, and by the individual-harm principle, their interests are of no relevance to my freedom to make a living." The accumulative interpretation of the harm principle would block this argument. The task of this chapter will be to see what can be said in defence of the accumulative interpretation.

In the air-pollution case there is generally no intention on the part of any polluter to bring about harm. Nor is there any collective intention involved, if for no other reason than that we cannot, even metaphorically, attribute intention to such a disorganized group. It might be thought that intention, or at least reasonable foresight, would be necessary for the existence of harm and for the application of either harm principle. But whereas intent or negligence may be necessary in order to find someone blameworthy, culpable, or at fault for doing a harm, I do not think that either is necessary in order to decide whether or not to "exercise power over a member of a civilized community" to "prevent harm to others." Consider the following unlikely case (it has to be kept unlikely in order to eliminate any expectation of reasonable foresight): Someone, going about his lawful ways, comes to a closed door that has a keypad-operated, electronic combination lock. He begins trying combinations at random. Unbeknownst to him and unforeseeable by him or by any other reasonable person, each combination is correlated to a living person. Entering any combination causes a person's death through a causal chain that I leave to the reader's imagination.[9] Three things are true here: First, the individual entering the combinations is, without doubt, causing harm. Second, the individual-harm principle will justify the state in regulating that individual's activity, that is, in interfering with the individual's liberty by stopping the button-pressing. Third, there are no grounds for blaming or punishing the button-pusher for what he is doing; we should more reasonably blame whoever designed such a dangerous lock. After the button-pusher has been apprised of the consequences of his actions, then he might reasonably be blamed or punished if he still continues. But neither negligence nor malicious intent is necessary for the application of the individual-harm principle. Consequently it cannot be an argument against the accumulative-harm principle that in cases of accumulative harm, the harms are neither intended nor recklessly disregarded.[10]

There is no conceptual connection between fault and harm, though there is between fault and harmful conduct. A harm is something like Feinberg's "set-back to interests," not a "set-back to interests which has a certain genesis." It is true that in the most familiar cases, harms and faults go together. But this is an empirical matter. In most cases in which an individual causes harm, the causal connection between the individual's activity and the harm will be commonly known, and the individual may reasonably be blamed for not foreseeing the causal consequences of the activity. There is, however, a conceptual connection between fault and the activity of harming. For instance, Feinberg thinks that the definition of "A harms B" must include reference to both fault and harm. Thus, A must act "with the intention of producing the consequences for B that follow, or similarly adverse ones, or with negligence or recklessness in respect to those consequences," and A's action must be "the cause of a setback to B's interests."[11] For Feinberg, the state may limit liberty only to stop the activity of harming, not to prevent harms. On the other hand, the accumulative-harm principle implies that the state may limit liberty only to prevent harmful consequences; it does not matter that the activities which generate the harm are themselves neither faulty nor the cause of the harm. Feinberg's harm principle, accordingly, cannot handle cases where individually harmless acts of polluting bring about harm only when a threshold of accumulation is crossed. "The harm principle in that case is of no use at all."[12] His harm principle cannot tell us whether or not a legislature is permitted to prohibit a polluting activity like copper refining, because it is only against the background of a preexisting state policy that polluting acts can be seen as harmful. He writes:

> How do we tell if a given refining operation causes harm? Only by determining whether its contribution to the accumulation of certain gases and materials in the ambient air is more than its permitted share. But we can only know its "permitted share" by reference to an actual allocative scheme, operative and in force.[13]

Feinberg's harm principle, limiting harming but not harms, does not by itself permit policies to prevent pollution and other accumulative harms to others.

The accumulative-harm principle has a familiar analogue in utilitarian thought. How do you prevent harm to a city lawn, where each would be better off if he or she could walk on it, but all would be worse off if the lawn were destroyed? An individual act of walking on the grass will cause no appreciable harm to the lawn. The grass will recover very quickly after it is crossed. Only after a certain threshold rate of grass-crossing is reached, a rate that will depend on the season of the year, the amount of rainfall, and so forth, will the lawn be damaged. Each individual act-utilitarian may reason that because his or her walk across the lawn will cause no damage, he or she is free to do so. The result will be no lawn. A society of rule-utilitarians will make out better. Reasoning that obedience to a rule such as "Keep off the grass" will have overall best consequences, the rule-utilitarian will not walk on the grass even though by doing so he or she would cause no harm.

The example of the utilitarian and the lawn can be made to illustrate a very important point about accumulative harms. Sometimes on city lawns you see "Keep off the grass" signs, sometimes you see no sign at all, and very occasionally you see the sign "Please walk on the grass." The latter sign might be put up by city officials (with a sense of humour) in large, little-utilized parks where few enough people come that it is a shame that their city habit of keeping off the grass prevents their harmless enjoyment of walking on it. In implementing the accumulative-harm principle to decide if non-neutral state intervention is necessary, attention must be paid to the actual empirical circumstances of the case. What are people likely to do on this lawn? It is not enough to simply ask, What if everyone were to do it? As Feinberg puts it,

> . . . we can ask of the most innocent and harmless actions imaginable, for example walking to the neighbourhood grocery to buy some provisions, what would happen if everybody did the same, and the answer would be that chaos would reign supreme. . . . In applying the harm principle, then, the legislator must acquire the best empirical information he can get about the readiness of persons generally (and also their opportunities and abilities) to act in the way whose prohibition he is considering.[14]

We must study the social circumstances of the case to determine what harm is done and what must be done to alleviate it. Accumulative harms are tied to their historical and social contexts. What starts out as innocuous (say the burning of coal to heat a house) becomes collectively harmful (the London fogs of the Victorian era). Regulation becomes, in that context and at that time, permissible by the accumulative-harm principle. But that, too, may change; London houses now have other forms of heating; there are few working fire-places left; coal is expensive, difficult to handle, difficult to get. Perhaps, now, what little coal is likely to get burned would do no harm. Similarly, an active state challenge to racist and ethnocentric attitudes is necessary in the context of a racist culture. However, should these measures succeed in reforming the culture, they would no longer be required.

NOZICK'S OBJECTION

Attention to actual social circumstances contrasts with two extreme positions we could take when applying the accumulative-harm principle. One extreme would be to consider what would happen if everyone engaged in the activity. This would be silly, because it would result in pretty much everything being forbidden. The opposite extreme would be to suppose that only one person engaged in the activity. We would be asked to imagine a state of nature, with persons living isolated, uncooperative lives – social and material conditions under which, of course, there can be no accumulative harms. I have in mind here arguments that have the structure of Nozick's defence of economic freedom under capitalism.[15] Nozick's concern with harms is confined to a libertarian concern with harms to personal security and liberty.[16] Can the independent employment decisions of capitalists amount to an accumulative harm to an unemployed worker? On the face of it, an employer's proposal of "Either work for me or starve to death" would appear to be a coercive threat and a harm to the voluntariness of the worker's choice. Against this view, Nozick advances a moralized account of coercion which holds that people cannot be said to coerce when they act within their rights. He argues that we have to look at the history of the choice situation and the morality of each of the events that led to it. He asks whether or not a worker, Z, works voluntarily if the sequential market exchanges between A through Y leave Z only the options of working or starving. Answer: "Z does choose voluntarily if the other individuals A through Y each acted [1] voluntarily and [2] within their rights" (p. 263). In order not to define "voluntarily" in terms of itself, this recursive definition depends on an initial clause in which "voluntary" does not appear. Nozick gets this by assuming that there is some time, t_1, back in the state of nature, at which A chooses independently of the actions of anyone else, and "if the facts of nature [limit A's alternatives], the actions are voluntary" (p. 262). Then at t_2,

B chooses voluntarily, given A's prior choice which was within A's rights. At t_3, C contracts voluntarily, given the shaping of C's choice environment by A and B, and so on down to t_{26}, when Z chooses voluntarily by the recursive definition. Hence A through Y cannot be said to have collectively harmed Z's interest in choosing between working and starving.

But this argument will not do as an argument against the accumulative-harm principle, because it basically begs the question. What does it mean for individuals to act "within their rights"? For the libertarian, all rights are rights to liberty, not rights to receive some benefit from others. Individuals act within their rights when they act within the bounds of their liberties. The limit of an individual's liberties is established by an interpretation of the harm principle. But which harm principle – individual or accumulative? Nozick's argument evidently presupposes the individual-harm principle. To Nozick, what it means for someone to act "within his rights" is for him not, by himself, to cause harm to others. Individually, each of A through Y causes no harm to Z's choice situation, so all are acting within their rights.

But what happens if we ask whether or not A through Y act "within their rights" according to the accumulative-harm principle? This time, suppose that A through Y are each putting nonharmful amounts of some pollutant into the atmosphere, and suppose that Z dies from accumulative ingestions of the pollutant. Suppose that each of A through Y starts polluting at their corresponding times and continues to do so thereafter. Finally, suppose the harm threshold is reached with G, the seventh polluter. A grievous harm, on anybody's interpretation, has been done to Z. But A, at t_1, did not do it. A, at t_1, does not cause harm to Z and is not part of an accumulative activity that brings about harm to Z. So A acts within A's rights. Neither A nor B does it at t_2; that is, neither A nor B causes harm to Z nor is part of an accumulative activity that causes harm to Z. So at t_2 there are no grounds for regulating either A or B. And so on up to G. Now the threshold into harm is crossed. At t_7, G's activity is part of an accumulative activity which brings about harm to Z. By the accumulative-harm principle, G does not act within G's rights. But, at t_7, neither does any of A through F. At t_7, though not before, their activities become accumulatively harmful. At, and after, t_7, what they do is part of an accumulative activity that brings about harm to Z, and consequently they no longer act within their rights. Nor do subsequent polluters H through Y. At, and after, t_7, the accumulative-harm principle permits regulation of A through Y to prevent harm to Z. Contrary to Nozick's recursive argument, A through Y are not acting within their rights, according to the accumulative-harm principle. The recursive argument works only by assuming that individual harms delimit what it is to act within one's rights.

Someone might raise this objection: "How can it happen that A through F, who were merrily polluting along, perfectly at liberty to do as they wished, should suddenly at t_7, through circumstances totally beyond their control, no longer be acting within their rights?" In general, the harmfulness of an activity is a function not only of the nature of the activity but also of the circumstances in which it is done. And circumstances change. Shooting a rifle at a target is a totally harmless activity until someone wanders between the shooter and the target. Shooting at stumps on Manhattan Island was once an innocuous activity, but now would be outrageously risky. A more general point is at issue here. The accumulative-harm principle enjoins us to examine the social context in which an activity takes place, at the point in history when we are considering regulating liberty to prevent harm. It is not appropriate to examine the social context of some other time, especially some hypothetical state of nature. We have to gather as much empirical information as we can about the workings of our social circumstances before we can decide on the limitations to our liberties that the accumulative-harm principle justifies. And we have to recognize that our circumstances, and therefore the extent of our liberty, will change.

The individual-harm principle yields a very odd result when applied to the pollution case. By the individual-harm principle, polluters A through Y are each acting "within their rights," and consequently Z "voluntarily" chooses to ingest a lethal dose of the pollutant. So Z commits suicide? Someone may, however, reply as follows: "The individual-harm principle is indeed adequate to stop pollution. We must focus on G, the threshold polluter. A through F are within their rights, but at t_7, G's additional pollutants cause harm and give grounds, on the individual-harm principle, for saying G is not within G's rights." This reply depends on identifying G as the proximate cause of harm, that is, on G being the last link in a chain of causes whose voluntary decision to pollute or not to pollute can cause or prevent harm to Z. Now, although being the proximate cause of harm may be relevant in legal assignments of blame and liability, it is not clear that it is relevant to the applicability of either harm principle. As argued earlier, neither malicious intent nor negligence need be present before an activity may be regulated to prevent harm to others. If so, then G's taking of the last "voluntary

81

decision" before the harm, being the last person who could prevent the harm, is not enough to make G the individual cause of the harm. Be that as it may, it is more important to recognize that the existence of a threshold, or proximate, cause of harm is an arbitrary result of how the situation is described. Suppose A polluted and then stopped, B polluted and then stopped, and so on; finally G pollutes, and Z dies from the accumulation of pollutants. Given this sequence of temporally discrete activities, we may have reason to identify G as the proximate cause. Instead, suppose, as in the earlier example, that A starts to pollute and continues to do so, B starts and continues, and so on; finally G starts to pollute, and Z dies from the resulting, continuously sustained level of pollutants. Yes, G voluntarily chooses to start polluting; but at the same time, A through F voluntarily choose to continue polluting. Whose intentional or negligent activity is the proximate cause of Z's death? Finally, suppose that A through Y all begin and continue to pollute together. Now who is the proximate cause? The individual-harm principle cannot be applied. The existence of a threshold polluter is an artifact of the abstractness of the example; actual history will be much more of a muddle. Sources of pollution will come and go, often contemporaneously. There will be a fuzzily defined period of history when this particular type of pollution will start to have victims. But there will be no threshold polluter, no individual cause of harm.

The sequential picture needed to make Nozick's objection work is particularly implausible as an account of the origin of cultural oppression. Sexism, racism, ethnocentrism, and classism have played roles in most liberal cultures for a long, long time. It is nonsensical to suppose a model in which first A says that women are ethically less important than men and then stops, then B says the same thing on another occasion, then C, and so on. The conditions which make Nozick's objection seem plausible simply do not apply to cultural oppression.

OTHER WORRIES

The result of allegiance to the individual-harm principle is that some interests may go unprotected. The interests of the victims of environmental or cultural pollution do not get considered when harm-preventing duties are allocated. Their interests do not get weighed because no individual harms them. Now, in actual fact, allegiance to the individual-harm principle is not as extreme as I have portrayed it. Legislatures and courts do attempt to prevent accumulative harms; they do regulate environmental pollution. Such regulation is justifiable by the accumulative-harm principle, even against the assertion of individual rights. Further, as I am trying to argue, the accumulative-harm principle is itself a defensible principle, and its application should be extended to the reform of a polluted culture. The contrary arguments of the libertarian presuppose the falsity of the accumulative-harm principle when they argue against it. But the principle may still engender other worries. The principle makes people liable for certain duties and obligations designed to protect others from accumulative harms – liable not in the tort-law sense of being at fault or in the criminal-law sense of having a guilty mind but in the theoretical sense of having no immunity from being assigned such obligations for the protection of others. The principle may seem to make a person liable to the imposition of (1) overly onerous duties for (2) his vaguely defined part in a collective activity which brings about harm because of (3) actions taken not only by himself but also by others. Let us look at these worries in reverse order.

Worry (3) is that the accumulative-harm principle makes a person liable to intervention because of the actions of other people. The individual's own actions may be harmless and would not be liable to regulation if others were not taking similar individually harmless actions. It appears that the individual is being penalized for what other people do. On this point we have strong intuitions; one person should not be penalized for the actions of another.

Worry (3) seems to lead directly to the denial of the accumulative-harm principle. But it misapplies our intuitions. Though polluters are penalized because others are taking similar actions, they are not penalized for the actions of others, but for their own actions – their own actions carried out in the context of others doing the same.[17] They are penalized for what they are doing because what they are doing is part of an accumulative activity which leads to harm. If they had been doing something else instead, no penalty would have been assigned. Their own actions are what they are responsible for and what they are penalized for. Their actions are prohibited and penalized, however, only against the background of a system of regulation designed to prevent accumulative harms.[18] Suppose we are considering several schemes of regulation designed to prevent the accumulative harm of pollution. The regulations state when and how much individual polluters may pollute, and they are backed by penalties. The import of the intuition that one person should not be penalized for the actions of another is that we should consider only schemes which assign penalties to those individuals who violate the regulations. Penalizing the family of a person who violates the regulations might be just as effective in preventing pollution as penalizing the violator himself. But if family members are not themselves violating the regulations, we have strong intuitions against penalizing them.

Worry (2) concerns who should be subject to such intervention. The easy answer, that the penalty should fall on those who are involved in an accumulative activity that brings about harm, raises a worry about lack of precision. Examples of accumulative harms divide into two categories: first, where individual members of the group all take actions of the same sort, and, second, where individuals take actions of different sorts which systematically result in the group doing harm. In the first category, membership in the group doing harm is defined by similarity of action. The harm is in the accumulation of some pollutant, for instance, and it is fairly easy to see who is putting that pollutant into the environment. In the second category, that of systemic harms, membership in the group is defined structurally.

Sexual harassment illustrates the systemic form of accumulative harm. In a world almost free of sexism, an act of sexist speech, conduct, or publication might merely elicit disgust and do no more than give offence. Under other circumstances, such as sexist speech by a male professor in front of a class, such acts might poison the learning environment for the women present. This would be an individual act of sexual harassment, and the individual-harm principle would license regulatory interference by the relevant authorities. But we can also imagine situations in which many small acts of sexist speech, conduct, and publication would bring about a poisoned environment for women, but with none of these small acts by itself being sufficient to create this harm. One *Playboy* centerfold displayed in a large workplace might merely attract vandalism, but a large number of such representations of women's bodies would make women employees feel disrespected. Differing acts of speech, conduct, and publication are elements in a structure of attitudes, policies, and discriminatory practices that can undermine a woman employee's self-respect and lead her to undervalue her projects. But it might well be impossible to identify who had done the harming, and legal redress could be very complicated.[19] It is only by their functional role in the harassing situation that actions can be identified as parts of an accumulative harm.

Similarly, pornography, as a cultural practice, reinforces men's false beliefs about sex and male dominance. It contributes to eroticising the submission of women, and indirectly to women's beliefs about their own self-worth. Yet the solitary consumption of pornography by one individual man may be totally harmless. It is the accumulative power of the whole system of production, distribution, and consumption which does the harm, a system of which the solitary consumer is but a small part. But if a culture of pornography is to be understood as a harm to both men and women, it will be an accumulative harm, not an individual one. The reform of a pornographic culture will involve identifying the functional elements of the system, considering the various interests involved, and targeting them with maximally equitable and minimally onerous state intervention.

Finally, worry (1) is that the harm principle will assign overly onerous burdens to individuals. Notice, though, that even the individual-harm principle does not, by itself, determine the nature of the duties which should be imposed to prevent the harm. Suppose a man is wildly flailing about with his fists. It is generally agreed that his freedom of movement should end a couple of inches from the body of any bystander. The pugilist is liable to the imposition of a duty which will prevent him from harming bystanders. But what duty? Many duties would succeed in preventing harm: Thou shalt not hit others. Thou shalt not flail about with thy fists. Thou shalt immediately commit suicide. Thou shalt present thyself to the nearest servant of the state for summary execution. And so forth. Only the first of these, however, is a contender, for though the individual-harm principle licenses the imposition of duties to prevent harm, it must be supplemented with considerations of justice and efficiency to determine what particular duties to impose. We have to weigh the interests of both the bystander and the pugilist in order to determine a fair allocation of duties. Clearly the last-mentioned in my list of possible duties would be grossly unfair to the pugilist. Consideration of the pugilist's interest in his personal security shows that the duty to submit to immediate execution would be too onerous under the circumstances. The point of either harm principle is to indicate when it is permissible to impose maximally equitable, minimally onerous harm-preventing obligations.

Similar comments apply to the accumulative-harm principle. The major task of the accumulative interpretation is to insist on consideration of the interests of those who are harmed by an accumulation of individually harmless activities. But its task is not to rule out consideration of the interests of the perpetrators. It is not legitimate to ignore the interests of either side. Further, there is a great deal of flexibility in the regulation of an accumulative activity; it is a mistake to think that the only solution is a blanket prohibition of the activity. For example, there is a story that one Oxford college solved the grass-crossing problem with a sign reading "Only alumni of this college may walk on the grass." This regulation permitted some use of the grass, but kept it below the threshold of harm. Similarly, to prevent accumulation of lead in the environment, we ban leaded gasoline, not cars; to prevent traffic jams, we insist that people drive on one side of the road – left or right in various jurisdictions – we do not ban driving; and to prevent the total breakdown of communication, we insist on rules of order in debate, not on complete censorship. Feinberg discusses the pollution case as follows:

> The legislative problem, then, is to control emissions so that the chemical accumulations remain below the harm-threshold, while restricting as little as possible the socially valuable activities that produce emissions as regrettable byproducts. A satisfactory solution requires not a simple criminal prohibition, modelled say on the statute against homicide or burglary, but an elaborate scheme of regulation, administered by a state agency empowered to grant, withhold, and suspend licenses, following rules designed to promote fairness and efficiency.[20]

As Feinberg makes plain, the regulation of accumulative harm is not a simple and straightforward matter. The accumulative-harm principle licenses a maximally equitable and minimally onerous intervention in the activity; it need not impose total prohibition. This first worry is particularly acute when we are considering the regulation of speech and other forms of expression to prevent cultural oppression. Freedom of expression is a very fundamental liberty, and total censorship is obviously too onerous a remedy. So the state is enjoined by the accumulative-harm principle to use strategies of reform which disrupt free expression as little as possible. I shall discuss such strategies in the next chapter.

I have tried, then, to give some defence of the accumulative interpretation of the harm principle. The accumulative interpretation allows us to protect interests that might otherwise get left out of consideration. It allows these interests to be considered not just as the goals of benign and enlightened public policy, but with an urgency equal to that enjoyed by any of liberalism's deepest principles. The arguments that might be brought against the accumulative-harm principle, and the worries we might have about it, do not turn out to have the force we expected. Many processes in social life have an accumulative structure:

the pressure of public opinion, the enforcement of social norms, the formation of gender identities, the effect of the capitalist economic system on the freedom of the worker, and, in particular, the cultural oppression that is the subject of this extended discussion. On the accumulative interpretation of the harm principle, we cannot simply ignore the harmful effects of these processes on the grounds that they are not the work of individuals. As they are usually interpreted, the boundaries of liberal state neutrality are demarcated by the prevention of individual conduct that would cause harm to others. But this interpretation of harm is too narrow. As we have seen, there are no good reasons for accepting only the individual interpretation of the harm principle. Accumulative harms, not individual harms, define the limits of state neutrality. If liberalism cannot accept this conclusion, it will fail to protect people from the harm of cultural oppression. In the next chapter, I shall discuss how a minimally onerous strategy for reforming an oppressive, inegalitarian culture challenges the liberal doctrine of state neutrality.[21]

5

LIBERALISM AND THE
REFORM OF CULTURE

A person's ultimate interest is in living as meaningful, worthwhile, and valuable a life as possible. Consequently, people have a highest interest in coming to know the good and a highest-order interest in implementing that knowledge. To implement their conceptions of the good, people require a fair share of the world's resources. What constitutes a person's fair share of the world's resources is the problem of distributive justice. To come to know the good, people require a cultural environment free of practices that would enculturate false and undermining beliefs about value. How to reform the cultural environment is the problem of liberation. Egalitarian liberal thought has neglected this second problem.

Human beings are essentially social. They are born, socialized, and enculturated into the inherited beliefs and ideas that make up a culture. Human beings are inescapably members of one culture or another. The value of people's cultural membership is ambiguous; its effects can be both beneficial and harmful. Liberals have recently, and quite rightly, emphasized the benefits of cultural membership. Nevertheless, forgetting that culture also has an oppressive side is wrong. We do not choose all the beliefs about value that make up our more significant ends. Either we take them up directly from what our culture presents or we arrive at them by deliberation on normative and factual background beliefs taken up unreflectively from our culture. The human capacity for critical reflection is finite, both for the philosopher in her study and for people leading busy and sometimes desperate lives outside academia. In an inegalitarian culture, many of the beliefs that people take up from their cultural environment are based on beliefs about the moral inequality of persons. Egalitarian liberalism must regard these beliefs as false. In a sexist culture, for example, women come to understand themselves as less deserving of access to certain opportunities than are men, and men, correspondingly, expect greater entitlements as compared with those of women. If people base their ends in life on these false evaluations, their highest-order interest in coming to know the good will have been harmed. Because contemporary egalitarian liberalism has implicitly become cognitivist about people's ends, it must accept that cultural oppression is a harm to people's highest-order interests. A culture does not have a determinate agent as a source, but is instead diffusely produced and maintained by the activities of its members. Thus cultural oppression is both a harm to a significant interest and a diffuse, collective, cumulative, environmental harm to that interest.

CULTURE AND EXPRESSION

A culture is sustained and perpetuated by the activities of its members. Some of these activities are solidified into the communications media, technology, and institutions of a culture, while others continually arise and pass away in the expressive behaviour of its members. Expressive behaviour, behaviour that individually or collectively transmits values, beliefs, and attitudes to members of the culture, is a wide category. At the individual level, one person has many ways of leading another to believe what she wants him to believe. Suppose she wants him to believe in ghosts. The most obvious, and least effective, method is speech; she can simply say, or write in a letter, that ghosts exist. She can, more effectively, lead him to believe in ghosts by her behaviour; she can act as though she has seen a ghost. Even more insidiously, she can utilize representations of ghosts; she can dress up as a ghost, or do tricks with lights in his garden after dark. Beliefs are transmitted not only by language but also by the perception of behaviour and representation. So it is with our beliefs about value. In critically reflecting on our ends, we initially employ a set of background beliefs that we have taken up from our culture. The content of these beliefs is determined by the social meanings prevalent in our culture. These background beliefs are not foundational. We likely shall revise them as we sporadically take up the slow task of reflecting on our values. We take up these background beliefs by a process that is more like perception than choice. Again, consider how one individual can transmit false beliefs in inequality to another. He can use speech; he can say that women are worth less than men, or he can give reasons based in physical features or social customs. He can transmit such a belief by his behaviour; he can show by the way he treats women how he thinks they ought to be treated. Or he can distribute representations of women in subordinate roles; he can show pictures of women enjoying being sexually dominated or provide magazines devoted to ways for women to please men. Expressive activities like this may be ineffective in transmitting beliefs by themselves. But when they are repeated over and over again, and come not just from one source but from every quarter, they form a relentless backdrop to people's ethical deliberation. This is roughly the technique of commercial advertising. An individual advertisement for the special value of some consumer good may be implausible by itself, but as shown by the billions of dollars worth of "empirical research" by advertisers, when advertising is continually repeated, it is successful in transmitting its message.

Joshua Cohen distinguishes three sorts of harms that expression can impose. First, when the harm is done just by what is expressed, we have a *direct* harm. Defamation is an example. Second, we have what he calls *environmental* harms:

> A second category of costs are "environmental." Thus expression may help to constitute a degraded, sickening, embarrassing, humiliating, obtrusively moralistic, hypercommercialized, hostile, or demeaning environment. It might, for example, combine with other expressive actions to contribute to an environment of racial or national antagonism, or to one in which dominance and submission are eroticised. Here the harm is not the expression by itself, since in the absence of other similar sayings the environment would not be degraded, hypercommercialized, or hostile; nor can we trace particular harmful or injurious consequences to particular acts of expression that help to constitute the unfavorable environment. Instead, the price of the expression lies in its contribution to making an environment hostile, for example, to achieving such fundamental values as racial or sexual equality.[1]

Third, when the expression persuades the listener to do something harmful, we have an *indirect* harm. The diffuse, accumulative harm done by cultural oppression fits into Cohen's category of "environmental" harms. It is important not to underestimate just how important these sorts of harms are, especially because there is no way to isolate what the expression's "contribution to making an environment hostile" is. But the harm done by a cultural environment which is hostile to the values of racial and sexual equality is a harm to significant, highest-order interests. The interpretation of the harm principle defended in Chapter 4 requires the liberal state to make some response.

I shall focus on the diffuse, accumulative harms brought about by expressions of inequality polluting our cultural environment, Cohen's category of environmental harms. That is not to say that the direct and indirect harms caused by expression do not pose important issues having to do with the limitation of freedom of expression. Consensus exists on the need to regulate some expression: assault or threats of bodily harm, child pornography, libel and slander, falsely crying "fire" in a crowded theatre, distributing recipes for homemade nerve gas. Controversy surrounds the need to regulate other forms of expression: hate speech, pornography, obscenity, incitement to revolution, "fighting words," expression inflicting emotional distress, and expression offensive by community standards. I do not propose to discuss the direct and indirect harms of expression, other than to note in passing that in all the controversial cases except the last I see the harms done as far outweighing the value of the expressive activities. I propose, instead, to discuss what strategy the liberal egalitarian state ought to pursue regarding expressive acts that do not, taken individually, fall into any category of regulated expression, but which, taken collectively, sustain an oppressive culture.

STRATEGIES OF REFORM

I see three strategies that an egalitarian liberal state might adopt regarding the reform of an oppressive culture. First is the *laissez-faire* strategy advocated by Rawls, Dworkin, and Kymlicka. This strategy holds that under conditions of equal basic liberties and material equality, the inegalitarian, oppressive aspects of culture will disappear. Second is the *censorship* strategy, under which the state should uphold equality by coercively regulating expressive activities that contribute to an oppressive cultural environment. Third is the *advocacy* strategy, under which the state should not interfere coercively with expression, but should employ non-coercive means, its economic and ideological power, to challenge false beliefs about moral equality. I shall argue that the laissez-faire strategy will prove ineffective, and because the advocacy strategy is less onerous in its requirements than the censorship strategy, the egalitarian liberal state should therefore adopt the advocacy strategy. Only if the advocacy strategy proves ineffective should it consider the censorship strategy.

The liberal state's laissez-faire attitude to culture is required by the doctrine of state neutrality. This doctrine forbids the state either to censor mistaken expression or to engage, directly or indirectly, in education campaigns against mistaken beliefs. The neutral state allows the development of what its defenders often call a "cultural marketplace," or a "free market of ideas." Defenders have also claimed that in the free market of ideas, false conceptions of the good will be driven out. Kymlicka writes:

Freedom of speech and association allow different groups to pursue and advertise their way of life. But not all ways of life are equally valuable, and some will have difficulty attracting or maintaining adherents. Since individuals are free to choose between competing visions of the good life, civil liberties have nonneutral consequences – they create a marketplace of ideas, as it were, and how well a way of life does in this market depends on the kinds of goods it can offer to prospective adherents. Hence, under conditions of freedom, satisfying and valuable ways of life will tend to drive out those which are worthless and unsatisfying.[2]

As I argued earlier, the analogy between a culture and a market is extremely misleading. In the ideal market, many vendors (speakers) each offer their wares (ideas about the good life) for selection by potential customers (members of the culture). A culture is less like a range of options offered for people's choice and more like a mechanism for controlling them. A better analogy than that between a culture and a market is the analogy between a culture and a maze. In the maze of ideas, people have the illusion that they are making choices, when in reality the maze is channelling them, as they work their way through it, toward a limited way of thinking. Nevertheless, the metaphor of the "cultural marketplace" guides the laissez-faire approach of the neutral state in its policies toward culture.

Kymlicka's view is overly optimistic. A statement of faith is not a very strong argument, as Kymlicka himself admits: "To some people this will seem an unwarranted naivety about the power of free speech in civil society to weed out cultural oppression."[3] Galston is much more pessimistic, and rather scathing about liberal optimism:

Social competition is no more reliably benign than economic competition. Indeed, a kind of social Gresham's Law may operate, in which the pressure of seductively undemanding ways of life may make it very difficult, for example, for parents to raise children in accordance with norms of effort, conscientiousness, and self-restraint. The easy assumption that only "undeserving" ways of life lose out in a liberal society is unworthy of serious social philosophy.[4]

Rawls has also become less optimistic about the view that deserving ways of life will win out and flourish in a liberal society:

But if a comprehensive conception of the good is unable to endure in a society securing the familiar equal basic liberties and mutual toleration, there is no way to preserve it consistent with democratic values as expressed by the idea of society as a fair system of cooperation among citizens viewed as free and equal. This raises, but does not of course settle, the question of whether the corresponding way of life is viable under other historical conditions, and whether its passing is to be regretted.[5]

Rawls's pessimism about the flourishing of valuable conceptions of the good should apply, *mutatis mutandis*, to the withering of false conceptions. If it is not clear that valuable conceptions will remain, then it also is not clear that false conceptions will disappear. The laissez-faire strategy cannot guarantee to rid the cultural environment of ways of life involving expressive activities that sustain beliefs in human inequality.

By implication, Rawls is saying that there is no way to get rid of cultural oppression "consistent with democratic values." Dworkin has offered several arguments that the laissez-faire strategy is the best available for liberals. He raises the question of why liberals should not actively reform the cultural environment by asking what is wrong with cultural paternalism:

> I have in mind cultural paternalism: the suggestion that people should be protected from choosing wasteful or bad lives not by flat prohibitions of the criminal law but by educational decisions and devices that remove bad options from people's view and imagination. People do not make decisions about how to live in a cultural vacuum. They respond in various ways to what their culture makes available by way of possibility and example and recommendation. Why, then, should we not try to make that cultural environment as sound as we can, in the interests of people who will decide to live influenced by it?[6]

He gives three answers to this question, none of which is satisfactory. First, he argues that to reform culture is to take away an important challenge to be faced by those seeking to live well:

> Living well would mean taking the best choices from a culled list, and paternalism would be indispensable rather than threatening to ethical success. But that view is not sensible: a challenge cannot be more interesting, or in any way a more valuable challenge to face, when it has been narrowed, simplified, and bowdlerized by others in advance, and that is as much true when we are ignorant of what they have done as when we are all too aware of it.[7]

This argument depends on Dworkin's view of value, in which a person gives value to her life by responding to the challenges that life presents her. But what about equality of challenge? Is it fair that some people should face harder challenges than others? To use Cohen's words, does not someone who is degraded, sickened, embarrassed, or humiliated by an "obtrusively moralistic, hypercommercialized, hostile, or demeaning environment" face a more difficult challenge in leading a good life than

93

one who is not? Does not a person who finds her submission eroticised, or one who faces a cultural environment hostile to racial equality, carry a heavier burden than one who does not? Does not someone whose self-respect is undermined, or who is led to undervalue her self-worth, face a harder challenge than one whose self-respect is bolstered and whose worth is valued properly? Dworkin responds that there are no independent grounds for determining what "circumstances are appropriate for people deciding how to live."[8] But that is wrong. Dworkin's liberal equality assumes the equal moral worth of persons. As argued in Chapter 1, this assumption transcends differences and disputes about the truth and falsity of conceptions of the good life. An inegalitarian cultural environment is the wrong circumstance for people deciding how to live.

In a second argument, offered in response to Catharine MacKinnon's argument that pornography contradicts the value of equality of opportunity for women, Dworkin concludes that combatting a polluted cultural environment requires only equality of access to shaping that environment:

> People's lives are affected not just by their political environment – not just by what their presidents and legislators and other public officials do – but even more comprehensively by what we might call their moral environment. How others treat me – and my own sense of identity and self-respect – are determined in part by the mix of social conventions, opinions, tastes, convictions, prejudices, life styles, and cultures that flourish in the community in which I live. Liberals are sometimes accused of thinking that what people say or do or think in private has no impact on anyone except themselves, and that is plainly wrong. . . . Exactly because the moral environment in which we all live is in good part created by others, however, the question of who shall have the power to help shape that environment, and how, is of fundamental importance, though it is often neglected in political theory. Only one answer is consistent with the ideals of political equality: that no one may be prevented from influencing the shared moral environment. . . . Of course it should go without saying that no one has a right to *succeed* in influencing others through his own private choices and tastes. Sexists and bigots have no right to live in a community whose ideology or culture is even partially sexist or bigoted. . . . In a genuinely egalitarian society, however, those views cannot be locked out, in advance, by criminal or civil law: they must instead be discredited by the disgust, outrage, and ridicule of other people.[9]

But this argument fails to address MacKinnon's original point that in our present culture and under our present distribution of resources, this strategy has failed:

So why are we now – with more pornography than ever before – buried in all these lies? Laissez-faire might be an adequate theory of the social preconditions for knowledge in a nonhierarchical society. But in a society of gender inequality, the speech of the powerful impresses its view upon the world, concealing the truth of powerlessness under that despairing acquiescence that provides the appearance of consent and makes protest inaudible as well as rare.[10]

So perhaps Dworkin does not mean that the equal-access strategy will work under our present distribution of resources and power. Instead, perhaps he means that the strategy will work under the egalitarian distribution of resources favoured by liberal equality.[11] But material equality cannot guarantee cultural reform. The reason stems from Galbraith's observation that the power to influence the cultural environment is associated not with individuals but with organizations.[12] Given an inegalitarian distribution of resources, one individual might control the discretionary resources needed to succeed in advancing his viewpoint in the communications media. However, given an egalitarian distribution, influence in the cultural environment would require the organized efforts of a large number of individuals. Equality of resources for individuals and freedom of association together do not guarantee that the friends of equality will be successful in organizing influential associations. Their success at cultural reform is especially unlikely, given the biased starting point created by an oppressive culture. Perhaps if we started with an egalitarian culture, then freedom of expression, freedom of association, and material equality could sustain it into the future. But if we start from an oppressive culture, it is less plausible that material equality will be sufficient to change it. The covert way culture acts on the individual also hinders the formation of organizations to challenge cultural oppression. People accept the values of their culture; they do not possess a different independent set of values from which to judge, or even be aware of, the need for reform. People who find their inequality natural are unlikely starting material for organizations to promote equality. Finally, oppressed groups may be small in size, and thus unable to support organizations of sufficient influence. Women have numerical equality to men, and under conditions of material equality they could support powerful movements for recognition of their moral equality. But numerical equality does not exist, for example, for gays and lesbians, who, given material equality, still might not be able to support sufficiently powerful organizations.

Dworkin's third argument is analogous to the argument that cultural oppression does not defraud its victims. He gives two reasons why it does not makes sense to talk of compensating people for false beliefs about value: One is that "there is the obvious problem that some official would have to make the decision about which ethical convictions were right and which were wrong." The second is that "no one could identify the resources he ought to have to compensate for mistaken beliefs he could not think mistaken."[13] Dworkin believes that people must take responsibility for the choices they have made, but that they should be compensated for unchosen circumstances. He argues that despite his admission that people do not choose their beliefs about value, they should not be compensated for arriving at false ones. Having false ethical convictions is not a handicap in the same way as being physically challenged:

> Liberal equality is designed for ethical liberals: it aims to make them equal in their circumstances, and it understands someone's circumstances as the set of opportunities and limitations he encounters in identifying and pursuing what he deems, after reflection, to be an appropriate life for him. Talents and handicaps are plainly circumstances in that sense. But convictions and preferences are plainly not. It would be incoherent for me to regard some ethical conviction I have – that the only important thing to do with my life is to create religious monuments, for example – as a limitation on the goodness of the life I can lead.[14]

Both these points have easy answers. The ethical convictions which are wrong are those that depend on false beliefs about the inequality of persons. The decision about their wrongness follows from the fundamental principles of egalitarian liberal theory and is not left to the whims of the bureaucratic bugbears of liberalism. The second point presents us with a false dilemma: the state must either adopt the laissez-faire strategy or compensate people for mistaken beliefs about value that they do not believe mistaken. But why is compensation the only alternative to leaving things alone?[15] We can never compensate a person for his accidental death, but that does not entail that we should do nothing to prevent it if we have the opportunity. Dworkin's dilemma is vitiated by a third option, which is for the state to prevent inegalitarian beliefs by challenging them actively and publicly.

STATE NEUTRALITY AND THE ADVOCACY STRATEGY

Three alternatives to the laissez-faire strategy are (1) for the state to participate actively in public forums on behalf of equality, (2) for the state to limit freedom of expression and censor inegalitarian expression, and (3) for the state to adopt both these strategies together. The first two strategies would act in different ways to prevent the cultural harm produced by expressive activities. The first, the advocacy strategy, would act on the beliefs and attitudes of both speaker and audience. It would endeavour to dissuade the former from the attitudes that led to the expressive activity, and to persuade the latter that beliefs in inequality acquired from the cultural environment are false and should be abandoned. The second, the censorship strategy, would act to force the expressive activities to cease, but would do little to change the attitudes behind the activity and little to challenge false beliefs already formed by the audience. Egalitarian liberals should be reluctant to adopt the censorship strategy without first trying to make the advocacy strategy work. Coercive intervention would violate the endorsement constraint of Locke and Dworkin, because the censorship strategy would not change the attitudes behind the expressive activities. By analogy to Williams's argument that people cannot decide to believe, people cannot be forced to believe. If someone comes to believe a proposition in full awareness that he is being forced to, and not because the proposition is true, then his attitude cannot really be belief because beliefs aim at truth. The censorship strategy would be more likely to cause resentment in the speakers and harden them in their attitudes. So adopting both strategies would undermine the gains of adopting the advocacy strategy alone. The advocacy strategy is the best interpretation of egalitarian liberalism.

However, the advocacy strategy requires that a severe modification be made to the liberal doctrine of state neutrality. Roughly, state neutrality holds that the state cannot use the superiority or inferiority of a conception of the good as grounds for pursuing one policy rather than another. More precisely, the doctrine of state neutrality has at least the following three variants:

(1) Neutrality of consequence: The state's policies should have the same consequences for every conception of the good.
(2) Neutrality of aim: The state should not intend its policies to favour, or to hinder, one conception of the good over another.
(3) Neutrality of justification: The state should not decide its policies using the correctness or incorrectness of any conception of the good as its reason.

Egalitarian liberals cannot endorse neutrality of consequence, for in the free market of ideas that state neutrality establishes, some conceptions of the good will fail to attract adherents, and their representations will disappear from the cultural marketplace.[16] The consequences of the free market of ideas are not the same for every conception of the good. Neutrality of aim collapses into neutrality of justification in a democracy. In a dictatorship, the state may aim to favour or hinder a conception of the good for no reason other than the whim of the dictator. However, if a democracy intends to favour or hinder a conception of the good, then it needs to give public reasons, and these reasons will presuppose that the conception of the good is correct or incorrect. So I shall take it that neutrality of justification is the most interesting variant.[17] Raz gives a formulation of this interpretation which he calls the "exclusion of ideals":

> Excluding conceptions of the good from politics means, at its simplest and most comprehensive, that the fact that some conception of the good is true or valid or sound or reasonable, etc., should never serve as a reason for any political action. Nor should the fact that a conception of the good is false, invalid, unsound, unreasonable, etc. be allowed to be a reason for a political action.[18]

Justificatory state neutrality, on a cognitivist interpretation, means that the state cannot pursue policies on the grounds that conceptions of the good are true or false.

State neutrality is a broader, more powerful doctrine than mere state recognition of a list of basic liberties.[19] A modern state is composed of much more than its army, police force, and judiciary. In a way corresponding to the classification of power into condign, compensatory, and conditioned that Galbraith proposed, the power of the modern state is rooted in the coercive, economic, and ideological state apparatuses.[20] The doctrine of state neutrality extends restrictions on state power from the coercive state apparatus to its economic and educational policies as well. The neutral state cannot outlaw being a hermit on the grounds that it is a waste of a life. As well, it cannot tax hermits differentially, offer them special subsidies for returning to society, grant money to associations formed to rehabilitate hermits, or run advertising campaigns that try to prevent young people from choosing a hermit's life style. The doctrine of state neutrality is broader in scope than the enforcement of basic liberties. It extends the scope of restrictions on state power to cover all policies and political decisions: coercive, fiscal, and educational.

Someone might observe that both the economic and ideological state apparatuses are indirectly coercive. Tax dollars support both, and libertarians have long argued that taxation is coercive. The state does not offer its citizens a choice about paying their taxes. Taxation is ultimately based on the coercive power of the state. So all state policies and actions are, in some sense, coercive. The doctrine of state neutrality extends the restrictions on state power to cover both directly and indirectly coercive interferences. Liberal egalitarians are not, however, uniformly against all indirectly coercive interferences with people. The theories of distributive justice of both Rawls and Dworkin need some form of taxation to achieve their different forms of equality of resources. Neither theorist thinks of taxation as a form of state theft. Instead, it is a device for ensuring that citizens get their fair shares, and it is legitimately backed up by coercion in the same way as are the basic liberties.

Neutrality is not just an auxiliary principle of egalitarian liberalism; it is a deep assumption of its theory of distributive justice. For example, Rawls argues for an egalitarian distribution of what he calls "primary goods" because primary goods are consistent with state neutrality. People can employ them to implement any permissible conception of the good. Allocating people money does not assume the superiority of any particular way of life; allocating them copies of *A Theory of Justice* assumes the superiority of a life of philosophical reflection.

The broad scope of the doctrine of state neutrality presents a problem for egalitarian liberal theory. The scope of state neutrality includes both directly coercive interferences with people's lives and indirectly coercive state economic and educational policies. However, egalitarian liberal arguments for toleration and neutrality are directed only against direct coercion and miss the indirect component. Rawls sums up his epistemological argument for tolerance among reasonable people thus:

> To conclude: reasonable persons see that the burdens of judgement set limits on what can be reasonably justified to others, and so they endorse some form of liberty of conscience and freedom of thought. It is unreasonable for us to use political power, should we possess it, or share it with others, to repress comprehensive views that are not unreasonable.[21]

Because, under conditions of reasonable pluralism, there is no way of reaching consensus on the truth of comprehensive beliefs, reasonable persons will think it unreasonable to repress other comprehensive doctrines. Whatever the merits of this argument, it does not follow as easily that reasonable people will think it unreasonable to use tax dollars to support their cause. Reasonable people may not find indirectly coercive state policies in support of their position to be as unreasonable as is direct coercive repression of opposition. So Rawls does not take the consequence of this argument to be state neutrality; he takes its consequence to be the liberties that underlie tolerance.

Dworkin's argument against coercive state paternalism is based on the endorsement constraint. Coercing someone into acting in accord with some conception of the good, even if it is the true one, cannot make his life go better for him. Prayer in the shadow of the rack is of no value to either god or supplicant. Again, this argument turns on the directness of the coercion. Suppose, instead, the person just pays his fair share of taxes, and the state then spends tax money on an advertising campaign to persuade him, and others like him, from their mistaken views. This is a paternalistic state policy that violates neutrality, but it does not violate the endorsement constraint. Neither of these foundational arguments for tolerance offered by Rawls and Dworkin is strong enough to capture the full scope of the doctrine of state neutrality.

The opposite of liberal state neutrality is state perfectionism. To the perfectionist, one conception of the good is superior to all others, everyone should adopt this conception of the good, and all other conceptions of the good are mistaken. According to the doctrine of state perfectionism, then, the truth of this shared conception of the good (and the falsity of all its competitors) is a good reason for state action. Religious states generally have this character. Totalitarian religious states were what the original liberals had in mind when they argued for toleration and state neutrality. Liberals deny state perfectionism. For Rawls, in a liberal state, people "do not use the coercive apparatus of the state to win for themselves a greater liberty or larger distributive shares on the grounds that their activities are of more intrinsic value. Perfectionism is denied as a political principle."[22] Liberals see state neutrality and state perfectionism as the only two principled options for dealing with culture. I shall argue that this is a false dilemma.

Though liberal state neutrality and totalitarian state perfectionism may be the opposites of one another, they do not exhaust the possibilities. Alternatives to state neutrality and state perfectionism do exist. I claim that the advocacy strategy is a better interpretation of egalitarian liberalism than is unqualified state neutrality. The advocacy strategy recognizes that citizens have a highest-order interest in knowing the good, undertakes to protect that interest from deceptive cultural practices, and will use the economic and educational state apparatuses to oppose inegalitarian cultural oppression. Accepting the core liberal principle of the equal moral worth of persons, it will oppose cultural practices falling into the following category: cultural practices that lead people to believe in the unequal moral worth of persons belonging to different groups, with people relying on these false beliefs about inequality in forming their beliefs about value. So, for example, an advocacy state should oppose commercial advertising that represents women in positions subordinate to men. It should do so because the representation of inequality is both false and part of a diffuse cultural sexism that leads women to false and undermining beliefs about themselves and their entitlements. The advocacy state, unlike the neutral state, can engage in the project of cultural reform.

The advocacy strategy conflicts with the doctrine of state neutrality regarding state economic and educational policies. The doctrine of state neutrality prohibits the state from adopting economic and educational policies based on the finding that some ethical beliefs prevalent in society are false. State advocacy follows from the limits put on state neutrality by the harm principle. Liberals regard beliefs in inequality as false, and these beliefs are harmful if prevalent in society. Beliefs in inequality are harmful *because* they are false, because their falsity undermines knowledge of the good. The state should prevent this harm, and one strategy of prevention is for the state to adopt economic and educational policies to challenge these beliefs in inequality, and to adopt these policies for exactly the reason that the beliefs are false. Liberal equality must recognize that actively advocating equality in public forums is a better response to the harm of cultural oppression than is a neutral stance.

The advocacy strategy does not collapse into totalitarian state perfectionism, because it recognizes that cognitivism about ends does not entail reductionism about ends. Value can be highly particular: different people, or even the same person in different contexts, may value different things, and their judgements may all be true. Of course it is true that we must universalize moral obligations to others; if committing murder is wrong for one person, committing murder is wrong for everyone. Yet it is not true that we must universalize personal evaluations; one person may judge that the most valuable way for her to earn a living is as a philosophy professor, while another person may judge that the most worthwhile thing he can do with his life is to become a farmer. The cognitivism about ends that leads to state advocacy does not entail that everyone shares, or ought to share, one end. Because personal value is highly particular, beliefs about value will often be false for many, though true for some. A belief that philosophy is the most valuable activity will be false for farmers, while true for philosophy professors.

One worry is that an advocacy state will become overly intrusive. This worry is out of place. The accumulative-harm principle, as discussed in Chapter 4, enjoins the state to prevent harms by the fairest and least onerous means possible. This constraint requires imposing duties that lead to the least disruption to people's lives. If the strategy of state economic and educational intervention in public forums can reform an inegalitarian culture without resort to the deployment of the coercive state apparatus, then this is what the harm principle requires. The grounds for intervention by the advocacy state are still limited, though less so than are the grounds for intervention by the neutral state. State advocacy says that state intervention is justified to oppose false and harmful cultural practices, but the criteria of false and harmful are stringent. For example, reasonable disagreement is possible regarding the existence of a god, and consequently nothing justifies state opposition to this belief. Other beliefs, while false, are not harmful. Someone's saying that the world is flat is not harmful, first because it is unlikely that anyone else will believe it, and second because even if someone else does believe it, serious harm to his reflections on his ends in life is unlikely to occur. Nor is a belief that redheads are inferior, though false, a harmful falsehood. It is not a component of any cultural practice that leads redheads to undervalue their projects. On the other hand, a belief that women are inferior to men is a component of sexist practices that do lead women to have false beliefs about their own value. Being part of an accumulative harm to people's knowledge of the good, it does give grounds for state opposition.

In an inegalitarian and oppressive culture, the egalitarian liberal state should take an active role opposing inegalitarian beliefs in public forums. Such opposition should involve vigorous educational efforts and active financial support for associations and groups striving to combat inegalitarian cultural practices. The advocacy strategy would not try to force people to believe in moral equality. The reasons raised by Locke and Dworkin would doom these coercive efforts at the start. Nor should it necessarily adopt a pro-censorship stance. The advocacy state should respect the basic liberties of thought and expression. It would nonetheless participate actively in public debate on the side of equality, contesting racist and sexist viewpoints both directly and indirectly. Consequently, the advocacy state occupies an intermediate position between the neutral state and the censorship strategy as an interpretation of liberal equality. The neutral state may neither infringe basic liberties nor use economic and educational policies to combat false ideas about inequality. The advocacy strategy will not infringe basic liberties, but will use all other policies to the same avail, whereas the censorship strategy would infringe basic liberties. Instead of coercing people, the advocacy state will persuade them. Final evaluation of ideas would be left to the public, in forums of deliberation outside the state. The state should not be impartial in these forums, but instead should be the major participant on the side of equality.

FREEDOM OF EXPRESSION

One way of reforming an inegalitarian culture would be to ban expressive activities that contribute to cultural oppression. This would violate one of the basic liberties: freedom of expression. The advocacy strategy, as an interpretation of liberal equality, does not adopt this approach, because the requirements of the censorship strategy are overly onerous. The advocacy strategy respects many of the reasons for being reluctant to countenance state interference with expression. This interpretation of liberal equality is not, however, absolutist about freedom of expression. Just as free expression serves important interests, an accumulation of expressive activities harms important interests. We must weigh these interests against one another. It is true that we cannot count the interest in expressing falsehoods very highly in this weighing. However, most of the expressive activities that sustain a culture do not have propositional content, and so we cannot call them true or false. Strictly speaking, pornographic images and racist behaviour have no truth value. As well, many expressive activities will be ambiguous in their import. Representations and behaviours cannot easily be singled out for censorship based on their propositional content.

So the advocacy strategy will use the state's economic and educational apparatuses to challenge inequality. It will do so on the grounds of preventing harm to people's highest-order interests. Now, one important characteristic of the doctrine of freedom of expression is that the harm principle does not constrain expressive activities in the way it does ordinary activities. Scanlon writes that "on any very strong version of the doctrine there will be cases where protected acts are held to be immune from restriction despite the fact that they have as consequences harms which would normally be sufficient to justify the imposition of legal sanctions."[23] Political leafleting often results in litter,

103

but littering is not an adequate ground for suppression of political activity. Expressive activities enjoy some immunity from the harm principle. Because the liberal tradition offers many arguments in favour of freedom of expression, it is worth examining them to see what objections they offer to the advocacy strategy.

Because of the high value of freedom of expression in the liberal tradition, liberals will insist on high standards of proof for the causality involved in the production of harm. They will insist on a "clear and present danger" of harm from the expressive activities and will interpret this rule stringently.[24] With an accumulative harm like the effects of a polluted cultural or natural environment, knowledge of the causal connections between act and harm is lost. We can carry out sociological investigations to show whether or not members of an oppressed group systematically think their own projects less valuable than those of other groups, or to show that their self-respect is lower, but we cannot trace the connection of these false beliefs to particular expressive acts. In contrast, we can trace the genesis of the false beliefs created by misleading advertising to their commercial source and rightfully force the advertiser to stop. That the chains of causality are hidden tells more strongly against the censorship approach than the advocacy approach. The censorship approach is likely to cause resentment in the censored, particularly as they can quite rightfully complain that they are doing no one any harm. Even the most insensitive of brutes can see the harm his fists do, but getting him to see how his wolf whistles help sustain a sexist environment will be a hopeless task. The advocacy strategy does not need to target any particular expressive act for intervention. Through state-subsidized ideological activity it attempts both to treat the symptoms of cultural oppression and to treat the inegalitarian attitudes which are responsible for the expressive acts in question. Because its effects are neither coercive nor targeted, liberals need not be so wary of the advocacy remedy for diffuse harms.

Liberals also stress the autonomy of the audience for expressive acts and hold audience members responsible for the offence they take or the beliefs they acquire. Offence is not the real issue. People can be asked to become less sensitive, grow thicker skins, ignore mere words, avoid or walk away from offensive situations, and so on. Nevertheless, this will not protect them from immersion in their culture. An inegalitarian cultural environment is sustained by acts that are, by themselves, innocuous or barely offensive. As well, what someone sees as offensive will depend on the values she has already developed. It is less worrisome that many women are offended by violent pornography than it is that some women and many men are not. It is the acquisition of the beliefs about value that underlie people's attitudes which is important.

The liberal tradition holds people responsible for how they interpret expressive activity and the beliefs they acquire from it. If membership in a culture leads someone to undervalue her projects, that is her fault; she could have believed otherwise if she had so chosen. Scanlon's early work on freedom of expression concluded that the "harms to certain individuals which consist in their coming to have false beliefs as a result of those acts of expression"[25] are not of the sort that could justify restriction of expressive activity. This reason was that "to regard himself as autonomous in the sense I have in mind a person must see himself as sovereign in deciding what to believe and in weighing competing reasons for action."[26] And so "the harm of coming to have false beliefs is not one that an autonomous man could allow the state to protect him against through restrictions on expression."[27]

Against this argument, the first point to make on behalf of the advocacy strategy is that it does not restrict expression. Instead, it acts to persuade a speaker promoting inequality not to speak further, and the audience not to believe the speaker. Because it persuades rather than coerces, the advocacy strategy does not violate the autonomy of either speaker or audience. The speaker might complain that it violates his dignity using his own tax money. Egalitarian liberals, however, should have little truck with a conception of human dignity based on the inequality of persons.

A second point is that this appeal to the ideal of autonomy is an appeal to a false ideal. It views expressive activity using the model of individual-to-individual communication under ideal conditions, like a discussion seminar with well-informed participants. But people do not decide their ethical beliefs as they choose a flavour of ice cream. Instead, as finite reasoners, they deliberate against a background of uncritically accepted beliefs about value, which makes autonomous formation of beliefs difficult. Scanlon's later work on freedom of expression accepts something like this conclusion regarding what he calls the "audience interest":

> Similarly, we have a tendency to assume that, having been exposed, an audience is always free to decide how to react: what belief to form or what attitude to adopt. This freedom to decide enables the audience to protect itself against unwanted long-range effects of expression. If we saw ourselves as helplessly absorbing as a belief every proposition we

heard expressed, then our views of freedom of expression would be quite different from what they are. Certainly we are not like that. Nonetheless, the control we exercise over what to believe and what attitudes to adopt is in several respects an incomplete protection against unwarranted effects of expression.[28]

Scanlon has to explain what is wrong with the formation of false beliefs through external influences, and to do so he has to confront the problem of wants based on false beliefs:

> Suppose that what the [subliminal] advertising does is to change us so that we both have a genuine desire for popcorn and will in fact enjoy it. One can still raise the question whether being affected in this way is a good thing for us, but an answer to it cannot rely on the claim that we are made to think that we have a reason to buy popcorn when in fact we do not. For in this case we will have as good a reason to buy popcorn as we ever do: we want some and will enjoy it if we get it.[29]

Wants based on false beliefs are still wants whose satisfaction brings subjective enjoyment. So the harm has to be to an interest that is not just a considered want:

> It is a bad thing to acquire certain desires or to be influenced by false reasons, and these things are bad whether or not they are brought about by other agents. . . . What we should want in general is to have our beliefs and desires produced by processes that are reliable – processes whose effectiveness depends on the grounds for the beliefs and on the goodness of the desires it produces. . . . The central audience interest in expression, then, is the interest in having a good environment for the formation of one's beliefs and desires.[30]

The central audience value is not autonomy, not deciding for oneself what to believe no matter what is presented or how. What we should want is to have true beliefs about value, based on reasons that justify the beliefs, and acquired by reliable processes. In other words, the central interest of members of the expression's audience is in *knowing* the good and, as a corollary, in not having a hostile, inegalitarian cultural environment.

The liberal tradition is also reluctant to allow state interference with expression because of its distrust of state power. Thus the liberal tradition has insisted on a clear demarcation of public and private realms and has resolutely restricted state activity to the public realm. The state can affirm equality by publicly upholding equality of resources and equal rights of citizenship, but that is as far as it can go. People can be offensive, demeaning, and critical in private; the state's job of affirming the equal worth of persons extends only to guaranteeing equal basic liberties and an equal share of primary goods.[31] However, domestic violence and exploitation occur in private, and though liberalism has traditionally turned a blind eye to their harms, recently egalitarian liberals have been trying to accommodate preventive measures by the state.[32] Much of the expressive activity that sustains culture occurs in private and is traditionally off-limits to the liberal state. Yet private expression that is harmless on a case-by-case basis can accumulate into harm, and the harm principle constrains privacy just as it constrains neutrality and liberty. The laissez-faire strategy to cultural reform confines the state to the public realm. If that cannot work, and we have seen reasons why it cannot, then the harm principle will license at least the intervention of the advocacy strategy.

The liberal tradition sees the state as an unreliable arbiter of expression, continually tempted to expand its power in various dimensions:[33] (1) Allowed to censor speech, and facing resistance, the state will be tempted to increase repression until the disliked speech is suppressed. This concern applies much more to the censorship strategy than to the advocacy strategy. Unlike its coercive role, the state's educational role is self-limiting; there is a limit to how much effort the state can expend to persuade its citizens before the effort becomes ineffective. Long before every second television advertisement is an earnest exhortation to treat others as equals, the viewers will have tuned out. Coercive repression is not similarly self-limiting. Any effective advocacy strategy will recognize its own limitations. (2) If the state is allowed to censor any speech, the liberal tradition worries, it will be on a slippery slope to censoring all speech it dislikes. This is why precise definition of the restricted categories of expression is important. The advocacy strategy does categorize the expressive activities which it challenges: those expressive activities which contribute to an inegalitarian cultural environment. Because expressive acts may have ambiguous interpretations, there can be some question that they so contribute. So the strategy of challenging audience attitudes, rather than targeting expressive acts, is fairer and less intrusive. The advocacy strategy is less drastic in its effects than the censorship strategy, so a certain amount of indeterminacy will be less dangerous. (3) Coercive regulation will affect other categories of speech. People will anticipate the effects of coercion and will be reluctant to speak their minds, especially if they are uncertain whether or not what they have to say is prohibited expression.[34] This will create an environment hostile to free expression. Again, the effects of the advocacy strategy are less drastic than the effects of the censor-ship strategy. The chilling effect of state-subsidized speech against in-equality is minimal and certainly far less than that of state punishment of speech favouring inequality.

The liberal tradition has opposed the censorship strategy on the grounds that the best way to combat false, inegalitarian expression is with more speech, not with coercion.[35] The advocacy interpretation ac-cepts this, but disagrees that the job can be left to debate in the free mar-ket of ideas. Instead, for reasons canvassed, it requires that the state ac-tively participate in this debate on the side of equality, both through moral education on its own account and by subsidizing private associ-ations opposed to inequality, in whatever mix is most effective. Egali-tarian liberals, worried that the cultural marketplace might lead to the loss of parts of the cultural structure, have argued for a very mild and very neutral economic intervention by the state. Discussing aid to cul-tural institutions, Dworkin says that "in general, aid should be given in the form of indiscriminate subsidies, such as tax exemptions for dona-tions to cultural institutions rather than as specific subsidies to particu-lar institutions."[36] The advocacy strategy drops the requirement that fiscal intervention be indiscriminate and overtly subsidizes expression that challenges inequality. Because some associations will effectively get larger shares of resources to promote their views, this strategy will appear to violate both Dworkin's equality of resources and Rawls's dif-ference principle. Nevertheless, the departure from equality will be fair and egalitarian, because even more important than equal economic re-sources to people's interest in leading as good a life as possible is the ex-istence of a cultural environment conducive to both equal levels of self-respect for people and equal chances for them to come to know their good.

A person's most fundamental interest is in leading as meaningful, worthwhile, and valuable a life as possible. People endeavour to satisfy this interest by forming and implementing their conceptions of what is good in life. Egalitarian liberals such as Dworkin and Rawls are plural-ists regarding people's conceptions of the good. They argue that people endorse a variety of ways to live a good human life, and they claim that political authority must be neutral among all reasonable conceptions of the good. However, in their laissez-faire attitude toward the "cultural marketplace," egalitarian liberals have ignored the power of cultural practices to interfere with the processes by which people form their conceptions of the good. Egalitarian liberal theory has slowly come to terms with the beneficial side to cultural membership in a multicultural society. But liberal theory is blind to the other, harmful side to cultural membership. Because of its implicit cognitivism about ends, egalitarian liberalism must recognize the harmful, oppressive side to cultural membership. To be faithful to their ideal of human equality and to deal with cultural oppression, egalitarian liberals must modify their interpretation of the doctrine of state neutrality in order to give the state a legitimate role in the reform of the cultural environment.

CONCLUSION

To be faithful to its vision of the moral equality of persons, egalitarian liberalism must modify its conception of state neutrality. This modification follows from the limitations that the harm principle puts on neutrality; the liberal state should make the most minimal interventions possible in civil society that are sufficient to prevent harms. Once liberalism recognizes the accumulative harm brought about by an inegalitarian cultural environment, it must see the state as having a duty to advocate reform of that cultural environment. In what follows, I shall first sketch what I think should be meant by a harm to someone's cultural identity, and why harms to identity also entail cultural reform. Then I shall briefly discuss some implications of the advocacy strategy by comparing it with Kymlicka's views on the toleration of inegalitarian minority cultures in a multicultural state. I shall conclude by discussing the proper egalitarian liberal response to prevalent attitudes toward the least advantaged.

The notion of "identity" is ambiguous. On the one hand, it can refer to the sets of characteristics by which people are recognized as who they are (e.g., as the child of such and such parents, born at such and such a time). On the other hand, it can refer to the set of characteristics by which an individual is recognized as a member of a group (e.g., someone's racial identity). Within this latter category there are two sorts of group identity. Group membership can be determined on the basis of characteristics over which the group's members have control and for which they can be held responsible. Such groups resemble associations and are characterized by members sharing some conception of the good and the right. Group membership can also be determined on the basis of characteristics for which the group's members cannot be held responsible. Racial groupings are of this sort, as are cultural groups. A cultural group is characterized by a range of options for defining the good life, together with the social meanings attached to these options. Members can be held responsible for which options they incorporate into their conceptions of the good, but having been born and brought up in a culture, they cannot be held responsible for the range of options with which they are presented, nor for the social meanings of these options. Cultural membership makes freedom possible by providing meanings to a range of options which form the basis of individuals' deliberations about the good. But cultural membership also limits, first by providing only a restricted range of options, and second by assigning meanings that restrict which options appear available to which members.

The other sense of identity, the set of characteristics by which someone is recognized as who she is, has a metaphysical sense – raising the problem of personal identity through time – and an ethical sense. Someone's identity in the ethical sense is defined by her conception of the good and the right. Rawls notes that when Saul of Tarsus saw the light on the road to Damascus and became Paul the Apostle, he did not thereby suffer a change in personal identity, nor a change in how he was to be regarded politically. But his ethical identity, as defined by how he thought he should lead his life, changed radically. Rawls writes:

> For example, when citizens convert from one religion to another, or no longer affirm an established religious faith, they do not cease to be, for purposes of political justice, the same persons they were before. . . . There is a second sense of identity specified by reference to citizens' deeper aims and commitments. Let's call it their noninstitutional or moral identity.[1]

A person's ethical identity is constrained by her cultural environment. No one can succeed in critically reflecting on all the social meanings provided by one's culture. This point is implicit in Walzer's characterization of a person's ethical identity: "Men and women take on concrete identities because of the way they conceive and create, and then possess and employ social goods."[2] Social goods are not bare physical things, or even multipurpose resources like money, but are life options as understood by members of a culture. So we can characterize the identity of a culture itself by the range of social goods it makes available. And we can recognize an individual as having a cultural identity if his conception of the good is drawn from the social goods of a particular culture. The characteristic harm that an oppressive cultural environment does to someone's identity is to provide social meanings that lead to false ethical beliefs, and thereby a set-back to her interest in knowing the good.

Someone's ethical identity should be distinguished from the identifications she makes. The notion of someone identifying herself with another person is drawn from psychoanalysis, where it suggests a strong psychological empathy with the other. Small children emotionally identify with the feelings of their parents. The sense of the notion has been extended; parents can be said to identify themselves with the accomplishments of their children. People frequently identify themselves with the groups to which they belong. A medical doctor may identify himself as a doctor and take pride in the respect accorded to doctors by society. In a racist society, on the other hand, someone may identify himself as a member of a race which the cultural environment portrays as inferior. Because of his emotional identification with his group, this portrayal will harm his self-esteem. The characteristic harm that an oppressive cultural environment does through a person's identifications is to diminish his self-respect.

Without denying the importance of the cumulative harm that an oppressive culture does to someone's self-respect, I wish instead to discuss the harm it does to someone's identity. In an oppressive culture, a person can acquire a false or bad ethical identity. Her ethical identity is her conception of the good and the right, her critical interests as constrained by her sense of justice. This is what characterizes her as an ethical being, and it is the reference point for her decisions about how to lead her life. Her understanding of the good and the right will be based on the social meanings of goods in her culture. If she is a member of a patriarchal culture, then she will find that one aspect of the social meanings of many goods will be that they should be distributed on grounds of gender. Because such grounds are arbitrary from a moral point of view, her conception of the good will be based on beliefs that egalitarian liberals must think false. This is a harm to her and, by extension, a harm to her identity. Reforming her cultural environment will eventually remove or mitigate this harm.

A different notion of someone's identity being harmed, however, is often used as an argument against cultural reform. On this notion, any successful change or even attempted change to a person's identity is a harm to him. For example, consider a man who has grown up in a culture which has inculcated, encouraged, and sustained his patriarchal attitudes. These attitudes run deep, so that within his conception of the good and the right it is entirely natural that women serve and defer to him, do his housework and look after his children. Because of his sex, he believes himself entitled to a larger share of those things that are necessary to a good life. Then, as the cultural environment becomes more egalitarian, the social world starts to change around him. He feels his identity threatened as his ethical convictions become increasingly contested, and there is less and less support and encouragement to sustain his attitudes. He feels harmed as he is pressured to revise his conception of the good and the right. He feels harmed because he feels he cannot revise his conception of the good without becoming a morally different person. But it is not at all clear that he is harmed. It is true that, as Rawls says, people believe that they cannot revise their conceptions of the good. People "may regard it as unthinkable to view themselves apart from certain religious, philosophical, and moral convictions, or from certain enduring attachments and loyalties."[3] Nevertheless, how things seem to people and how things really are may be two quite different things. Just because it seems to the man in the example that he cannot revise his convictions, it does not follow that in fact he cannot.

The argument that in fact he cannot revise his convictions will depend on a stronger claim about the relationship between convictions and identity. It will require the assumption that certain convictions are essential to his identity. This appears to be Sandel's view when he writes that "those qualities most plausibly regarded as essential to a person's identity – one's character, values, core convictions, and deepest loyalties, for example – are often heavily influenced by social and cultural factors."[4] The implied argument is that if we change cultural factors, then we will change core convictions. If we change core convictions, then we will change something essential to a person's ethical identity. So if we change the cultural environment of the man in the example, we risk changing the person that he is, and this constitutes a harm to him. But this conservative view assumes too strong a connection between convictions and ethical identity. While it is essential that a person have some ethical convictions, some deeper self, in order to make choices, it is not essential that he have some particular conviction or other.[5] His ethical convictions must have some continuity over time or he will have an "identity crisis," but that does not mean that his convictions cannot change gradually without destroying him as a person. By way of analogy, a boat can be rebuilt gradually over time, plank by plank, yet remain the same boat. In fact, the man in the example is in a harmed state prior to the cultural change, since his convictions are based on false, inegalitarian beliefs. He is benefitted, not harmed, by egalitarian cultural reform that challenges and changes him. He may not like the process, it may seem to threaten his sense of self, but his conception of the good will nonetheless improve. However, it is essential that the man be persuaded, not forced, to believe in the moral equality of persons, for, as we saw earlier, by analogy to Williams's argument that people cannot choose to believe, a forced assent is not a real belief. If his interest in knowing the good is to be benefitted, he must truly change his beliefs. Persuasion, not force, is the method of the advocacy strategy toward cultural reform.

Egalitarian liberals are close to recognizing the need for the advocacy strategy. To show how close, I shall compare it to the strategy Kymlicka suggests the liberal state should adopt regarding illiberal minority cultures. I have been assuming that each state has only one societal culture of which its citizens are members and that it is this societal culture which is oppressive and in need of reform. This assumption is false for many liberal democratic states. Canada, for example, was originally composed of many national cultures – aboriginal, French, and English – and has since been enriched, through immigration, by diverse other ethnic cultures. Much of the discussion of the role of cultural membership in liberal theory has arisen from the problem posed by multicultural states. Some minorities within the liberal democratic state are illiberal or inegalitarian. By an illiberal minority, I mean one whose social practices coercively restrict the basic liberties of its members. By an inegalitarian minority, I mean one whose pervasive social meanings, values, and attitudes are inegalitarian. Usually, illiberal minorities will be inegalitarian in their dominant attitudes, whereas inegalitarian minorities may rely on non-coercive means of controlling their members and thus may seem liberal on the surface.

I contend that the egalitarian liberal state should adopt the advocacy strategy toward any inegalitarian culture, be it a minority culture or the majority societal culture. For comparison, we can extrapolate Kymlicka's strategy for dealing with illiberal minority cultures to inegalitarian cultures. The harms posed by illiberal cultures are more apparent and more urgent to liberal eyes than are the harms of inegalitarian cultures. Kymlicka develops his strategy for state response to illiberal minorities by analogy to how liberal national governments should deal with illiberal national governments. In both cases, he believes, "there is relatively little scope for legitimate coercive interference."[6] Attempts to forcibly impose liberal principles from the outside will cause resentment and lead to unstable conditions unless the principles are internalized by members of the culture. Kymlicka notes that in the nineteenth century, John Stuart Mill thought liberal states should spread liberal principles by colonizing illiberal countries. Contemporary liberal states, however, have tried to spread liberal principles to illiberal countries without the use of force, through "education, persuasion, and financial incentives."[7]

In essence, liberal states should adopt the equivalent of the advocacy strategy toward illiberal states. Illiberal minorities are unjust, but imposing liberalization from the outside will not lead to a stable solution. Enduring liberalization can come only from internal reform. Kymlicka writes:

> This does not mean that liberals should stand by and do nothing. A national minority which rules in an illiberal way acts unjustly. Liberals have a right, and a responsibility, to speak out against such injustice. Hence liberal reformers inside the culture should seek to promote their liberal principles, through reason or example, and liberals outside should lend their support to any efforts the group makes to liberalize their culture. Since the most enduring forms of liberalization are those that result from internal reform, the primary focus of liberals outside the group should be to provide this sort of support.[8]

Kymlicka would extend the strategy of the liberal state toward illiberal foreign states to the strategy of the liberal state toward illiberal domestic minorities, because "there are many analogous opportunities for a majority nation to encourage national minorities, in a non-coercive way, to liberalize their internal constitutions."[9] An illiberal minority that restricts its members' activities thereby harms its members. The harm principle would justify the liberal state in intervening coercively. Nevertheless, the best strategy for a liberal state to pursue in dealing with illiberal minority cultures is something akin to the advocacy strategy.

The harm done by a minority which coercively restricts the basic liberties of its members is obvious to the liberal. The harm done by an inegalitarian culture, minority or majority, is just as real, though less apparent. The egalitarian liberal state should extend the strategy of non-coercively encouraging the reform of illiberal minority societies to the reform of inegalitarian minority and majority cultures. It should encourage reform through "education, persuasion, and financial incentives."

The educational curriculum should be permeated by the egalitarian liberal view of the moral equality of persons; there should be no room in the curriculum, except as cautionary tales or historical curiosities, for teaching that people's worth depends on grounds that are arbitrary from a moral point of view. Equality should not play a merely negative role in education, determining only what should not be taught. The curriculum should both inform about and give positive value to the experiences and ways of life of groups whose member have historically been treated as inferior. It should teach how persons, no matter what

115

their group membership or their natural abilities, should treat one another with respect.

In the wider culture outside the education system, the egalitarian liberal state should actively persuade people to its view of the moral equality of persons and contest any opposing, inegalitarian conceptions. At a deeper level, it should foster egalitarian social meanings and shared understandings. Persuasion can be done directly, by speeches, advertising campaigns, and so on, or it can be done indirectly, by financial support of groups and associations advocating equality. The latter strategy may prove more effective than the former, but both strategies violate neutrality as it is currently understood by egalitarian liberals. In particular, the indirect strategy involves the state in distributing additional resources to an association whose shared conception of the good and the right it regards as true. This truth, the moral equality of persons, is at the heart of egalitarian liberalism. However, the state does not give associations advocating equality additional resources to reward them for their beliefs, but to support their activity in changing an oppressive cultural environment. This cultural environment is an obstacle facing members of oppressed groups as they strive to learn their good, so the state is justified, on equality grounds, in directing additional resources to reforming it.

In his discussion of the grounds for equality, Rawls started from the settled assumption that inequalities based on caste, inheritance, and race were unjust. Such grounds were arbitrary from a moral point of view. He then extended this reasoning to a critique of meritocracy; natural ability as a ground of differential treatment is just as arbitrary and unjust. This reasoning can be extended further to critique forms of gender and heterosexual privilege and to characterize the false assumptions of an oppressive culture. But the cultural meanings that underlie and justify our current capitalist economic system are heavily meritocratic and classist. Many people find it natural to suppose that those gifted with the natural abilities that the market happens to demand should receive disproportionately large shares of the resources which make a good life possible. Many think it just that those lucky enough to inherit capital goods should have better lives. Our consumerist, commercial culture is pervaded by inegalitarian assumptions about appropriate rewards to merit and property ownership that egalitarian liberals must see as false. Meritocracy and the ideology of private property compete with liberal equality as a theory of justice. It is not at all clear that an egalitarian system of distributive justice can be established in a society in which it is contradicted by the prevailing assumptions. Nor is it clear that an egalitarian liberal state would be stable if there were powerful and pervasive attitudes continually undermining it.

This point is important, because egalitarian liberals often seem to assume that cultural reform will follow as a natural outgrowth of basic liberties and egalitarian economic justice:[10] If everyone has equal resources with which to express their opinions, and equal freedom to do so, then inegalitarian components of the cultural environment will wither away. Egalitarian beliefs in the ideological superstructure will follow egalitarian reform of the economic base. The conventional strategy of the egalitarian liberal political movement has been to win control of the state democratically, implement egalitarian distributive justice, and then allow cultural reform to follow naturally. I think, however, that it is entirely possible that the process must go in the other direction. In order that egalitarian economic reform not appear tyrannical, the ideological battle must be won first. An egalitarian liberal state will not be able to implement its egalitarian economic program without first convincing its citizens that its program is just. If citizens are to accept economic reform, they will need first to be convinced that distribution on the grounds of natural ability or inheritance is unjust and that being poor is not a mark of fecklessness. This will involve the state in contesting the inegalitarian social meanings of many goods, and in the project of cultural reform, prior to achieving economic equality.

The foregoing remarks have implications for the role of egalitarian liberals, as individuals and members of a political movement. If some degree of cultural reform has to precede state-sponsored reform, then egalitarian liberal citizens need to participate actively in changing how people think about equality. It follows, too, that the egalitarian liberal movement should ally itself with other egalitarian movements for social change which are contesting the prevailing social meanings.

None of us is totally free of our oppressive cultural environment. All of us base our conceptions of the good on assumptions that appear natural and unexceptional, but which are sometimes inegalitarian and false. Because of our finitude, solitary critical reflection is of only limited help. We can come to know our good only in a cultural environment purged of inegalitarian social meanings. Ethical knowledge is a collective undertaking, and cultural reform is its essential project.

NOTES

PREFACE

1. John Stuart Mill, *On Liberty*, in John Gray and G. W. Smith, eds., *J. S. Mill – 'On Liberty' in Focus* (London: Routledge, 1991), p. 26.

CHAPTER 1: EQUALITY, TOLERANCE, AND CULTURAL OPPRESSION

1. Ronald Dworkin, "Foundations of Liberal Equality," in *The Tanner Lectures on Human Values* (Salt Lake City: University of Utah Press, 1990), p. 13.
2. Dworkin, "Foundations of Liberal Equality," p. 111.
3. John Rawls, *Political Liberalism* (New York: Columbia University Press, 1993), pp. 48–58.
4. Rawls, *Political Liberalism*, pp. 60–61.
5. Rawls, *Political Liberalism*, p. 19, and *A Theory of Justice* (Cambridge: Harvard University Press, 1971), pp. 504–512. Compare Rawls at *A Theory of Justice*, p. 19: "It seems reasonable to suppose that the parties in the original position are equal. . . . Obviously the purpose of these conditions is to represent equality between human beings as moral persons, as creatures having a conception of their good and capable of a sense of justice."
6. Rawls, *Political Liberalism*, p. 1, and numerous other places.
7. The moral equality of persons is an assumption common to most modern ethical traditions, teleological and deontological, though it is subject to different interpretations in each. Even non-anthropocentric views have not denied moral equality; they have just extended it to animals and to plants. See, for example, Peter Singer, *Animal Liberation* (New York: Avon Books, 1975), and Paul Taylor, "The Ethics of Respect for Nature," *Environmental Ethics* 3 (1981), pp. 197–218. To find a view that denies moral equality, we need to look at an ecocentric ethic like Aldo Leopold's land ethic: "A thing is right when it tends to preserve the integrity, stability, and beauty of the biotic community. It is wrong when it tends otherwise." "The Land Ethic," in *A Sand County Almanac* (New York: Ballantine, 1970), p. 262; originally published by Oxford University Press, 1949. J. Baird Callicott comments: "The land ethic manifestly does not accord equal moral worth to each and every member of the biotic community; the moral worth of individuals (including, n.b., human individuals) is relative, to be assessed in accordance with the particular relation of each to the collective entity which Leopold called 'land'." "Animal Liberation: A Triangular Affair," *Environmental Ethics* 2 (1980), p. 327.
8. Note that Rawls is not a skeptic about ethical beliefs, nor does he take all be-

liefs about value to be false. He writes: "Political liberalism does not question that many political and moral judgements of certain specified kinds are correct and it views many of them as reasonable. Nor does it question the possible truth of affirmations of faith. Above all, it does not argue that we should be hesitant and uncertain, much less skeptical, about our own beliefs. Rather, we are to recognize the practical impossibility of reaching reasonable and workable political agreement in judgement on the truth of comprehensive doctrines. . . ." *Political Liberalism*, p. 63.

9. Ronald Dworkin, "In Defence of Equality," *Social Philosophy and Policy* 1 (1983), p. 24.

10. Dworkin, "Foundations of Liberal Equality," p. 22.

11. Rawls, *Political Liberalism*, pp. xvi-xvii.

12. Dworkin, "Foundations of Liberal Equality," p. 117.

13. Of course, if the monarchist were to press her case not just through speech, but through terrorist action, the liberal state would respond. Such a response, however, is justifiable on grounds that have nothing to do with issues of neutrality and tolerance.

14. See Rawls's discussion of the limits to tolerance and the toleration of the intolerant in sections 34 and 35 of *A Theory of Justice*, pp. 211–221.

15. John Stuart Mill, *On Liberty*, in John Gray and G. W. Smith, eds., *J. S. Mill – 'On Liberty' in Focus* (London: Routledge, 1991), p. 26.

16. Susan Sherwin, *No Longer Patient: Feminist Ethics and Health Care* (Philadelphia: Temple University Press, 1992), pp. 13–14.

17. Will Kymlicka, *Contemporary Political Philosophy* (Oxford: Clarendon Press, 1990), ably defends Dworkin's version of egalitarian liberalism against all challengers.

18. Kymlicka, *Contemporary Political Philosophy*, p. 257.

19. Rachel Carson, *Silent Spring* (Greenwich: Fawcett Publications, 1962), p. 169.

20. Joel Feinberg, *The Moral Limits of the Criminal Law, Volume One: Harm to Others* (Oxford University Press, 1984), pp. 225–232.

21. Marilyn Frye, "Oppression," in *The Politics of Reality: Essays in Feminist Theory* (Freedom, CA: Crossing Press, 1983), pp. 4–5.

22. J. K. Galbraith, *The Anatomy of Power* (Boston: Houghton Mifflin, 1983), pp. 5–6.

23. Galbraith, *The Anatomy of Power*, p. 29.

24. *A Discourse on Political Economy*, trans. G. D. H. Cole, cited in J. P. Day, "Threats, Offers, Law, Opinion and Liberty," *American Philosophical Quarterly* 14 (1977), p. 263.

25. Galbraith, *The Anatomy of Power*, pp. 25–26.

26. Sherwin, *No Longer Patient: Feminist Ethics and Health Care*, p. 21.

27. Galbraith, *The Anatomy of Power*, p. 2, quoting Max Weber, *Max Weber on Law in Economy and Society* (Cambridge: Harvard University Press, 1954), p. 323.

28. Iris Marion Young, "Five Faces of Oppression," in T. E. Wartenberg, ed., *Rethinking Power* (Albany: State University of New York Press, 1992), p. 180.

29. Michel Foucault, "The Subject and Power," *Critical Inquiry* 8 (1982), p. 781.

30. Michel Foucault, *The History of Human Sexuality, Volume I: An Introduction* (New York: Vintage Books, 1978), p. 95.

31. Michel Foucault, "Two Lectures," in C. Gordon, ed., *Power/Knowledge* (New York: Pantheon Books, 1980), p. 97.
32. There is controversy whether or not it is legitimate to use the concept of power when there is no determinate agent who is exercising the power. In my paper "Social Power and Human Agency," *Journal of Philosophy* 86 (1989), pp. 712–726, I give a technical defence of the view that power can exist without determinate agency.
33. Jon Elster, *Political Psychology* (Cambridge University Press, 1993), p. 11.
34. Will Kymlicka, *Liberalism, Community and Culture* (Oxford University Press, 1989), pp. 164–165.
35. Bernard Williams, "Deciding to Believe," in *Problems of the Self* (Cambridge University Press, 1973), p. 148.
36. Dworkin, "Foundations of Liberal Equality," p. 108.
37. Kymlicka, *Liberalism, Community and Culture*, p. 165.
38. Clifford Geertz, "The Impact of the Concept of Culture on the Concept of Man," in *The Interpretation of Cultures* (New York: Basic Books, 1973), p. 44.
39. Geertz, "The Impact of the Concept of Culture on the Concept of Man," p. 45.
40. Geertz, "The Impact of the Concept of Culture on the Concept of Man," p. 50.
41. Feinberg, *Harm to Others*, pp. 31–45.

CHAPTER 2: LIBERALISM AND THE EPISTEMOLOGY OF VALUE

1. John Rawls, *A Theory of Justice* (Cambridge: Harvard University Press, 1971), p. 440.
2. Rawls, *A Theory of Justice*, p. 178.
3. This is not Rawls's analysis. He thinks that to support self-respect, "it normally suffices that for each person there is some association (one or more) to which he belongs and within which the activities that are rational for him are publicly affirmed by others." *A Theory of Justice*, p. 441. It would follow, for example, that the self-respect of women is adequately supported only if every woman is a member of some association that publicly affirms women's equality. The union of these support groups must then include at least the set of all women. Only if there is no cultural inculcation in women of a belief in the naturalness of women's inequality will all women publicly affirm equality. To achieve this condition, liberal society would need to actively challenge the social transmission of a belief in inequality. Rawls, however, does not agree with this conclusion. He does think that "self-respect is secured by the public affirmation of the status of equal citizenship" (p. 545), but he also believes that this is accomplished by the public affirmation of equal basic liberties for all. *Political Liberalism* (New York: Columbia University Press, 1993), pp. 544–546. The issue will then turn on the interpretation of the "equal moral worth of persons." If to have equal moral worth is simply to have equal basic liberties, then the public affirmation of equal basic liberties will suffice to publicly affirm equal moral

worth. If there is more to moral equality than having equal basic liberties, then Rawls's position becomes a questionable empirical prediction.

4. Charles Taylor, *Multiculturalism and "The Politics of Recognition"* (Princeton University Press, 1992), pp. 25–26.

5. Rawls, *A Theory of Justice*, p. 547.

6. John Locke, *A Letter Concerning Toleration*, in John Horton and Susan Mendus, eds., *John Locke – 'A Letter Concerning Toleration' in Focus* (London: Routledge, 1991), p. 33.

7. Ronald Dworkin, "Foundations of Liberal Equality," in *The Tanner Lectures on Human Values* (Salt Lake City: University of Utah Press, 1990), p. 50.

8. Dworkin, "Foundations of Liberal Equality," p. 50.

9. These examples are from Dworkin, "Foundations of Liberal Equality," pp.75–86.

10. Will Kymlicka, *Contemporary Political Philosophy* (Oxford: Clarendon Press, 1990), pp. 203–204.

11. Richard Taylor, *Good and Evil: A New Direction* (London: Collier Macmillan, 1970), p. 259.

12. Dworkin, "Foundations of Liberal Equality," p. 79.

13. Ronald Dworkin, "Liberal Community," *California Law Review* 77 (1989), p. 486.

14. Edmund Gettier has shown that the account of knowledge as justified true belief needs supplementation: "Is Justified True Belief Knowledge?" *Analysis* 23 (1963), pp. 121–123. If someone correctly infers a true belief from a false but justified belief, then he will have a justified true belief that is not knowledge. Knowing whether or not I should search for love may depend on knowing of my circumstances whether or not someone loves me, and knowing of myself whether or not I love someone. With regard to knowledge of my circumstances, A's words and behaviour may justify me in believing that A loves me, when in fact A is deceiving me and A's love is false. Meanwhile B loves me, but never shows me that love. I correctly infer that someone loves me from my justified belief that A loves me. Thanks to B, this justified belief is true. But I do not know that someone loves me. With regard to my self-knowledge, my feelings of lust for A may justify me in believing that I love A, when in fact my lust is not love, and I do not love A. The deep intimacy I have with my friend B amounts to real love, but I do not recognize this. I correctly infer that I love someone from my justified, but false, belief that I love A. Thanks to my intimacy with B, this justified belief is true. But I do not know that I love someone. My knowledge of my ends can be undermined by factors over and above whether or not my ends are true, endorsed, and justified. Various theories of how to revise the traditional account of knowledge to deal with Gettier examples have been proposed. Explanation: Alan Goldman, *Moral Knowledge* (London: Routledge, 1988), and *Empirical Knowledge* (Berkeley: University of California Press, 1988). Defeasibility: Keith Lehrer, *Theory of Knowledge* (Boulder: Westview Press, 1990). Reliability: Alvin I. Goldman, *Epistemology and Cognition* (Cambridge: Harvard University Press, 1986). Tracking: Robert Nozick, *Philosophical Explanations* (Cambridge: Harvard University Press, 1981); cf.

Kymlicka's claim that "liberty helps us come to know our good, to 'track bestness', in Nozick's phrase." *Contemporary Political Philosophy,* p. 204.

15. In another context, Dworkin appears to recognize something like the justification component of the knowledge constraint on ethical judgements. He has written about the concept of a moral position: "What must I do to convince you that my position is a moral position? . . . I must produce some reasons for it. This is not to say that I have to articulate a moral principle I am following or a general moral theory to which I subscribe. Very few people can do either and the ability to hold a moral position is not limited to those who can." "Liberty and Moralism," in *Taking Rights Seriously* (Cambridge: Harvard University Press, 1977), p. 249.

16. John Stuart Mill, *On Liberty,* in John Gray and G. W. Smith, eds., *J. S. Mill – 'On Liberty' in Focus* (London: Routledge, 1991), p. 54.

17. Michael J. Sandel, *Liberalism and the Limits of Justice* (Cambridge University Press, 1982), p. 58.

18. For discussion, see David Brink, *Moral Realism and the Foundations of Ethics* (Cambridge University Press, 1989), ch. 2.

19. David Gauthier, *Morals by Agreement* (Oxford University Press, 1986), p. 49.

20. David Hume, *A Treatise of Human Nature,* ed. L. A. Selby-Bigge (Oxford: Clarendon Press, 1888), pp. 413–418.

21. For example, see Stanley Benn, *A Theory of Freedom* (Cambridge University Press, 1988), pp. 22–42.

22. Joseph Raz, *The Morality of Freedom* (Oxford: Clarendon Press, 1986), p. 141.

23. See James Griffin, *Well-Being: Its Meaning, Measurement and Moral Importance* (Oxford University Press, 1986).

24. Brink, *Moral Realism and the Foundations of Ethics,* p. 64.

25. Dworkin, "Foundations of Liberal Equality," p. 9.

26. Dworkin, "Foundations of Liberal Equality," p. 23.

27. Dworkin, "Foundations of Liberal Equality," p. 43.

28. Dworkin, "Foundations of Liberal Equality," p. 44.

29. Dworkin, "Foundations of Liberal Equality," pp. 39–40.

30. Dworkin, "Foundations of Liberal Equality," pp. 44–45.

31. Rawls, *A Theory of Justice,* p. 408 and n. 10, p. 408.

32. Rawls, *A Theory of Justice,* p. 417.

33. Rawls, *A Theory of Justice,* p. 417.

34. Rawls, *A Theory of Justice,* p. 433.

35. Rawls, *A Theory of Justice,* p. 419.

36. Rawls, *A Theory of Justice,* p. 31.

37. Rawls, *A Theory of Justice,* p. 481.

38. Rawls, *Political Liberalism,* p. 82.

39. Rawls, *Political Liberalism,* p. 85.

40. John Rawls, "Social Unity and the Primary Goods," in Amartya Sen and Bernard Williams, eds., *Utilitarianism and Beyond* (Cambridge University Press, 1982), pp. 164–165.

41. Ronald Dworkin, "In Defence of Equality," *Social Philosophy and Policy* 1 (1983), p. 26.

42. Will Kymlicka, *Liberalism, Community and Culture* (Oxford University Press, 1989), p. 166.

CHAPTER 3: THE MORAL EQUALITY OF PERSONS

1. On the idea of seeing Robert Nozick's *Anarchy, State, and Utopia* (New York: Basic Books, 1974) as egalitarian, see Will Kymlicka, *Contemporary Political Philosophy* (Oxford University Press, 1990), and Amartya Sen, *Inequality Reexamined* (Oxford University Press, 1992).
2. A good introduction to the literature on egalitarian theories of distributive justice is G. A. Cohen's "On the Currency of Egalitarian Justice," *Ethics* 99 (1989), pp. 906–944.
3. S. I. Benn and R. S. Peters, *Social Principles and the Democratic State* (London: George Allen & Unwin, 1959), p. 108. I am following their discussion here of relevant grounds for difference (pp. 107–122).
4. John Rawls, *A Theory of Justice* (Cambridge: Harvard University Press, 1971), p. 504.
5. Rawls, *A Theory of Justice*, p. 512; John Rawls, *Political Liberalism* (New York: Columbia University Press, 1993), p. 21. This limitation in scope, together with a tendency to confine justice to a particular political society and ignore the plight of distant people and the interests of future generations, is one of the principal areas in which egalitarian liberalism needs criticism and extension.
6. Rawls, *A Theory of Justice*, p. 505.
7. John Rawls, "Social Unity and Primary Goods," in Amartya Sen and Bernard Williams, eds., *Utilitarianism and Beyond* (Cambridge University Press, 1982), pp. 164–165; *Political Liberalism*, p. 74.
8. Rawls, *Political Liberalism*, p. 19.
9. Rawls, *A Theory of Justice*, p. 19.
10. Rawls, *A Theory of Justice*, pp. 103–104.
11. Rawls, *A Theory of Justice*, p. 312.
12. I do not see that Rawls would resist these extensions for race and gender. On racial discrimination, see *A Theory of Justice*, p. 19, and on race, sex, and cultural background, see p. 99.
13. Two other characteristics of people which are arbitrary from a moral point of view are the spatial and temporal locations of their birth. Samuel Black points out that the moral arbitrariness of where someone is born can ground an argument for international social justice, in "Individualism at an Impasse," *Canadian Journal of Philosophy* 21 (1991), pp. 347–377. Gregory Kavka points out that the moral arbitrariness of temporal location can ground an argument for justice toward future generations, in "The Futurity Problem," in R. I. Sikora and Brian Barry, eds., *Obligations to Future Generations* (Philadelphia: Temple University Press, 1978), pp. 180–203.
14. Marilyn Frye, "Oppression," in *The Politics of Reality: Essays in Feminist Theory* (Freedom, CA: Crossing Press, 1983), pp. 7–8.
15. Karen J. Warren, "The Power and Promise of Ecological Feminism," in Christine Pierce and Donald VanDeVeer, eds., *People, Penguins, and Plastic*

Trees, 2nd ed. (Belmont, CA: Wadsworth, 1995), p. 214; originally published in *Environmental Ethics* 12 (1990), pp. 125–146. Warren extends the scope of the argument from arbitrariness to the natural world: "Even if humans are 'better' than plants and rocks with respect to the conscious ability of humans to radically transform communities, one does not *thereby* get any *morally* relevant distinction between humans and non-humans, or an argument for the domination of plants and rocks by humans" (p. 215).

16. Rawls, "Social Unity and Primary Goods," pp. 168–169.
17. This interpretation of Rawls's argument is due to Cohen's "On the Currency of Egalitarian Justice," pp. 914–916.
18. Rawls, *A Theory of Justice,* p. 312.
19. Ronald Dworkin, "What Is Equality? Part 2: Equality of Resources," *Philosophy and Public Affairs* 10 (1981), pp. 283–345.
20. Cohen, "On the Currency of Egalitarian Justice," pp. 915–916.
21. Rawls, *A Theory of Justice,* p. 31.
22. Amartya Sen, "Equality of What?" in Sterling M. McMurrin, ed., *The Tanner Lectures on Human Values 1980* (Cambridge University Press, 1980), pp. 197–220, and Dworkin, "Equality of Resources."
23. Will Kymlicka, *Multicultural Citizenship: A Liberal Theory of Minority Rights* (Oxford: Clarendon Press, 1995), p. 83.
24. Michael Walzer, *Spheres of Justice* (New York: Basic Books, 1983), pp. 7–8.
25. Walzer, *Spheres of Justice,* pp. 8–9.
26. I have borrowed the device of using as an example the subculture of academic philosophy from Nathan Brett's unpublished manuscript, "Multiculturalism and Equality," though I employ it differently. I have used the example not because I think philosophers are an oppressed group but because I assume it to be close to the reader's heart.
27. I am here following Raz's discussion of cultural membership in his chapter "Multiculturalism: A Liberal Perspective," in *The Ethics of Well-Being* (Oxford: Clarendon Press, 1994), pp. 153–175, and in particular the section entitled "The Case for Multiculturalism," pp. 160–163.
28. Rawls, *A Theory of Justice,* p. 31, quoted earlier.
29. Walzer, *Spheres of Justice,* p. 313.
30. Walzer, *Spheres of Justice,* p. 313.
31. Ronald Dworkin, "What Is Equality? Part 1: Equality of Welfare," *Philosophy and Public Affairs* 10 (1981), p. 201 [word missing in original].
32. Rawls, *A Theory of Justice,* p. 102.
33. Rawls, *A Theory of Justice,* p. 548.
34. Walzer, *Spheres of Justice,* p. xiv.
35. Walzer, *Spheres of Justice,* p. 9.

CHAPTER 4: NEUTRALITY AND THE HARM PRINCIPLE

1. John Stuart Mill, *On Liberty* (London: Penguin, 1974), p. 68.
2. Charles Larmore, *Patterns of Moral Complexity* (Cambridge University Press, 1987), p. 43.
3. For a discussion of this ambiguity in the interpretation of Mill's harm prin-

ciple, see David Lyons, "Liberty and Harm to Others," *Canadian Journal of Philosophy: Supplementary Volume V* (1979), pp. 1–19.

4. This is Joel Feinberg's definition in *The Moral Limits of the Criminal Law, Volume One: Harm to Others* (Oxford University Press, 1984), pp. 33ff.
5. Joseph Raz, *The Morality of Freedom* (Oxford: Clarendon Press, 1986), p. 208.
6. Feinberg, *Harm to Others*, p. 228.
7. I defend this claim in detail in "Individual Acts and Accumulative Consequences," to be published in *Philosophical Studies*.
8. Raz, *The Morality of Freedom*, p. 416.
9. Virginia Held gives an example like this, except that it is a one-shot case: "If an individual flips on a light switch and, by a mechanism of which he could have no knowledge, causes an explosion that kills a child, he could be said to be responsible for flipping the switch, but not for causing the child's death." "Can a Random Collection of Individuals Be Morally Responsible?" *Journal of Philosophy* 67 (1970), p. 472.
10. We are familiar with harms involving neither intent nor negligence in cases of strict liability, e.g., statutory rape, or the movement of dangerous goods. We are familiar with harms without causation, as in acts of omission or failure to take the appropriate care. We are even familiar with harms involving neither cause nor defect; as the law once stood in Canada, the driver of the getaway car in a robbery unintentionally involving murder would have been liable for murder the same as the actual killer. (I am indebted to Arthur Ripstein and Nathan Brett for this last example.)
11. Feinberg, *Harm to Others*, pp. 105–106.
12. Feinberg, *Harm to Others*, p. 230.
13. Feinberg, *Harm to Others*, p. 230.
14. Feinberg, *Harm to Others*, p. 226.
15. Robert Nozick, *Anarchy, State, and Utopia* (New York: Basic Books, 1974), pp. 262–265.
16. Nozick endorses Locke's state-of-nature harm principle: "The bounds of the state of nature require that 'no one ought to harm another in his life, health, liberty or possessions' (sect. 6)." *Anarchy, State, and Utopia*, p. 10. The section reference is to Locke's *Second Treatise of Government*.
17. I owe this point to Ann Decter's suggestion.
18. Compare the earlier discussion of Feinberg on copper refining, permitted shares, and allocative schemes.
19. In some cases, collective sexual harassment may take place in an institutional context, e.g., a workplace, and it may be possible to attribute the harm to the institution, e.g., the company. This artificial person, the company, may then be assigned a duty to prevent the harassment by regulating the behaviour of its employees. This strategy disguises the collective nature of the harm by creating an individual, a legal fiction, to do the harm. But the strategy will work only where there is enough organization and collective decision making to justify attributing a duty to the corporate person. In other cases of collective sexual harassment, e.g., on the street, this strategy is not available.
20. Feinberg, *Harm to Others*, p. 229.

21. This chapter is a revised version of my paper "Accumulative Harms and the Interpretation of the Harm Principle," *Social Theory and Practice* 19 (1993), pp. 51–72.

CHAPTER 5: LIBERALISM AND THE REFORM OF CULTURE

1. Joshua Cohen, "Freedom of Expression," *Philosophy and Public Affairs* 22 (1993), p. 231.
2. Will Kymlicka, "Liberal Individualism and Liberal Neutrality," *Ethics* 99 (1989), p. 884.
3. Will Kymlicka, *Contemporary Political Philosophy* (Oxford: Clarendon Press, 1990), p. 257.
4. William Galston, *Liberal Purposes: Goods, Virtues, and Diversity in the Liberal State* (Cambridge University Press, 1991), p. 96.
5. John Rawls, *Political Liberalism* (New York: Columbia University Press, 1993), p. 198.
6. Ronald Dworkin, "Foundations of Liberal Equality," in *The Tanner Lectures on Human Values* (Salt Lake City: University of Utah Press, 1990), p. 83.
7. Dworkin, "Foundations of Liberal Equality," p. 84.
8. Dworkin, "Foundations of Liberal Equality," p. 84.
9. Ronald Dworkin, "Women and Pornography," *The New York Review of Books* (October 21, 1993), p. 41. This article is a review of Catharine MacKinnon, *Only Words* (Cambridge: Harvard University Press, 1993).
10. Catharine MacKinnon, "Not a Moral Issue," in *Feminism Unmodified* (Cambridge: Harvard University Press, 1987), p. 155.
11. See Ronald Dworkin, "What Is Equality? Part 2: Equality of Resources," *Philosophy and Public Affairs* 10 (1981).
12. J. K. Galbraith, *The Anatomy of Power* (Boston: Houghton Mifflin, 1983), pp. 54–71.
13. Dworkin, "Foundations of Liberal Equality," p. 110.
14. Dworkin, "Foundations of Liberal Equality," p. 108.
15. Cultural oppression is not an issue of the redistribution of resources to compensate people for cultural handicaps. David Dyzenhaus writes as follows: "Suppose the issue is not redistribution of an economic resource, but of a resource which, while it may be crucial to have in place for equality's sake, might be difficult to think of in redistributive terms. I mean the kind of cultural resource that is lacking when the following situation obtains. A dominant group not only prefers that another group be treated as less than equal, but, through its dominance, has brought it about that those preferences have solidified into social practices that legitimize and maintain a situation of cultural inequality. Moreover, such practices amount to an ideology; their building blocks are the expression and reexpression of opinions that the situation of inequality is normal, legitimate, and so on. The preferences many men have to live in a patriarchal social system – the ideologies of patriarchy in practice – is the important example for our purposes." "Pornography and Public Reason," *The Canadian Journal of Law and Jurisprudence* 7 (1994), p. 267.

16. Kymlicka, "Liberal Individualism and Liberal Neutrality," p. 884.
17. Dworkin, in his article on liberalism which brought the doctrine of state neutrality to the fore in liberal thinking, wrote that neutrality "supposes that political decisions must be, so far as it is possible, independent of any particular conception of the good life, or of what gives value to life. Since the citizens of a society differ in their conceptions, the government does not treat them as equals if it prefers one conception to another, either because the officials believe that one is intrinsically superior, or because one is held by the more numerous or more powerful group." "Liberalism," in *A Matter of Principle* (Cambridge: Harvard University Press, 1985), p. 191. Also compare Kymlicka on "justificatory neutrality" which "requires neutrality in the justification of government policy." "[Justificatory neutrality] allows that government action may help some ways of life more than others but denies that government should act in order to help some ways of life over others. The state does not take a stand on which ways of life are most worth living, and desire to help one way of life over another is precluded as a justification of government action." "Liberal Individualism and Liberal Neutrality," p. 166. Rawls doesn't like to use the term, but allows that two doctrines of neutrality are consistent with political liberalism: ". . . the state is to secure equal opportunity to advance any permissible conception [of the good]," where a permissible conception is one that respects the principles of justice, and ". . . the state is not to do anything intended to favor or promote any particular comprehensive doctrine rather than another, or to give assistance to those who pursue it;" *Political Liberalism,* pp. 192–193.
18. Joseph Raz, *The Morality of Freedom* (Oxford: Clarendon Press, 1986), p. 136.
19. Contra the libertarians, liberal egalitarians argue that some liberties are more significant than others. My freedom of expression is more important than my freedom to drive the wrong way up Lexington Avenue. [Ronald Dworkin, "What Rights Do We Have?" in *Taking Rights Seriously* (Cambridge: Harvard University Press, 1977), p. 269.] That London traffic lights restrict my freedom of movement is less important than that Albanian law restricts my freedom to worship as I please. [Charles Taylor, "What's Wrong with Negative Liberty," in Alan Ryan, ed., *The Idea of Freedom* (Oxford University Press, 1979), pp. 182–183.] Rawls argued for the priority of a particular set of basic liberties because these basic liberties are instrumental to people forming and pursuing their conceptions of the good. He gives the following list of important basic liberties: ". . . political liberty (the right to vote and to be eligible for public office) together with freedom of speech and assembly; liberty of conscience and freedom of thought; freedom of the person along with the right to hold (personal) property; and freedom from arrest and seizure as defined by the concept of the rule of law." [John Rawls, *A Theory of Justice* (Cambridge: Harvard University Press, 1971), p. 61.]
20. L. Althusser, "Ideology and Ideological State Apparatuses (Notes towards an Investigation)," in *Lenin and Philosophy and Other Essays,* trans. B. Brewster (London: New Left Books, 1971), pp. 123–173. Althusser classes some associations as part of the ideological state apparatus that liberals would put in civil society.

127

21. Rawls, *Political Liberalism,* p. 61.
22. Rawls, *A Theory of Justice,* p. 329.
23. Thomas Scanlon, "A Theory of Freedom of Expression," *Philosophy and Public Affairs* 1 (1972), p. 204.
24. For discussion, see Rawls, *Political Liberalism,* pp. 348–356.
25. Scanlon, "A Theory of Freedom of Expression," p. 213.
26. Scanlon, "A Theory of Freedom of Expression," p. 215.
27. Scanlon, "A Theory of Freedom of Expression," p. 217.
28. Thomas Scanlon, "Freedom of Expression and Categories of Expression," *University of Pittsburgh Law Review* 40 (1979), pp. 524–525.
29. Scanlon, "Freedom of Expression and Categories of Expression," p. 526.
30. Scanlon, "Freedom of Expression and Categories of Expression," pp. 526–527.
31. Recall the discussion of Rawls's theory of the bases of self-respect in Chapter 2.
32. For example, Susan Moller Okin, *Justice, Gender, and the Family* (New York: Basic Books, 1989), and Kymlicka, *Contemporary Political Philosophy,* pp. 247–262.
33. See Scanlon, "Freedom of Expression and Categories of Expression," p. 534, and Cohen, "Freedom of Expression," p. 233.
34. Cohen, "Freedom of Expression," p. 233.
35. Cohen, "Freedom of Expression," pp. 232–233.
36. Ronald Dworkin, "Can a Liberal State Support Art?" in *A Matter of Principle* (Cambridge: Harvard University Press, 1985), p. 233.

CONCLUSION

1. John Rawls, *Political Liberalism* (New York: Columbia University Press, 1993), p. 30.
2. Michael Walzer, *Spheres of Justice* (New York: Basic Books, 1983), p. 8.
3. Rawls, *Political Liberalism,* p. 31.
4. Michael J. Sandel, *Liberalism and the Limits of Justice* (Cambridge University Press, 1982), p. 74.
5. Will Kymlicka, *Liberalism, Community and Culture* (Oxford: Clarendon Press, 1991), pp. 52–58.
6. Will Kymlicka, *Multicultural Citizenship: A Liberal Theory of Minority Rights* (Oxford University Press, 1995), p. 167.
7. Kymlicka, *Multicultural Citizenship,* p. 166.
8. Kymlicka, *Multicultural Citizenship,* p. 168.
9. Kymlicka, *Multicultural Citizenship,* p. 168.
10. "Liberals tend to believe that cultural oppression cannot survive under conditions of civil freedom and material equality." Will Kymlicka, *Contemporary Political Philosophy* (Oxford: Clarendon Press, 1990), p. 257.

INDEX

Priscilla
and the
Snow Fort

Pat LaMarche
Bonnie Tweedy Shaw

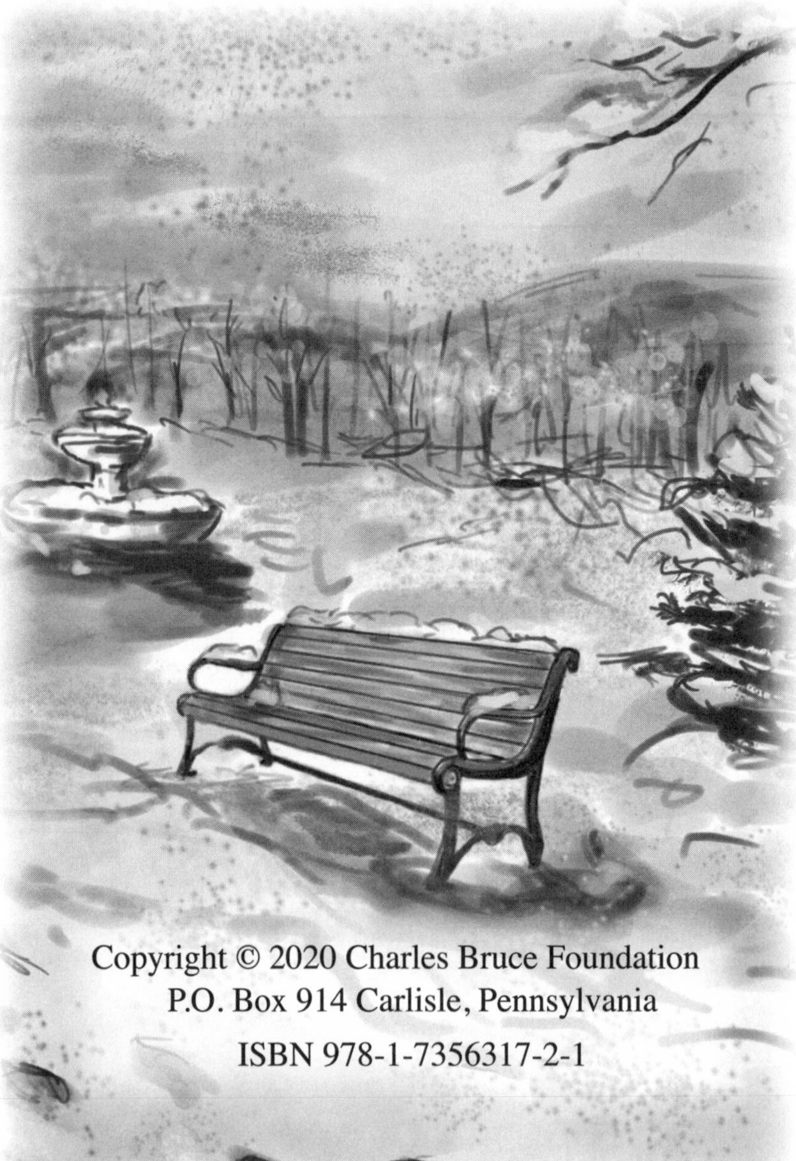

P.O. Box 914 Carlisle, Pennsylvania

ISBN 978-1-7356317-2-1

For Ron Lang

a humble, kind and joyful man
I was so fortunate to have in my life.

Table of Contents

CHAPTER 1

The Protector of the Realm

Tomas knocked quietly on his grandmother's door. "Bela," he called softly, "Can I come in?"

A gentle voice from behind the door replied, "Of course, Nieto."

Tomas opened the door and crossed the darkened room to his grandmother's bed.

Bela set her book down and slid over to make room for Tomas to sit. "Have a seat, Nieto. Have you decided to tell me what is wrong. It's been a long time since you were too distracted to eat supper." Her voice got a little louder as she said, "I can't remember the last time Hugo didn't eat."

"We are both very sad, Bela." Tomas voice cracked as he spoke. "I wasn't going to tell you. But I am so worried about Hugo now. I've never seen him like this. Someone needs to help." Tomas felt like he might cry but he pressed onward, "I know I shouldn't ask you this. But, I absolutely can't help myself. If I tell you what is wrong, you have to promise you won't tell Mama and Papa."

Bela did not want to keep secrets from her son and daughter-in-law. When she moved in to help with the parenting of her three fine grandchildren, the adults agreed they would do it together. No secrets.

Still, Bela could tell that something earth-shattering had happened. Bela counted herself lucky that her granddaughter was somehow spared by whatever was bothering the boys. Bela suggested a compromise, "I tell you what," she offered. "You tell me what's happened. If it's not life-threatening or dangerous, I'll see what I can do to help."

Tomas grabbed her hand, "Thank you, Bela, thank you."

"But wait. I'm not finished," Bela sensed his relief but continued with the conditions of her secret keeping. "If you tell me something that I feel is dangerous to your well-being, you and Hugo must go to your parents and tell them too. I will not tell on you. You will tell on yourselves."

Tomas stared at his hands. He was still clutching his grandmother's hand. He thought back to the scene in his bedroom. Hugo, across the room, on his bed. Unwilling to talk. Unable to eat.

"I guess you have a deal," Tomas replied.

"Wow," Bela sighed, "This must be a very big problem if you are willing to take such a chance. Hurry and tell me now. Do it before I get too scared to learn what happened."

Tomas told Bela the whole story. He told her about walking home through the park instead of around it. He told her how he'd met Priscilla in the park. He mentioned seeing her feeding squirrels, chipmunks and robins. Straight out of her

hand! He told her about the other
kids: Jeff, Beth, Maggie and Jillian.
The posse as Jillian's mom called them.
He told her that Hugo had been against Tomas
visiting the park. He explained that Hugo would find him in
the park and drag him home. For a long time Hugo scolded
him. But then, when Hugo needed something from Tomas, he
started going to the park with him. Hugo agreed to keep an
eye on Tomas in exchange for help doing his math homework.
Tomas told his grandma that, in addition to Maggie's baby
sitter who stayed with them, Hugo had become a guardian of
the little group.

"He was so good at watching over us, Priscilla named him
the Protector of the Realm," Tomas face beamed with pride
when he explained about his big brother's lofty title even
though his eyes remained dull with sadness.

Bela listened quietly to Tomas' story of sneaking off to the
park with his brother. They had never blatantly lied to their

parents and their grandmother, but they had left many things out of the conversations over the last few months.

Bela cleared her throat and said, "So you kept these tea parties and UNO games a secret from your family. Why? Because you thought we would tell you that you couldn't go back? You didn't trust your parents and me to trust you?"

Tomas nodded slowly and then bowed his head until his chin nearly touched his chest. Without looking up, he whispered, "Yes. We didn't trust you to trust our judgement. I guess that is true."

Bela put her arms around him and pulled him close to her. "Well, we are a lot older and wiser than you two are. Although, you may be right about our decision. We might have jumped to a conclusion that hanging around in the park with strange grownups is a bad idea. You say there's a street musician too? An older man."

Tomas loved being hugged by his grandmother. She always smelled of lavender and her hugs warmed him even when he didn't know he was cold. Keeping his face pressed up against her, he answered, "Yeah, Vinny. He's not really an older guy. He's like a college kid."

Bela kept holding her grandson closely, wondering how many more years he would let her have these long hugs. "So if you've worked this secret afternoon routine out so well, why tell me now? Something must have happened or you two wouldn't be so entirely miserable."

Tomas picked his face up from her robe and looked into her eyes. "She's gone, Bela. Nobody can find her. Her stuff is

4

gone. Everything. Nobody saw her leave. Not even Vinny."

The minute Tomas told his terrible truth, he burst into tears. Bela hugged him back close and rocked him, singing one of his favorite bedtime songs to him. When his weeping subsided she spoke to him again, "So this is why Hugo is so devastated. The Protector of the Realm couldn't protect the Princess of the Park."

Bela sat her grandson up straight, held his shoulders and looked into his eyes. "You and I must go to Hugo now. We must talk to him and help him deal with this."

Tomas stood up as his grandmother swung her legs out of the bed.

"What about Mama and Papa?"

Bela moved toward the door. "One thing at a time," she answered. "Your parents aren't going to be as upset as you think they will. We have a big lesson to learn about trust going forward, maybe. But right now, the most important thing is Hugo."

Tomas nearly shouted at his grandmother. "That's not true. The most important thing is that Priscilla is missing."

Bela reached over and rested her hand on Tomas shoulder, "I know you care about Priscilla. And it's plain you've thought she was the most important thing all along. That's why you were dishonest with us. But in this house she is not more important than your brother. We are going to see Hugo now, and we are going to make sure he is okay. Because your Bela is the original protector of the realm."

CHAPTER 2

Car Full of Tears

Ken couldn't remember seeing Beth and Jeff so miserable. Even leaving Uncle Mike and Aunt Trudy's place had an upside. No more living with relatives meant no more getting yelled at just for being ordinary human beings who take up space and eat the rest of the peanut butter and jelly.

Remembering their short stint staying in his brother and sister-in-law's mobile home, Ken thought about that night that Trudy went to slather jam on her English muffin and found the jar had only a whisper of jelly left in it. Boy, she was angry alright, Ken reminisced in his head. She started yelling about having too many mouths to feed.

Ken recalled his brother coming to his rescue, "Now Trudy, Ken gets home from work late and the kids get hungry. You can't expect them to eat nothing in the afternoon after school." Trudy just fumed all the more. Mike continued, "What happened to Ken's EBT card? I thought he gave you all his food stamps to buy groceries."

Trudy drew a deep breath and wheezed it back out bitterly. She sneered, "Well, he and those kids shouldn't get that food.

We should. After all, if we're housing them, the least he can do is feed us. If they want to eat here too then he should..." and she really emphasized the word should, "he should buy extra groceries. If they want to eat here, they can go shopping. Those food stamps should be for us."

Mike was no match for Trudy. She laid down the law and she laid it down thick. Mike looked at his brother, Ken, rounded his shoulders and muttered, "But Trudy, we need to help them. If he gives you the food stamps and then uses money to buy more food, he won't be able to save enough to get a place to live."

Trudy's neck turned the color of boiled lobster. She seethed at her husband, "Don't those kids get free lunch at school? Let them eat there."

Months later, sitting next to his grieving children, Ken shook his head as if he could loosen the bad memories. Those were rotten times, but they weren't as rotten as losing Priscilla.

They didn't just lose her. She'd vanished. Gone without a trace. If not for all the love she'd left behind it would have been like she never existed in the first place.

After Vinny told Priscilla's posse that she was gone, Beth and Jeff raced to the warehouses to wait by the car for their dad. Luckily his shift ended a little early and he got to the car earlier than usual.

Ken walked up, expecting the twins to be bebopping around the car like they often did. Instead, he found them sitting together in the back seat, with their heads hanging down. Jeff was sniffling but Beth was full blown crying. If Ken hadn't

8

heard her sobs, he might have thought the kids too had disappeared. No radio blaring and no parking lot dancing, just a back seat filled with two puffy-faced, red-eyed, crumpled-up children.

"Heyyyyy, what happened to you guys. You look awful." Ken put his key in the door lock to let himself into the front seat. Neither of the twins answered. Ken reached his hand around to the back door lock and unlocked it too. Then he pulled open the passenger side rear door and said, "Scoot over, let me sit down."

Beth wiped her nose on her sleeve then scooted over to the middle. Ken reached for his handkerchief and handed it to his daughter. "Here. Blow your nose. You'll get your sleeve all nasty."

Beth took the hanky and did as she was told. Then she wiped her eyes. The motion was pointless. Her eyes just made more water as she thought about her missing friend.

Ken tried to keep his tone light as he searched for the reason for all the tears, "You know the Lady of the Laundry should be more careful with her sleeves. What would Priscilla say?"

"Oh Dad," shrieked Beth as she buried her face in her father's shirt.

Stunned by her response, Ken held his daughter close. "Hey Jeff," he turned his attention to his more composed child. "How about you let me know what's going on here. Please Jeff, find your words. You're literally scaring your old man half to death." Ken nearly started crying himself. Seeing his kids in such agony was more than frightening.

Ken continued, "Seriously, you two act like someone died," Ken looked imploringly at his son hoping he'd explain what was wrong.

Jeff just looked up, his eyes swollen and dark. He whispered, "Oh gosh Dad, I hope not. It's just so awful. She's gone. I suppose she could have died. We don't know. This is almost worse."

With that Beth wailed all the louder. She shoved her brother hard against the door and said, "No, Jeff. No! She's not dead and if she did die, that would be worse than anything."

"She who," Ken asked. But Ken knew who. So he added, in the softest voice he could muster, "Did something happen to Priscilla?"

Getting the whole story out of the Lord and Lady of the Laundry – as Priscilla had named them when they helped her wash her clothes – proved more difficult than it should have been. When the sobs subsided, the message was actually quite simple. Priscilla had vanished without a trace.

CHAPTER 3

Next of Kin

It took a fair amount of convincing but Maggie finally got her dad to agree. He promised her that he'd call all the local hospitals. Shewan didn't want him to do it. Not only because he had no answers to most of the important questions a family member should know – starting with Priscilla's last name and ending with her date of birth.

Shewan told Gabriel not to bother trying at all, "I hate to say 'I told you so.' But I told you so."

Gabriel asked his wife, "What harm could it do to try?"

Shewan mused, "It encourages these little delusions of hers when you play along with this mysterious imaginary friend's disappearance. Of course Priscilla's gone. The Princess of the Park has vanished into thin air because she never existed in the first place."

"Shhhh," Gabriel hushed his wife, "You'll wake up Maggie."

But Gabriel needn't have worried. Poor Maggie cried herself to sleep so bitterly that nothing was going to wake her, not for hours.

"Look, Shewan, let me make these calls. I'll be done in a few minutes and then we can try and hatch a plan to help Maggie with this grief she's feeling. Her friend might not have been real, but her sorrow sure is."

Shewan agreed with that point completely, "Poor Magdalena. I think the appearance and disappearance of her little friends up at Nilan National Park finally broke the spell. When she realized Beth wasn't real, she accepted that she'd invented Priscilla as well. You make those phone calls. I'll make us some tea."

Gabriel started with the police. He figured if they didn't know anything, he could try the hospitals. To no one's surprise, the police could not help him. The police wouldn't even start looking for a missing person without knowing her full name, an accurate physical description and approximately when she disappeared.

Gabriel tried to get them to bend the rules, "Look, I'm not asking you to tell me if you have some random ordinary person in custody. I'm asking if you have an elderly woman who dresses herself out of the dumpster and parades around acting like royalty. I'm pretty sure you'd know if you picked up someone that fits that description! You don't have to tell me where she is, just if you have her and if she's safe."

The dispatcher was not amused.

"Look sir, if you want to report that someone matching this description committed a crime, then maybe I can send a few officers around to take your statement. If they think the offense is serious enough, they might start looking for her.

Mind you, falsely reporting a crime is a crime itself, sir."

Gabriel started to feel a little the way Maggie must've when Shewan doubted her. He was pretty sure the dispatcher didn't believe him. Politely he asked, "Look, if someone had a mental illness and they wandered off, you'd go looking for her wouldn't you? There wouldn't have to be a crime, necessarily, would there?"

The dispatcher had a mechanical way of talking that didn't tell Gabriel anything about her mood. From her tone he didn't know if she was mad or bored or even if she was paying close attention. Through the phone Gabriel heard, "Sir, if you'd like to report a missing person, I need to know how long they've been gone and at least a first and last name. We can't just contact the bus stations and ask for someone using only a first name."

Gabriel lost his temper, "You can't?" He hollered. "You seriously can't call and say there's a woman, answers to Priscilla and she thinks she's a princess. Dresses the part too. You can't do that?"

The dispatcher responded with one word, "No."

Gabriel shouted, "Well, why not?"

The reply was brief, "Sir, what if she's changed her clothes? We really need that last name. Good night." She disconnected the call.

Gabriel sat there staring at the phone in his hand. Shewan walked back into the room with his tea. "Here, no caffeine. I think you're wired enough."

Gabriel stared at his phone and took the magnetic list of emergency numbers off the refrigerator. He ran his index finger down over the directory of first responders. Time to try the hospitals, he thought. He looked at his wife, "Thanks Hun, I doubt there's enough chamomile in the world to calm my nerves tonight."

Shewan kissed his forehead and went upstairs to read.

Gabriel punched ten numbers onto the phone pad and waited for someone to answer.

"Mount Hope General. If this is an emergency please hang up and dial 911. How may I direct your call." Gabriel recited his plea to the operator.

By the end of the evening, Gabriel had called five area hospitals and two county facilities. Every one of them told him the same thing. Hospital, federal and state regulations prohibit the sharing of information with anyone not designated by the patient.

Gabriel asked each of them – his tone sounding more desperate with every new number he called, "What if the person is unconscious? Then they can't give you consent to talk to me. Can't you just tell me if you have someone there who is unconscious?"

The answer was always the same, "No. Very sorry. No consent, no disclosure. Good luck."

When Maggie woke the next day, Gabriel would have to tell her that there was no record of Priscilla the Princess of the Park. He would make sure she knew that it wasn't necessarily because Priscilla didn't exist, but because they didn't have enough information or the permission to ask.

Gabriel knew that Maggie had plans to meet her friends at the park. She told her parents that she was supposed to give the other kids a full report about the hospitals and police. Poor Maggie wouldn't have much to tell them. Nothing, in fact.

Gabriel picked up his tea and walked to the bottom of the stairs. He could see light on the top landing coming from under his bedroom door. He walked up to the hallway and glanced down the hall to Maggie's closed door. She had absentmindedly left the key in the lock when she went to bed. He saw it sticking out with the purple ribbon hanging down. "Poor kid was so distracted she forgot to take the key out," he said to no one.

Gabriel tapped softly on the door to the room he and Shewan shared. He went in and closed the door behind him. He spoke softly, "The sitter, Lani will be taking Maggie to the park tomorrow, right?"

Shewan nodded in agreement.

Gabriel knelt down in front of the chair where Shewan sat reading and put his head on her lap. "I think it might be time
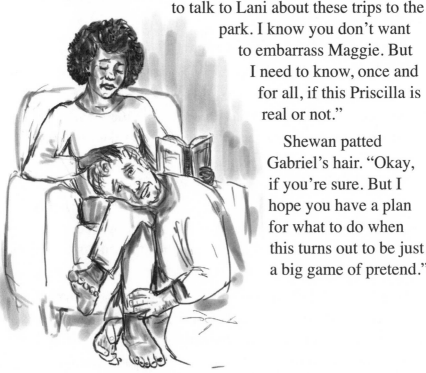
to talk to Lani about these trips to the park. I know you don't want to embarrass Maggie. But I need to know, once and for all, if this Priscilla is real or not."

Shewan patted Gabriel's hair. "Okay, if you're sure. But I hope you have a plan for what to do when this turns out to be just a big game of pretend."

CHAPTER 4

Visiting the Legos

The children had grown so quiet in the back seat that Ken had to keep checking them in the rearview mirror to convince himself they were still there.

Beth and Jeff each sipped occasionally from the bottles of ginger ale Ken had given them. He told them it would help calm them down. It seemed to be working. Ken read somewhere that kids' brains reacted to sugar the way adult brains react to anti-depressants. He thought he'd break the ice by bringing that little tidbit up in conversation.

"Hey, you two seem to be doing a little better. Do you think it's the ginger ale? I read somewhere that sugar can have a calming effect on kids' brains."

Jeff piped up in a little more animated tone then Ken had expected, "Yeah, Dad. I guess that's true. Priscilla told us that humans evolved such big brains because they became friends with bees. The honey aided brain development in children."

Ken steeled himself for a new wave of tears when Jeff mentioned Priscilla's name. But none came. Maybe they're getting over the initial shock, Ken thought to himself.

Ken decided to try and discuss Priscilla's disappearance a little more. He wanted to help if he could. He needed more information. "So you said the other kids all left the park with jobs to do. Jillian's parents were there and they were going to go out looking for her in other parks and at shelters."

This time Beth answered, "Yeah, but they won't find her. Priscilla wouldn't go to a shelter."

Ken met her eyes in the rear view mirror. Beth seemed to smile and frown at him in the same moment. Ken whispered, "Gosh, Beth, you look so much like your mom sometimes." He pressed on, "Magdalena said she'd get her dad to call hospitals. So that's good. What about Tomas?"

Jeff took a big drink of ginger ale. After swallowing he answered, "I don't think Tomas could do anything, Dad. He's a mess. I don't think he could have made it home if Hugo hadn't been there to hold him up. I mean it. Hugo practically had to carry him."

"Poor kid," moaned Ken.

Jeff continued, "Those other kids don't understand like we do, Dad. I'm upset and I'm worried, but we disappear on people all the time. We got nowhere to live. When you got nowhere to live, sometimes you've got to hide. It makes me think she's somewhere. She just can't tell us where. Not yet, anyway."

Beth heard her brother's words and her face brightened a little. She agreed with him, "Yeah Jeff, like that time we disappeared on Magdalena at Nilan National Park. I never thought she might have wondered what happened to us."

Ken, still worried but grateful to see his kids feeling hopeful, changed the subject. "Hey," he said, "I've got an idea. Let's grab a pizza and head to our storage unit. It gets dark so much earlier these days, now that winter's almost here. We can pretend to go get some things and just spend the night with our stuff. If I move some of the boxes around, I think I can pull out our sofa and we can all lay down on it tonight. We can even have a picnic in bed!"

The idea didn't inspire the cheers, hoots and howls it would have on a different day, but the kids looked much happier all the same.

Jeff asked, "How easy do you think it would be to find the Legos? Do you think we could play with them for a little while."

Beth supported her brother by anticipating their father's next question. "We don't have very much homework, Dad. In fact, we have so little homework we could do it in the morning while we wait in the cafeteria after you drop us off."

On this particular day, Ken wasn't the least bit worried about their homework and he liked Beth's idea just fine. "Great plan, Beth. I know that you have a bit of time every morning because I go to work so early. So let's just have pizza, play with Legos and relax on our old couch tonight."

Ken pulled over the side of the road and called their favorite pizza parlor. He ordered cinnamon twists for dessert. He and the kids drove in silence to *Four Corner Pizza* and then out old route 11 to that Safe Stuff Storage facility. Ken drove to the back of the parking lot and turned left after the last row of interconnected garage units. Big signs at the end of each set of storage bays displayed an enormous letter of the alphabet and a notice that read, *This Facility is for the Temporary Storage of Inanimate Objects. No Pets Allowed. No Overnight Lodging.*

THIS FACILITY IS FOR STORAGE OF INANIMATE OBJECTS. NO PETS ALLOWED. NO OVERNIGHT LODGING

Ken paid $85 a month to secure everything that he and the kids still owned after losing their apartment. Ken knew he could get arrested if he was found living in the storage shed. But one night every now and then wouldn't hurt anything.

Ken pulled up next to Unit G 21. He hopped out of the car and unlocked the shed. The garage door slid up on the runners and recessed over their heads. Beth and Jeff unbuckled their seatbelts and leapt onto the pavement. Beth ran to her dad and attacked his waist, hugging him tightly. "Thanks for bringing us here, Dad. This was a good idea."

Beth, Jeff and Ken all moved boxes and then the cushions off of the couch. Ken pulled the sofa sleeper insert handle and like magic, a cozy bed appeared.

"Here's your queen-sized bed for the night," Ken bowed at the waist and presented it to the children. Jeff looked at his dad and softly said, "Queen sized bed, makes me think of the Princess of the Park. You think we'll ever see her again, Dad?"

Beth's fragile happiness turned to fear. Ken hurried to answer the question before her good mood disappeared completely, "Yes, I do." He responded in a resolute tone. "I absolutely do. Priscilla likes the park. I think she'll want to go back. But more importantly, Priscilla loves you and your friends. She won't stay away forever."

Ken pulled more boxes out of his way. "In fact, just last week, when I went to the park to meet her, she promised she'd babysit you guys each day after school. She wanted me to work more overtime. That doesn't sound like a woman who was planning to leave everyone. Forever. Without so much as a word."

The little trio hugged each other tightly. They all agreed. Priscilla would be back.

Ken took clean sheets, blankets and pillows from a plastic storage bin and together they made the bed. Ken reached up to the highest set of boxes and pulled down the one with lettering on the side that read, "Kids' Room." He set the box on the bed for Beth and Jeff to paw through. Ken walked to the car, grabbed the pizza, dessert and juice boxes and placed them on a box near the unfolded sleeper.

"Let's use this carton for our dining table, shall we?" Ken smiled, "You two unpack the Legos if you want. I'm going to drive Martha down past the surveillance cameras and park her on the street. Then I'll sneak back up here through the bushes – just in case the owners watched us drive in. They'll see the car leave and we won't have to worry about getting in trouble tonight. When I get back, we'll eat."

Preoccupied with their toys and the memories inspired by being with their own things, Beth and Jeff nodded in agreement. Ken turned on the battery operated lantern and kissed his children on the top of their heads. He reminded them, "I'll only be a few minutes. I'll close the door while I'm gone. When I come back, I'll knock twice before I open it. So you know it's me." With that Ken left. He pulled the rolling garage door down behind him.

24

CHAPTER 5

Sergeant Justus Brown

Sergeant Justus Brown strolled quietly into the squad room. He didn't often stop by the station mid-shift, but he'd forgotten his thermos and a whole shift without hot coffee just wouldn't work for this man. The Sarge loved quiet nights – so long as he could stay awake.

Passing by the dispatcher, Justus waved to the woman behind the bulletproof glass. "Pretty quiet out there, aye Sarge?" she asked.

"The quietest," he responded. "Had to come back for my coffee. I left it on the bench in the locker room. How are you tonight, Devera?

"I'm good. My hip's a little sore, but that's what I get for driving a desk 12 hours, four nights a week."

Justus found his thermos right where he left it. He made a quick stop at the vending machine. He reached into the side pocket on his left pants leg and grabbed five quarters. A minute later he held a package with two blueberry toaster pastries in a flimsy foil pouch.

He walked by Devera one more time on his way back out to his squad car. He almost made it to the front door when Devera called to him.

"Hey Sarge, one more thing."

Justus turned around trying to catch the crumbs that were falling from his lips. Failing his task miserably, crust fragments landed on the tile floor in the entryway of the police station. "What is it, Devera?" his voice muffled by a mouth full of tart.

"Didn't you say that if I ever heard anything about some old lady princess I was to let you know."

Sergeant Justus Brown dropped his snack and stared blankly at her. He bent down to pick up the fallen food. He stood up dragging his forearm across his lips, wiping crumbs from his face.

"Yeah, Devera, yeah I did. What happened? Did you hear anything? Did someone bring her in? Where is she? Is she in holding?"

Justus peppered Devera with so many questions she almost couldn't get the words out to answer him.

"No, no. Sorry. She's not here. It's just that some guy called. Gabriel something. I have it right here. Got his number too. He called asking if we'd locked up some old lady who acts like a princess and dresses the part too. Wanted to know if we hadn't arrested anyone like that, then maybe

26

we'd transported someone fits the description to a hospital or something. I told him I couldn't divulge that…" Before Devera could finish her story, Sergeant Justus Brown was up the corridor, around the corner and in the dispatcher's room with her.

He threw the rest of his vending machine food in the trash can and looked straight into Devera's eyes. "Devera," he said firmly, "Give me that guy's information. Please. And make it quick."

CHAPTER 6

The Post Office

Vivian walked around the side of her bright blue custom van. She brushed her hand down the side of her vehicle as she approached the rear passenger side and opened Jillian's door. Vivian looked at her fingers. Not a speck of dirt. Jillian was unbuckling her seat belt when her mom called out to her, "There's not even road grime on this van. How often does your dad wash this thing?"

Jillian didn't answer.

Vivian knew the answer to her question as well as she knew that her heartbroken daughter wouldn't answer it. Jillian's glum mood didn't stop her mom from trying to chitchat. Vivian was worried about Jillian. But her kid was a talker. She just had to get her started. Vivian knew that sooner or later Jillian would open up and express herself.

Vivian opened the tailgate and removed Jillian's wheelchair. She tried again. This time she decided to say something a little less superficial, "I think your dad washes it so often because it cost so darn much. If he's making that big an investment, he wants it to look nice."

Jillian had turned her swiveling rear seat toward the parking lot. She stared at her mom. The corners of her mouth turned up, but her eyes were still dark and sad. Jillian thought about the day they had all picked out the van that her dad promised he'd get for her. Edgar constantly reminded Jillian that he wanted one with "All the bells and whistles." Vivian pushed the chair alongside the open door. Jillian artfully hopped out of the van and into her wheelchair.

"I know Dad bought this van for me. It has 360 degree interior wheelchair turning radius and 57 inches of headroom. He even purchased the extra hand control package." Suddenly, Jillian was chatting up a storm, "He said that he spent so much on the van, he might as well get one I can drive in six years – because the vehicle loan won't even be paid off by the time I get my learner's permit."

Vivian smiled at Jillian, happy to watch the little girl who loved electronic gadgets grow more animated. *Get that kid talking about anything with a motor and you can pull her out of her doldrums for a bit*, Vivian thought. She felt quite pleased with the outcome of her conversational fishing expedition.

Jillian reached into the van and pulled her backpack off the floor of the back seat.

"Is that heavy? You want me to grab it?" Vivian asked.

Jillian shook her head, "No, I got it." After she placed the backpack on her lap, she resumed her discussion of the family's expensive van, "You know. I was fine climbing in and out of our old car. I appreciate that you and dad don't

30

have to help me in and out anymore, but…" Her words tapered off.

Here it comes, Vivian thought, here come her real thoughts.

"Go on," Vivian encouraged.

"It's just that for what you and Dad have for a car payment, we could have rented a small apartment."

Vivian knew what her daughter was getting at, but she wanted her to say it.

"We already have a place to live," Vivian replied.

"Well, we could have gotten a place for someone else to live. Someone who doesn't have a home or an extra $621 a month."

"Oh my goodness. What was your father thinking telling you how expensive the van payment is?" Vivian's face flushed.

"We worked on the payments together," Jillian answered. "Dad said that this is as good a time as any to start learning about compounded interest and accrued debt. It was fun. Although I don't think either of us could have done it without the calculator on my tablet. Zero percent interest for the first 18 months. Dad said that's how they suck us in."

"Suck you in, huh." Vivian clasped her hands behind her back and stared down at her daughter.

Jillian smiled her first real smile of their conversation, "Dad said you'd scold him for using that expression. But yeah, they suck you in with the no interest, then start raising the rate while you pay. Second 18 months is one and a half percent. Then we pay four percent for the last three years. It took us a while to figure it out. With our trade-in on the old car, it came out to $621 a month." Jillian grabbed her water bottle from the side pouch, took a quick swig and kept talking, "So after a while I got to thinking about it and I went on Craig's list."

"Craig's list!" Vivian exclaimed. "Who on earth told you about Craig's list."

Jillian rolled past her mom's comment and kept talking. "Do you know there are studio apartments in this town for what we pay for this van? Of course that doesn't include utilities. They could run another hundred, or more even. There are people who don't have that kind of money, Mom." Jillian had been coasting along beside her mom as they headed across the parking lot to the post office. She brought her chair to a sudden stop and shouted, "Think about it, Mom! Some people don't have as much money to live on as we spend on our van!"

Vivian stopped when Jillian did. "I know, sweetheart. Do you know that you yell sometimes? I know this is upsetting. But we have to find better ways to deal with our frustration. That's why we are here, isn't it."

Jillian looked up. Vivian's heart broke when she saw that she'd deflated her daughter a little. Jillian continued with a more restrained tone, "I know, Mom. It's not your fault. I know you promised to help Priscilla if we ever find her." Jillian's darkened eyes filled with tears. She brushed one away, "I'm either angry or sad, lately. I can't make up my mind. I can't even tell which emotion is taking over until it does."

"Well, all these emotions are new to you at your age. You'll get used to managing them. Most kids don't know some of the hard truths you've been learning the last few months," Vivian tried to speak words of comfort. Vivian believed they could talk all day, now that the floodgates had opened. But fall was nearly over and she could feel winter blowing into town. "Let's finish this conversation in the post office, shall we? I'm getting cold."

Vivian and Jillian moved hurriedly through the frosty air. Once inside, they approached the counter where Rose Marie, their very favorite postal clerk, stood waiting for them.

"Well hello, Viv and Jill, how are you two today? Mailing packages to the grandparents again?'

"No, not today," Jillian answered as she unzipped her backpack. "I have some posters here and I'm wondering if you would hang them up. Or if you'd let us hang them up."

Rose Marie started to tell her imploring customers that it was against United States Postal Service regulations to hang playbills of any kind... but then she glanced down and read the poster.

In big bold letters at the top, the word MISSING was written in a child's neatest handwriting. Under that was a picture of a woman Rose Marie had seen dozens of times. Usually Rose Marie walked by her in the park. But from time to time Priscilla would wander a few blocks from her throne to check her post office box or buy an envelope that already had a stamp on it. Keeping a book of stamps or a box of envelopes didn't make any sense for a woman who kept all her belongings under a park bench. Rose Marie remembered this old woman telling her how grateful she was that the post office sold single envelopes already stamped.

As Rose Marie stared at the woman's face, remembering their interactions, she realized the woman hadn't been in for a while.

"Oh my," Rose Marie gasped, "She's missing? Are you sure? Maybe she moved away. I haven't seen her around here in a while either. Let me ask my husband. He works up back." Rose Marie called over her shoulder into the sorting room. Past the boxes stuffed and ready to be shipped somewhere far from their little town worked a crew of package sorters and letter carriers. "Gary! Gary!" She called, "Check box 117. I'm pretty sure it's 117. Check it and see if anyone's gotten the mail."

Jillian shifted nervously in her seat. She hadn't expected to learn any clues to Priscilla's disappearance at the post office. It made sense though that Priscilla would have a post office box. How else would she get her mail? Gosh, thought Jillian, Priscilla's mail has a safe home, even though she doesn't.

After about 30 seconds Gary poked his head around the corner. Just his head. If the rest of him was behind the counter, Jillian and Vivian couldn't tell. He looked at his wife, "Hey, babe. Nope, it's full to overflowing. Doesn't look like anything's been picked up for a while." Then he looked past her and saw who was asking. "Oh hey, Jill and Viv. That your mailbox? You know we can't give you the mail if you don't have your key. You'll just have to come back when you do."

Rose Marie answered for them, "No, it's not their box. Thanks though, Gary. No wonder I love you so much." Gary grinned then waved the sentimental comment away and disappeared back into the sorting room.

Vivian thanked Rose Marie, "Aw, it was good of you to find that out for us. How nice that you two get to work together."

Impatient to get the job done, Jillian interrupted her mom, "You see, Miss Rose, we have these fliers. Our phone number is at the bottom about twelve times. People who might have seen Priscilla, or have some information about her, can tear off our phone number and give us a call. We're afraid something has happened to her. She wouldn't just move away or take off. We really miss her and I'm a bit worried."

Vivian added, "More than a bit, really."

Rose Marie reached under the counter top and brought up a sign that read, *Next Window Please*. She looked over at her coworker and said, "Michael, I'm taking my smoke break." Michael looked away from his customer and replied, "Ok. Uh wait, Rose Marie, you don't smoke."

Rose Marie had already disappeared from the counter. In a moment she stood by her friends. She whispered in a low tone, "Look girls, we can't hang posters here. Uncle Sam won't allow it. But if you give me a fistful of those fliers, Gary and I will hang them up when we leave tonight. We can get the whole west side of the square on our way home."

Jillian pulled a stack of papers out of her backpack and handed them to her friend. "Do you need a staple gun? We only have one, but Mom can take me to get another."

Gently taking the posters from the child's hand Rose Marie smiled as she replied, "Nothing to worry about, we have all that stuff here. We'll get these notices up easy-peasy." She leaned over and hugged Jillian and then patted Vivian on the back, "You make sure you let me know if you get any leads. I'm going to worry now."

"Thanks so much, we sure will," Vivian told the kind woman. Then she turned Jillian's chair and wheeled it toward the door. "We'll let you know as soon as we find out she's safe. You have a nice day. We have a lot more posters to get up around town before this day ends."

38

CHAPTER 7

Priscilla is a Person of Interest

G abriel went inside with Maggie when he dropped her off at school. He explained to her teacher that their family had been going through some things and she might be out of sorts for a day or two. Mrs. Tarrant asked if she might help in some way. Gabriel rested his hand on his daughter's shoulder and answered, "No. I think everything will be okay. If she seems too upset, just give me a call and I'll come back over."

Then Gabriel addressed his answer more to Maggie than to her teacher. He turned to his daughter and added, "Mrs. Tarrant is a great listener, Maggie. If you get upset you should just tell her what is bothering you. You can never have too many good grownups on your side."

Mrs. Tarrant crouched down and looked into Maggie's eyes. "I'm here if you need me. Why don't you go put your things away for now, but if you want

39

anything you come let me know." Maggie nodded, then walked to the coat hook to hang up her things.

"You're the best, Nancy." Gabriel smiled then shrugged. "I hope she's okay." The two grownups shook hands and Gabriel looked at his watch, "Oh darn, I'm going to be late. Thanks, Nancy, for this and for all you do for these kids."

Later, after his morning meeting and before he started working on his new project, Gabriel sat at his desk thinking. The night before had been rough and in the morning, Maggie woke up in a gloomy mood. That didn't surprise anyone. Gabriel told her all about the phone calls he'd made. Even though he didn't have any new answers about Priscilla, Maggie seemed to feel better knowing he had tried. Gabriel thought that the sleep had done them both at least a little good. Besides, he thought, no news is good news. If something bad had happened to a woman living in the park, it certainly wouldn't stay secret for long.

"If there ever was a woman who lived at the park," Gabriel said aloud to himself as he fumbled the note paper with Lani's phone number on it. He took his cell phone from his jacket pocket. "Time to ask the babysitter if there's an old lady in the park, or if – like Shewan says – 'Magdalena made the whole thing up.'" He'd only pressed the first two numbers when the phone started ringing in his hand.

Gabriel read the display aloud to himself, "Blocked." He harrumphed, touched the answer icon and then placed the phone against his ear. "Hello," he said.

A man's voice on the other end spoke slowly and clearly,

"Hello. I'm looking for Gabriel Prosser. This is Sergeant Justus Brown. I was on duty last night when you called and spoke to the dispatcher. But she didn't tell me about your call until mid-shift. That's basically the middle of the night and I didn't want to wake you."

Gabriel shuffled the phone to his left hand to free up his writing hand. He grabbed a pen and paper. He wanted take notes so he could tell Maggie everything the sergeant said, word for word.

"This is just grand, Sarge. I'm so excited you called. I mean, if you considered calling in the middle of the night then that must mean you found her." Gabriel's voice was shaking. He couldn't wait to tell Maggie that they'd found her after all. Maybe I won't wait until school gets out. Maybe I'll go right over there. Maggie will be so thrilled. Thoughts were flying through his head. I hope she's okay. What if something bad has happened? Gabriel articulated his fears, "She's alright, Sarge, isn't she? The princess is okay, right?"

The officer on the phone interrupted, "Well, actually, no, sir. You see, I can't tell you that. I mean, I don't know. I'm just calling to get a little information on the woman you claim disappeared from the park. At this point the most I can tell you is that she's a person of interest."

Crestfallen, Gabriel stared down at the blank paper on the desk before him. "Gosh," Gabriel sighed, "That's a shame. What does that even mean? A person of interest. I was hoping this was good news." Thinking to himself, this has to be how Maggie feels when no one believes her. Gabriel continued, "What do you need to know?"

41

The sergeant grilled Gabriel for what seemed like hours. He peppered him with questions about the woman that his daughter called Priscilla. Finally Gabriel said, "I'm sorry Sarge, but I don't know what you're after. I've told you everything I know. Now I need you tell me something. Is this Priscilla woman real? Or is she a figment of my kid's imagination?"

After a long pause the officer replied, "Please, call me Justus." He exhaled loudly and resumed talking. "Do you think I could meet your daughter? I'd love to ask her some questions, too. I'd love to meet these other kids you say that she hangs out with at the park. Perhaps the sitter too, if you don't mind."

Gabriel thought about it for a few minutes, glanced at his schedule on the desk and suggested a meeting time, "Well, Justus, tomorrow's Thursday and that's a park day for the little posse. I'll take off from work. You can meet us at the park tomorrow. I can definitely make sure that Maggie and the sitter get there. But I have a feeling the whole crowd might be there too. If Priscilla's real as she seems, a whole bunch of kids are going to head back to the park hoping she shows."

"That'll be fine, just fine," Justus Brown responded. "I'll see you then."

The sergeant disconnected the call. Gabriel finished plugging Lani's phone number into his cell and pressed the call button. His call went straight to voicemail, "Lani, this is Gabriel, Maggie's dad. I wanted to talk with you, but you're probably still in school. Look, don't bother calling me back. I'll meet you at the park tomorrow for your regular shift with Maggie. If Charlie your boyfriend is around, ask him to come along too, please." Gabriel was about to end the message but then he thought Lani might think she was in trouble. He added, "It's nothing about you. We think you do a great job. I just have a few questions and maybe Charlie can help with some of the answers."

CHAPTER 8
The Posse Returns

Sergeant Justus Brown pulled his squad car up to the northwest side of the park. Unfastening his seat belt, he hit the ignition button silencing the vehicle's engine. Sergeant Brown popped open his door and wearily pulled himself out, stepping onto the sidewalk. Tapping the side of the microphone clipped to his shoulder, the sergeant radioed dispatch, "two zero seven, dispatch. I'll be ten seven for 60 minutes." The radio crackled and a woman's voice responded, "Ten four, two zero seven, enjoy your lunch."

Justus rolled his eyes and turned to walk into the park. He'd already eaten his lunch. He did it while looking after the crosswalk leading to Mitch Snyder Elementary and Middle Schools. The crossing guard had reported a few speeding vehicles the last two afternoons, so he set up a mini speed trap. Eating on duty was a little outside regulations, but he had no choice. The sergeant needed to use his lunch hour to meet with Gabriel and find out what he and a bunch of little kids might know about the princess.

The walk to the fountain area was chillier than he anticipated. Justus always felt so overheated in his bullet proof vest. Every beat cop who worked on his squad wore one. He made sure that they did. So he always wore his too. Lead by example he thought as he pulled his winter gloves out of his pants' right pocket. The vest kept his body warm but his arms and hands got cold when the weather turned.

Justus walked to the bulletin board by the park restroom. There was a drawing of the princess and a request for help from anyone who might know what had happened to Priscilla, the Princess of the Park. The bottom of the paper had phone numbers on tear-away strips. A few of the numbers had been torn off already. "Hmm," Justus mused to himself, "I wonder if anyone has seen her and called. I guess the kids will tell me when they get here."

Justus thought he'd be early. He wanted to get to the area where Parks and Rec had mentioned seeing Priscilla's things before the others got there. He didn't want them... What did Gabriel call them? The posse? He didn't want the posse waiting for him while he looked around.

While the sergeant searched the area, he reminded himself to play it cool, "Remain calm so they don't suspect that you know the princess better than they do."

Justus hadn't noticed that he was speaking out loud as a young man with a guitar came up from behind. "You know Priscilla?" Vinny asked.

The sergeant whipped himself around and extended his hand. "Well, hello there." The sergeant looked at the musician

46

from the top of his head down to his feet. "You must be
Vinny, the street musician. Parks and Rec told me all about
you."

Vinny didn't flinch. He also didn't shake the sergeant's
hand. He responded without hesitation, "Oh, they did, did
they? Did they tell you that they keep trying to run Priscilla
out of here? Did they tell you that they try to take her things
away but I stop them? Well, I did until this last time. Are they
the ones who got her? Did they make her leave?"

"They say they're not," the Sargent responded. "Let's start over again. I'm Sergeant Justus Brown. But I'm not here on official business so you just call me Justus. I used to know the princess a number of years back when she was a much younger woman. I lost track of her and I'd like to make sure she's okay."

Vinny stared into the policeman's eyes looking to see if he could find trouble brewing behind his story, "I don't know why you didn't start looking for her until she was gone. You could have seen her here in the park any old day until she disappeared. Why didn't you come see her then?"

Justus rested his gloved fists on his utility belt and sighed, "Well, Vinny, that's a long story. I'll keep it short for now by telling you that the princess didn't like it when I came around. I kept an eye on her from a distance. Just to keep her safe."

"Ha!" Vinny laughed. "That's funny. I guess that didn't work very well. She's gone. Besides, if Priscilla didn't want you around then maybe I shouldn't be talking to you, either."

Justus understood Vinny's concern. Vinny couldn't know for sure if Justus legitimately wanted to help. Technically it wasn't illegal to live in the park, but lots of folks in town didn't like her doing it and they called the police regularly to complain. "Look, Vinny. Some guy called the police department looking for her. Said his kid plays with the princess here in the park. That's how I found out she might be in trouble. He's hoping she comes back to see the kids. If she does and I see that she's okay, I'll go away again. But if she doesn't and you all really want to find her – having a cop on

48

your side might help, right?"

Vinny nodded his head. He ran his hand through his hair and answered, "Okay, you can hang around to see if she comes back today. But if she doesn't and you start looking for her – you are going to keep us in the loop. You report back to us. Not the other way around. If we see you putting in a good faith effort. If you prove to us that you aren't one of those cops that wants to clear her out the park, then maybe we'll tell you what we know too."

Justus extended his hand again. This time Vinny shook it. "You have a deal, Vinny."

"We have half a deal," Vinny responded. "If by some wonderful twist of fate the princess does return today and she wants you gone. You go."

The sergeant nodded.

Vinny looked past him, "Here come the kids now."

A small group gathered around the county van while a little girl in a wheelchair was lowered to the sidewalk. Two grownups waited by the side of the vehicle next to an older woman, a big boy, a little boy, and some twins.

When Jillian rolled over to meet her parents all the other kids rushed to hug her. Even Hugo stepped up to her chair and patted her on the shoulder. Jillian spoke to everyone, "Hey, these are my parents, the Hoovers. They're cool with you calling them by their first names, Edgar and Vivian. The kids all murmured their hellos. Then the older woman spoke up. "Hello kids and Edgar and Vivian. I'm Tomas' and Hugo's

49

grandma – they call me Bela." She gave a warm smile and continued, "I'm cool too, so you can all call me Bela." The little group chuckled.

Beth spoke next, "This is so great that we have so many grownups here to help us. Our dad couldn't get off work today. But he told us to give him an assignment and he'd help any way he could."

Jillian's mom asked, "Should we go over and see if that policeman knows anything?"

Jillian answered, "We will in a minute, Mom, but that's Maggie walking this way with the guy. I bet it's her dad." Jillian waved her arm high over her head and yelled, "Hi, Maggie!"

The little group huddled close together. Bela turned and asked the twins, "You are Beth and Jeff, right? Tomas told me all about the Lord and Lady of the Laundry. I see that you don't have any mittens on. I love to knit. Shall I make you some?"

Jeff answered, "Gee, Bela. That would be so nice. I think we have some but we didn't know it would be so cold this afternoon. So we didn't bring them."

Bela smiled, "Well, I'll make you some no matter what. Children who play outside can never have too many mittens."

Gabriel and Maggie approached the posse. Maggie ran over and hugged Jillian. Once Jillian had re-introduced her parents, Maggie introduced her dad to the crowd and gave them a full report, "My dad called the police. I guess that's him over there. He also called the hospitals but they wouldn't tell him anything. It doesn't help that we don't know Priscilla's last name."

Tomas muttered, "Yeah, I never thought about asking her what her last name was. That would have been smart."

Vivian responded, "Jillian has been telling us that part of your special relationship with Priscilla was that you respected her uniqueness. Asking her for her last name – if she hadn't volunteered the information – might have been a little like prying."

Hugo spoke, his voice heavy with sadness, "Priscilla didn't like anyone to stick their nose in her business. She took care of herself and didn't need anyone fussing over her or putting that at risk."

Gabriel reached down and took Maggie by the hand. He looked at his new friends and spoke, "I don't know much about this police guy, except he seems willing to help. We can't get information from hospitals or group homes but maybe he can."

Jillian interrupted Gabriel, "We tried... Oh, sorry, I didn't meant to cut you off."

"No, go ahead," he said.

"Well, my mom and I hung up posters all over town. We've gotten about ten calls. But no one knows anything. They have been asking us what we know."

"Which ain't much," Hugo added.

"No, it ain't, Hugo." Jilllian replied.

Gabriel motioned with his free arm toward the sergeant and Vinny, "Shall we go over and see what we can learn from the officer. It doesn't look like Priscilla's come back. Maybe he knows more than we do."

The posse – having grown much larger than before Priscilla disappeared – walked over to talk to Vinny and the policeman. Introductions went around again. Gabriel stared at each child and adult as they said who they were and how long they'd known Priscilla. He leaned over and kissed Maggie on the cheek. Then he turned his face toward her and she kissed him back. While her lips were close to his ear she asked, "Hey Dad, what was that for?" Gabriel whispered, "I'm just so proud of you. No matter how many times your mom or I doubted the existence of Priscilla the Princess of the Park, you never got mad or treated us rudely."

Maggie reached over to hug her father's neck. "It's ok. I had a feeling you always believed me. And Mom's got such a wild imagination, only she could come up with a crazy story of a kid who pretends there's a princess living in the park."

Lani and Charlie walked up just as the introductions ended. Gabriel looked at Justus and explained, "These two are Maggie's sitter and her boyfriend."

"I'm Sergeant Justus Brown," the officer addressed the group, "But as I've mentioned already to Vinny and Gabriel, I'm not here on official police business. I've known the princess for a long time and like you good folks, I just want to make sure that nothing bad has happened to her. If we work together on this, we might be able to find the princess real soon."

Justus turned to Jillian. He had one of her flyers in his hand. "I understand you and your folks have been hanging the flyers. Is that your phone number on the bottom?"

Edgar responded, "It's my cell number, Sergeant. Sorry. I mean Justus."

Justus smiled, "Have you gotten any leads?"

Vinny reached over and touched Edgar on his arm. "Don't answer that yet. Before you all walked over, Justus made me a promise. He promised to meet us here every Thursday and give us a report of what he knows."

Tomas let out a groan, "Every Thursday? That sure sounds like this is going to drag on for an awful long time." Hugo put his arm around his little brother's shoulders. Bela smiled a brokenhearted smile as she watched the boys shared sadness bring them closer.

53

Vinny went on, "Well maybe it won't come to that. But if it does, he has promised that he will give us whatever information he finds. And if we decide he's reliable, we'll start giving him information too."

Jillian's mom chimed in, "How'd you kids all get to be so suspicious of everyone. I noticed it in Jillian but you all have it. You don't trust the police to help us?"

Jeff coughed. He thought he might not be able to say what he was thinking but at the same time, he knew he had to explain, "Vivian. It feels weird calling you by your first name, but if you say so." Vivian nodded. "You see, the police have a job to do for the town or the city. Even national park rangers have a job to do for the park."

Beth listened while Jeff explained the facts of life without a home – the way his own dad had explained them to him. Jeff continued, "The job they do for the town or the national park has a lot to do with protecting property. Isn't that right?"

Jeff looked at the sergeant and the sergeant nodded.

"Well, when it's their job to protect property, sometimes that means that they protect it from people who aren't going to do it any harm but they don't own it either. And if they don't own it, they can't sleep on it without paying money they might not have. So the police sometimes arrest those folks." Jeff looked at his feet, "Sometimes they don't. Sometimes they just tell them to get lost."

Vinny took back the conversation, "That's right, Jeff. That might be what happened to Priscilla. Some of the cops might have run her off. We don't know if that's the case. But Justus here is going to find that out. And if he comes back with some good information for us, we'll tell him what we know."

Maggie let go of her dad's hand and walked over by the officer. She looked up at him with giant tears in her eyes. "Mr. Justus, sir. Please tell us if you find her. We won't be mad at you if someone arrested her or ran her off."

Hugo yelled out, "Speak for yourself!" Bela shushed him.

Maggie went on, "We just want you to let us help. My parents said we can raise money to pay her bills – if she owes money to the park. We just want our friend back."

The sergeant got down on one knee. "If the princess got herself locked up, I promise to tell her this. And I promise that I'll ask her if you all can help. But if you know the princess, you know she might tell me not to tell you that I found her. Then what do I do?"

Edgar answered for the group, "You tell us anyway. My brother's an attorney and we'll get him to help her. You tell Priscilla that she's got a lawyer that wants to see her. That's how we'll make contact. We'll leave you out of it."

Sergeant Justus Brown thanked everyone for their concern. He promised to drop by the park each Thursday afternoon at 3:00 sharp and call sooner if he learned her whereabouts. As he turned to walk back to his squad car, Tomas called out, "Hey Sarge, you said you've known Priscilla a long time. You're not that old. Did you know her when you were a kid like us?"

The sergeant turned around and smiled, "Yes, I did, Tomas. I knew her when I was very little, in fact." Then he turned back again and kept on walking.

CHAPTER 9
Play Dates

Magdalena stomped through the deep snow all along Hempstead Avenue. She looked back over her shoulder and saw the hollow impressions left by her high steps. Maggie noticed that if she picked her foot straight up after stepping down she could leave a line of odd little boot holes that marked her path. The street had been plowed but fluffy white snow still clogged the sidewalks. Maggie enjoyed watching the tiny curbside snow removal machine – but she hated what it did to the freshly fallen white stuff. Maggie thought about how she liked leaving tracks behind her. Maggie thought, *I wish Priscilla had left some tracks. I'd give anything to follow them and find out where she went.*

Maggie sighed and turned up the walk toward Jillian's house. The path to the front door had been shoveled but a thin layer of new-fallen snow crunched under Maggie's boots when she walked. *Shoveling takes the silence out of the snowstorm*, she thought. *I couldn't hear my steps at all when the snow was deep.*

Maggie walked up the wheelchair ramp and crossed the deck to Jillian's front door. Without thinking, she stood up on her tiptoes and grabbed the steel knocker on the front door. It was shaped like a lion's paw. When she used it to knock, she imagined she was shaking hands with a giant cat.

Maggie brought the lion paw down against the door with three solid bangs. Within seconds, she heard motion inside the house. Jillian's front door swung open and the warmth from inside rushed out – inviting Maggie to enter.

"Hello, Maggie."

"Hello, Edgar. Thanks for letting me come over and play." She replied.

"Any time, Maggie. It's always a pleasure." Jillian's dad said with a smile, "Here, c'mon in and stamp your feet in the boot box. You look like a snow person!"

"Oh, it's the perfect snow for snow-people, Edgar. You think Jillian would want to come out and make one with me?" Maggie asked.

"I think she might just love that. Why don't you take off a couple of layers and run down to her room and ask her." Edgar helped their visitor remove her hat, gloves and overcoat. Then Maggie pulled off her boots. She left them in the boot box.

Before Maggie could tear off down the hall, Edgar grabbed a suspender on her snow pants and held her in place. He laughed and asked, "Hey did you wear only one sock?"

"Aw, gee," Maggie giggled. She looked down and saw one

little bare foot next to one with a big fluffy sock. "It must be in my boot." Maggie found her sock and hopped down the hall, calling back behind herself, "I'll put it on in Jillian's room."

Edgar smiled as he watched Jillian's friend navigate the distance to his daughter's room on just one foot. He marveled at her agility. He didn't feel sorry for himself because he had a daughter who couldn't walk, run or hop. Most of the time he didn't think about it at all.

But some days, when other kids came around, Edgar thought about the difference between his daughter and a child without her challenges.

While Edgar and Vivian made choices based on his daughter's disability, they didn't resent those decisions. Their lifestyle made daily routines easier for Jillian. They bought a house with all the rooms on one floor. They built ramps to both the front and back doors.

They installed railings in all the bathrooms. Jillian used a wheelchair on regular days and had a special sled for getting around in the snow. Edgar and Vivian could afford all the things their little girl needed. Edgar felt lucky they had enough money to make life easier for Jillian. Even the new van they purchased, though more expensive because it accommodated her disability, wasn't a financial hardship.

Still, seeing the way Maggie effortlessly adapted to losing her sock, Edgar wondered how much simpler life would be for Jillian if she were just able to walk.

Vivian crept up behind her husband and putting her arms around his waist she asked, "Sure is nice to have Maggie over to visit so often, isn't it?"

Edgar turned around to return the hug. He answered, "Yeah. Those two got pretty close spending all their time with Priscilla in the park. They formed quite a friendship."

"Speaking of Priscilla. Any word?" Vivian stepped back from Edgar to look into his eyes.

Edgar wrinkled his forehead and sighed, "Not that I've heard. Sergeant Brown, Justus, I mean. He still shows up at the park every Thursday. But from what Gabriel tells me, he's got no leads. I don't have any clients this Thursday afternoon, I thought I'd join them in the park and get any smaller details that the sergeant might not share without a little prodding."

Vivian smiled, "Time to see for yourself, huh?"

"Something like that." Edgar answered. "It's kind of hard to imagine that an eccentric little old lady could be gone for – what is it now? She disappeared the week before Halloween and it's already the first week of January. Nine weeks is a long time to be missing."

The couple hugged again as Jillian wheeled up the hallway with Maggie on her lap. On top of Maggie's lap sat one of the world's happiest kittycats.

Edgar and Vivian both chuckled warmly. "Hey, what's the weight limit for that chair?" Edgar asked playfully.

Jillian ignored his silly question and asked, "We're headed out to play in the snow. Is my sled ready, Dad?"

"It's right where you left it at the bottom of the ramp, M'lady." Her dad bowed. The whole posse and all their respective grownups continued referring to each other with their royal hellos and goodbyes and bows and curtseys. "You're one lucky kid, I'll say. It's snowed practically every day since you got that sled for Hanukkah. Non-stop winter fun, for sure."

Jillian's eyes sparkled, "Yeah, this has to be the best year for sledding of my whole life!"

Vivian leaned down and kissed both girls on the forehead, "Your whole life, huh? That's not a long time when it comes to recorded snowfall history. You two head out and play. I'll wait an hour to start dinner. Maggie, can you stay for dinner? We're having home-made macaroni and cheese. Edgar will drive you home after because it's dark too early now for you to walk home."

"Homemade mac and cheese!" Maggie rubber her tummy and licked her lips, "I would never turn down homemade mac and cheese. Shewan will totally understand. Can I use a phone to call home and ask?"

Edgar pulled out his cell phone, brought up his contact list, made a selection and handed the phone to Maggie. Maggie smiled when she read the name on the screen, it read, "Lady Maggie's Mom."

Jillian finished pulling on her snowsuit while Maggie got permission to stay for dinner. When Vivian helped her daughter with the snow pants, Jillian leaned over to kiss her mom's forehead and whisper, "Some evening, would it be okay to invite the entire posse over for dinner?"

Vivian finished buttoning the straps over Jillian's shoulders. She answered, "Now that is a wonderful idea! Should we invite their grownups too?"

"Sure." Jillian agreed, "Let's have a play date after school for the posse and the parents can come to dinner after."

The girls went out the back door. Jillian rolled her chair down the ramp and hopped out of her seat and onto the sled. Maggie grabbed the rope at the front and started pulling Jillian around the back yard. The girls giggled so loudly that Edgar and Vivian could hear them from inside the house.

"Edgar."

"Yes."

"When you're at the park on Thursday, invite the others to dinner Tuesday. Nine weeks is long enough. I want to get to the bottom of this if I can."

Edgar looked over at the woman he loved and asked, "Justus too?"

"Justus too."

CHAPTER 10
Saving Stories for Prescilla

Tomas waited at the westside exit of Mitch Snyder Middle School. That door was directly across from the eastside exit of Mitch Snyder Elementary School. Unless plans changed, when he left school at the end of the day, Tomas would find Hugo patiently waiting for him.

Not this time.

Tomas didn't handle disappearances well – not since Priscilla vanished in the fall. In this case, Hugo probably wouldn't disappear permanently, even though Priscilla seemed to have. But Hugo not being where he was supposed to be alarmed his little brother. Tomas remembered the rules Bela had made. If either he or his big brother didn't show up at their meeting place – the remaining child was supposed to walk back into their own school's main office and get the secretary to call home.

"It's too cold to wait out here anymore, anyway." Tomas muttered to himself. He turned around and went back inside.

Tomas walked in the elementary school office and found

Mrs. Patterson teaching a first grader to tie his shoes. "I know I could do it for you, Max. But if you learn to tie them yourself, you won't wander around dragging your laces behind you looking for help."

The little boy Mrs. Patterson called Max offered no response. He just concentrated on the task she had given him. He had one shoe tied. A little anyway. The knots looked so loose he'd be getting more practice in a few minutes when it came untied again.

Still, Mrs. Patterson encouraged him. "That's great, Max. Do you remember the rhyme?"

Max whispered softly as he pulled the loops up on his second shoe, "Bunny ears, bunny ears, playing by a tree. Criss-crossed the tree, trying to catch me. Bunny ears, bunny ears, jumped into the hole, popped out the other side beautiful and bold."

"Perfect," Mrs. Patterson squeaked with delight. "Now run along and keep an eye on those shoes, you might have to tie them a few times before they stick."

Tomas couldn't help but smile seeing how kind and patient the school secretary was with that really little kid. He called out to her, "Hey, Mrs. Patterson."

"Oh Tomas, I'm glad you're here. I was about to send someone outside to fetch you. Mr. Ramos called from the big school. He's got your brother in his office. He wants me to send you over there too."

"Mr. Ramos?" Tomas asked. "He's the vice-principal, right? Did Hugo do something wrong?"

"I'm sure I don't know," Mrs. Patterson answered. "I just give messages, I almost never get the back stories."

Tomas thanked the secretary and walked back down the hall to the east wing exit. Once through the door the wind bit at his nose and cheeks. "Brrrr," he said to himself. "I think it got even colder while that kid tied his shoes. I hope Priscilla's inside somewhere."

There he was, thinking about Priscilla again. Earlier that week, Tomas asked his grandmother when he'd stop worrying about his old friend, the princess of the park. Bela told him that he might never forget her – especially not in the bad weather when living outside would be such a frightening thought.

The cold made Tomas rush along the walkway. He pulled open the west wing door and went inside the middle school. He walked up the warm hallway to the offices in the center of the building. A gentleman he didn't know looked over the counter at him and asked, "What can I do for you?"

"I'm Tomas Saenz. I'm looking for my brother, Hugo."

"Oh, yeah, he's in there." The gentleman motioned with his thumb, up and over his shoulder. He pointed to the office behind him. "I guess your grandmother's on her way down here to get him. You too, I imagine."

Tomas swallowed slowly and whispered, "Oh gee, is he in trouble?"

"Sure looks that way," the man replied. "I think you can go in there and wait with him."

Tomas walked around the counter and slipped silently into the office on the other side. There sat Hugo in a big armchair across from a gigantic wooden desk. Behind the desk sat an empty office chair.

"Hugo," Tomas whispered even more quietly than before, "Are you in trouble? What are you doing in here? They told me Bela is on her way."

Just then the man from the outer office walked in and sat behind the desk.

Tomas looked stunned, "Are you the vice-principal?" he asked.

"Yes, I'm Mr. Ramos. Your Bela is here. She's hanging up her coat. You can take your coat off too, Tomas. And have a seat against the wall over there. We'll save the other seat in front of my desk for Mrs. Saenz."

Bela walked into the office and put a kiss on Tomas head as he walked by her to the chairs at the back of the room. Then she walked over and kissed Hugo on the top of his head too. "Hello, Bela, I'm very sorry," Hugo murmured. Bela sat down beside him and took his hand in hers. She stared across the desk at the man who had summonsed her to school.

Tomas shifted in his chair. He had never seen Bela so quiet when meeting a new person. She seemed almost unfriendly. *She's on our side!* He thought, feeling a sense of relief and pride – even without knowing what side they were actually on.

Mr. Ramos cleared his throat. "Mrs. Saenz, your grandson got into a fight today at school." Bela never let go of Hugo's hand. She stared at the man speaking. She had no expression on her face. Bela had no intention of engaging with the man. He had demanded she come to the school but he couldn't force her to talk.

Mr. Ramos went on, "We are going to suspend him for three days."

Bela sat there. Still silent.

"Mrs. Saenz, do you speak English? I speak Spanish if that would make this easier."

That did it. Bela had something to say. "Si, Senor. I speak English."

67

"Well, good. The way you sat silently without a response, I thought maybe you didn…"

Bela interrupted Mr. Ramos, "Where is the other child? The other half of the fight? Why isn't he here? Did he get suspended?"

Mr. Ramos responded, "Well no, we have a webcam on the playground and it shows the two boys talking and then, BLAM, out of nowhere, Hugo pops the other boy in the nose."

"Out of nowhere you say? No provocation, no bullying by the other boy?" Bela took a deep breath and continued, "Mr. Ramos, did you know that Hugo went to the nurse after the fight? Did you know that Mrs. Hashko let Hugo call me because he was so upset? Do you know that I know the other side of this story, already? I wonder, Mr. Ramos, do you know what that boy said to Hugo?"

"Well, no, Mrs. Saenz, in cases like these where there is one-sided physical contact we don't need to know the story. You can't think brute force is okay. You can't believe that Hugo should go unpunished because somebody said something, no matter how out of line it might have been." Tomas didn't realize the he was smiling until Mr. Ramos yelled, "What are you smiling at young Mr. Saenz?"

Bela continued undeterred, "Don't smile, Tomas. This isn't funny. We are dealing with a man who thinks it's just fine to say mean things about little old ladies who have no home and who have to live outside. We are dealing with a school official who doesn't even care if another kid tells your brother that he hopes that little old lady – our friend – dies in the snow."

Tomas' mouth fell open and he stared blank-faced at his grandmother. Oh yeah, she's protecting the realm, all right, he thought. Bela stood up and turned to look at the boys, "Hugo, Tomas, get your coats on, we're leaving." Then she looked back at Mr. Ramos. He too looked stunned by her anger and forcefulness. "Hugo is not suspended. You may find a different way to punish him for fighting. I've never approved of fighting and I'll have a chat with him and his parents when we get home. But you will not deny my grandson three days of math, science, reading and his other studies because you forgot to teach basic human decency to the children in the school yard." Bela turned on her heel and left the room. Both boys hurried to catch up with her.

Bela and the boys walked home in silence. Just before they got to the stairs at the apartment complex, Hugo spoke. "Bela, before we go inside and talk to Mama and Papa, I want to tell you that I'm sorry. I'm sorry you had to come to school. I'm sorry I embarrassed you and I'm sorry I hit that kid. Even if the little jerk had it coming."

Bela stopped. Hugo stopped. Tomas, looking down as he walked, smacked into his older brother. Hugo smiled and hugged his brother. "Look out, you knucklehead! You need to look where you're going before you smack into somebody who doesn't like you as much as I do."

Bela liked the difference Priscilla had made in her grandsons.

Bela looked at the boys and accepted Hugo's apology,

"Thank you for apologizing, Hugo. I can only imagine how hurt you were when that other child insulted your friend and wished her dead! Who is bringing children up that way?" Hugo shrugged, not sure if his grandmother was asking a real question or not.

Bela continued, "There won't be any big ordeal upstairs with your parents. They already know the story and we all agreed that your violent outburst will cost you your screen time for two weeks. No more hitting. Arms are for hugging. Not hurting." With that the older woman hugged her grandsons tightly.

Then Tomas spoke, "Bela, can I tell you something?"

Bela kept hugging and said, "Sure, of course. I hope it's not more drama. I've had my fill for today."

Tomas responded, "No. It's just something I would have told Priscilla if I had been lucky enough to see her today. We used to tell each other the favorite part of our day."

Hugo ruffled his brother's hair, "It better not be me losing screen time, you little brat."

Tomas laughed, "No. You weren't even there. Today I watched Mrs. Patterson teach a little kid how to tie his shoes. It was so cute. She was so patient."

Tears welled up in Tomas' eyes. Hugo hugged him, "I miss her, too."

Bela squeezed them both close to her and said, "I miss her, too. And I never met her. She makes me want to be a better listener. You boys keep teaching me the things she taught you, ok?"

The brothers agreed. Then Bela, Tomas and Hugo all walked into the building arm in arm to go home.

CHAPTER 11

Life Goes On

As winter wore on, Priscilla's disappearance had a lasting impact on the posse. Maggie and Jillian spent all the time they used to spend in the park together at each other's houses. The girls were well on their way to becoming lifelong best friends. Hugo and Tomas grew closer to their grandmother. They learned to cherish their time with her. The brothers missed Priscilla and Bela understood. She didn't try to replace Priscilla but she did try to learn the things that Tomas and Hugo loved about her. One day Bela told Tomas and Hugo, "I'm toying with the idea of asking Priscilla – when we find her – to make this old grandma the Princess of the Bodega."

Most of the grownups became friends, too. Bela kept in regular contact with Vivian, Edgar, Shewan and Gabriel. Shewan eventually recovered from learning that Priscilla really did exist. It took more than a minute for her to accept the news. It unsettled Shewan to learn that an old woman really did live on a park bench with squirrels. It saddened Shewan to think of a person old enough to be a grandma fishing her clothes from a dumpster. Like many others who'd never met Priscilla, Shewan wanted to deny Priscilla's harsh reality.

After all, Priscilla's story was intimidating and worthy of denial.

What really set Shewan back was forgiving herself. She had spent the better part of a year accusing her daughter of lying. Shewan had a lot of apologizing to do. Gabriel told her to tell Maggie how she felt. So she did, "Maggie, I can't explain how bad I feel about rolling my eyes and scoffing at you every time you mentioned Priscilla. I'm embarrassed and sorry and I hope you can forgive me."

Maggie was generous and kind with her mom, "I got mad at you when you did it. But I never stayed mad. I knew there was a princess of the park. That was enough. So I forgave you every time you teased me. I didn't save any of those feelings. They're gone. It's fine now." Maggie added, "It's sad though that she had to disappear to become real. I'd rather have her back in my life. I wouldn't care if you never believed me."

Shewan knew this was true. The size of her daughter's loss only made her earlier actions more regrettable.

The newest addition to the group, Sergeant Justus Brown, kept in regular contact with the posse. Every Thursday like clockwork, Justus parked his squad car by the park and went inside to meet Gabriel and any other of the parents who might have questions and the free time to ask them. Ken never went, of course. Ken didn't have the kind of job that allowed a person to step out for even a minute. Ken had to call in sick and lose a day's pay to go to parent/teacher conferences or bring the twins to the doctor.

Ken, Beth and Jeff fell away from the rest of the posse. They still missed Priscilla as much as any of them, but living without a home isolated them. The twins couldn't invite the other kids over to play the way Jillian and Maggie did. Beth and Jeff loved their dad as much as Tomas and Hugo loved their Bela, but he worked all the time. When the weather turned colder the kids couldn't wait for their dad by the car anymore after school. The twins started going to the library until their dad left work. They'd hide out in the back of the kids' section and read books, hoping nobody asked him where their parents were. Children under twelve weren't supposed to use the library on their own.

One day the children's librarian, Bonnie, walked up to them. She'd figured out – around the third time she saw them there – that they didn't have a grownup with them. She let a few weeks go by, then decided she had to do something. It really was against library policy to allow children under twelve to visit without a parent or guardian.

Kids aren't the only people with nowhere to go when it's too hot or too cold to be outside. The Dorothy B. Porter Library belonged to a network of libraries across the nation that had social work training for the staff. Libraries provided refuge to many who had nowhere else to go. Everyone who worked there learned how to help people experiencing homelessness.

One afternoon Bonnie approached the twins. Beth and Jeff looked to be holding each other up on either side of a beanbag chair. Sitting with their backs against each other they read silently. They were the ultimate bookends.

Bonnie spoke softly to the children, "Hey there. We have a few snacks in the community room downstairs. I'm about to

take my break. Want to get a carton of milk or a cookie with me?"

The twins knew they were busted. This librarian lady didn't even ask it was okay with their parents for them to leave the kids' section. Jeff and Beth knew, that she knew, they didn't have parents with them.

Beth spoke first, "I am kinda hungry."

The twins put the books they were reading back on the shelf and walked downstairs with Bonnie. Inside the community room, they got their snacks. They sat at a table in the middle of the room munching on cookies. Bonnie got right to the point. "It's nice down here cause we don't have to whisper. I've seen you kids here at the library since it turned cold outside. I notice you leave each night about six. Is that because somebody picks you up?"

The children nodded.

Bonnie pulled some papers out of a book she'd been carrying. "We have a referral service here at the library.

There's an after-school program at the YMCA for bigger kids who aren't babies and don't need daycare, but still shouldn't be alone. If you like, I can refer you for it."

The twins just stared at her. Beth put down her cookie and sipped on her water bottle.

"You'll still get to come to the library a couple of times a week. But you'll do other things too." Bonnie added hopefully, "They even go to the trampoline park every now and then."

Beth and Jeff remained silent. Neither looked excited. Neither looked eager. No emotion showed on their silent faces.

Bonnie pressed on, "Look, I can fill the paperwork out if you give me a few answers. I just need your names and ages. I can list your address as ours – here at the library." Bonnie emphasized that point just like she'd learned in her training, "You won't have to tell me where you live to qualify. They let us do that for the young people the librarians recommend."

Jeff relaxed a little – very little. "Our dad picks us up at six, usually. Can he answer those questions for you?

Bonnie thought to herself, Nobody's better trained to deal with unnecessary questions than kids with nowhere to live. I can always tell a kid with a house. They're willing to talk about themselves. Kids without one – they could keep state secrets.

"Sure, I can talk to your dad. Or, if you promise to bring it back, I can give you the form to fill out – he can bring it to me signed tomorrow – when he comes after you. That way he can think about the idea."

Beth and Jeff exchanged glances.

Jeff started to speak but Bonnie cut him off.

"One more day without a grownup won't make much difference. Now that we know each other, just check in with me when you get to the library tomorrow. Promise me you won't leave without saying goodbye and we will let it slide this last time."

Bonnie and the kids finished their snack in silence. When she finished putting her wrappers in the trash, Beth took the referral form and put it in her backpack.

Jeff looked up at the librarian as they left the room, "Are we going to have to leave the library now that you know we don't have a grownup?"

Bonnie looked around the hallway and put on her biggest smile. She winked at the twins as she pretended to reprimand them, "Hey, how'd you two get down here. This is for employees only. You better run back upstairs and finish those books you were reading before some other kid checks them out."

The kids smiled at Bonnie for the first time. She lowered her voice and reminded them, "Don't forget your form, or to say goodbye when you leave. Run along now."

CHAPTER 12
The Pike Motel

Ken drove Martha the Volkswagen up to the front door of the Dorothy B. Porter Library. He would have left the car running but she was low on gas. Ken got paid every other week. But that meant eight more days until he could budget more for fuel. Ken had to tighten the Kritzell family belt tighter than he ever had before. He peered out of the car and into the children's reading room window. He saw his children, still hunkered down, noses firmly planted in books. He checked the time on his phone. 5:50 p.m. Ken was early. Work let out early. The company gave workers far fewer hours after Christmas. The warehouses shut down one full shift. Everyone working overnights got sacked. Ken felt lucky he didn't get laid off when the holiday season ended.

Ken turned his gaze away from the library. He stared through the windshield at nothing. It had been months since he sat on the bench with Priscilla and told her that he and the kids would have a home soon. She knew better. He could see it in her eyes. "And now almost half of my savings are gone," he whispered to himself. "It's only January. We got at least two bitter cold months to go."

He remembered Priscilla telling him to take all the overtime he could. He would have too, if she hadn't disappeared. Nearly November when they met, Priscilla promised Ken she'd keep an eye on the kids. That would have been a big help through the busiest shopping – and shipping – season of the year. Priscilla keeping the children with her in the park would have freed up a lot of time for Ken to work.

"What happened to your realm, Princess? Your throne is empty and my kids have nowhere to go."

Maybe Ken could have saved his last few weeks' paychecks and gotten the apartment on Pomfret Street if the weather hadn't turned so nasty, bitter and cold. When Priscilla disappeared he and the twins had run off to comfort themselves by visiting their things in the storage shed for a night. The night turned into a week. Then two weeks. It was difficult. There were no bathrooms and they lived in fear of getting caught. The kids toughed it out – washing up in the school restrooms before most of the other kids got there.

But a couple weeks into their stay the temperatures dropped. They woke up one morning in the storage shed shivering. Beth spoke and her voice cracked, "Dad, I can see my breath."

"So I bit the bullet. I had no choice. I got us a room at the Pike Motel out on the turnpike," he explained to himself. "What a fleabag the place is." He hung his head, "But it's warm and we have a bathroom."

The rear passenger side door opened and a cheerful, "Hey

82

Dad!" broke up the gloom.

"Hey guys," Ken shouted back. "Hop in quick and I'll fire this puppy up."

Beth slid across to the seat behind her dad. Sitting in the back seat had gotten considerably easier since they moved so many of their belongings into the hotel room.

Jeff hopped in after his sister, "Okay, Dad. Let's go!"

The Kritzells drove two and a half miles out of town. The turnpike had no sidewalks for the kids to walk along. The school bus would have dropped them off at the motel but Ken would have had to file a change of address with the school. Ken decided against that for two reasons. He didn't like some of the characters he saw hanging out at the strip malls and rundown motels along the way. He also didn't want anyone to know they weren't living with Mike and Trudy anymore. Ken reasoned, If we have to start living in the car again this spring, I'll just have a whole lot of explaining to do.

Living with Uncle Mike and Aunt Trudy had been their cover story so long – it'd last a little longer.

Jeff pulled Martha in the space in front of room 101. It looked like it was room 10 because one of the numbers had fallen off the door and nobody replaced it. If a person looked closely they could see the discolored paint from where the missing one had been. Nobody ever visited, so it didn't really matter what they called the room.

The kids jumped out of the car and ran to the door. Ken followed them, fumbling for the key. Beth and Jeff jogged in place and rubbed their mittened hands together. "Hurry up, it's cold," they hollered in unison.

Once inside Beth and Jeff pulled off their outerwear. They put their boots in the boot box so they didn't track snow through the small hotel room. The twins shared the double bed furthest from the door and window side of the room. They never pulled the curtain open. Ken asked them to leave it closed. The motel walkway passed right in front of the room and while there was no law against raising children in a hotel room, Ken didn't like the idea of people knowing much about their living situation.

Besides that, the mechanism that pulled the curtain back had broken long before the Kritzells took up residence. The first night they stayed there the flimsy drapery hung from the rod at a 45 degree angle. "Nothing a little duct tape won't fix," Ken muttered when he taped the curtain shut.

Ken Kritzell had quit smoking the day he found out Edna was expecting. He remembered agreeing with his wife that kids shouldn't grow up around cigarettes. Ken had to shake his memory of that day out of his head every time he opened the hotel room door.

The smell of stale cigarettes overpowered any other scent that tried to survive in the room. Even pizza smelled and tasted a little bit like smoke just minutes after delivery.

"Why does the room always smell so bad?" Beth asked about the second week they stayed there. "Maybe if we washed the bedspreads, we could get rid of the smell."

Ken rocked his head, "Nah, that won't work." He surmised, "The walls are so thin, that's not an old smell you're noticing. That's new smoke seeping through the flimsy paneling from the rooms on either side."

Beth's eyes widened, "Are we going to get lung cancer from secondhand smoke?"

Ken shook his head, "No, I don't think so. We won't be here that long. But we'd definitely die of a bad lung freeze if we slept in Martha or the storage shed any longer." Ken hugged his daughter, "We just have to pick our battles, Beth. Tonight our battle is with the cold."

85

At the back of the hotel room coat hangers hung from an exposed bar. The kids clumsily hung their coats up and took turns using the restroom. The door shutting off the toilet/shower area from the hand sink didn't close all the way. It gave a little privacy, but couldn't be locked.

After the kids finished washing their hands they hopped on their bed and waited for their dad to give them dinner instructions. They had a hot plate and a tiny refrigerator. The fridge held so little, Ken had to shop for milk and cold cuts at least twice a week. Against the wall across from the two double beds, the fridge stood next to a long low bureau that held the TV and the hot plate. Beside the bureau were cases of canned goods Ken had gotten from the food bank. They had plenty of ravioli, some potted meats and assorted canned vegetables. All of it tasted pretty bad but the Kritzells had grown used to it. Bad smells, bad tastes, they were just part of motel living.

Ken walked over to the stack of canned food, "What'll it be, tonight? Chili, chili or chili?"

Beth shouted out, "I think I'll have the chili."

Jeff chimed in, "Not me! I want the chili."

Ken picked up the can opener, "Wise choice, Lord and Lady. Chili it is." He motioned to Jeff with the can opener, "Can you get the plates and silverware? And see if we have any of those taco chips left."

Jeff jumped up and went to the hand sink. Underneath it the Kritzells kept all their kitchen items. Ken had toyed with the idea of using paper plates. The limited storage space

combined
with the added expense,
convinced him to bring some of
their kitchen items from the storage bin.
They just scrub everything in the bath tub after dinner. The
tiny vanity sink barely had room for washing silverware.

"Yippee," bellowed Jeff, "We have a whole bag of corn
chips."

Ken smiled, "Well, what do you know about that? We now
have a two-course meal. Go ahead and open the chips while I
heat up the chili. I want to talk to you two about something."

The kids started munching. Beth drank from her water
bottle, finished chewing and said, "We have something to
discuss too."

The twins told their father about Bonnie and her offer to
let them use the library address to apply for an afterschool
program.

Ken frowned, "So she knows we ain't got a home."

Beth answered, "She figured it out on her own, Dad. We didn't tell her."

Jeff added, "Or she guessed. Doesn't really matter though, she's right."

Ken thought while he ladled hot chili onto three plates. "What do you guys think? If she outed you today and said you could come there unescorted one more time..." Ken paused, "that means you won't be allowed to sit alone in the library anymore after tomorrow."

The twins agreed.

Jeff offered his thoughts, "This Bonnie seems to understand secrets. I think she'll keep ours. I think we should let her enroll us at the YMCA. We'll get to go swimming. Jimmy Griffith, he's a fifth grader, he goes there and he even takes Karate. The paper says you have to pick us up by 7 p.m."

Ken nodded his head, "That wouldn't be any problem. I agree. If you two are okay with it, I'll fill the paperwork out. When I get you tomorrow evening, I'll bring it in and sign it."

Beth dipped a chip in her chili, "What did you want to talk about, Dad?"

"I met a nice lady yesterday," the kids cut him off with silly noises and teasing comments, "Oh, you met a nice laaaddyy, huh?"

"No. You two little comedians! Not like that," Ken's cheeks flushed. "She's a social worker. Reverend Matthew from the parking lot ministry told her where I worked. She waited for me to get out of work this evening and offered to help us apply for a housing program."

Beth stopped chewing and wiped her lips on her napkin, "Can she get us a house? For real?"

Ken answered, "Well, not a house. But an apartment. There's a big problem though."

Jeff rolled his eyes, "Of course there is. Why did you even talk to her?"

Ken looked at his son, "I had to try. We can't keep living here. I had almost enough money saved for a place but now half that's gone because this dingy hotel room cost $393.60 per week – with the discount. Remember when we did the budget together. I take home about $420 a week, and I have to keep dipping into our savings to buy gas, food, shampoo, dish detergent, car insurance, the cell phone. We're just lucky Martha runs so smooth. One bad car repair bill and we wouldn't be able to afford these luxury digs."

Jeff pushed his food away and lay back down on the bed. Ken walked over and picked up his plate, "Here, let me move this to the bureau until you want it back. You might kick it off the bed if you sit up quick."

Beth kept swirling her chip around in her chili. "What's the problem? Can we fix it?"

"Miss Stacie says we can."

Beth smiled. The idea of a home settled into her mind, "What do we do?"

"Miss Stacie says we have to get homeless."

"What?" Jeff shouted.

Ken stared at him and shrugged.

Jeff lowered his voice and continued, "We aren't homeless now?" Jeff gestured around the room pointing to their meager environment. "What does Miss Stacie call this? We don't even have a bathroom door that closes all the way. Or a kitchen table. We live in a hotel room. That's not a home."

"Well, I pay for it and we live here. So they say it's a home."

"So what do we have to do? Go back to living in our car?" Beth asked.

"No, that won't work either. Not well anyway." Ken explained, "We have to prove we're homeless. We don't really have a way to do that when we're living in the car. Besides, it's just too cold for outdoor living. Miss Stacie says there's a mission we can go to and they will vouch for us having no home."

"A mission," Jeff whispered. A tear ran out of the corner of his eye and down onto the bed. "Every day our lives just get worse and worse."

Ken crawled in between Beth and Jeff on the double bed. He hugged Jeff. Beth put her plate on the side table and climbed on Ken's back. "Dad sandwich!" She hollered.

Ken spoke softly to his children, "Things really do keep going from bad to worse for the Kritzells, don't they? Honestly, I thought we could get things under control. I

90

thought we'd hit rock bottom when we left Uncle Mike's place and started living in the car. But then the cold weather hit and boom! New bottom." Ken cleared his throat. "I have to find a way out. I have to take a step to stop this downward slide we're on. Maybe letting Miss Stacie help us will make the difference." He pulled his head up off the pillow to see the kids' faces. "We're paid here until Sunday. Miss Stacie says she can do an intake with us at Bethlehem Mission Sunday morning. You have several days to think about it. But I think we should give it a try."

CHAPTER 13

Searching for the Princess

Justus Brown stopped by the vending machine and
purchased two packages of his favorite toaster pastries.
One for now and one for later, he thought. *This could be
a long night*. Justus had spoken with his unit commander
about having an On Call night. Justus wouldn't be working.
Not officially. But he'd be in uniform and driving his squad
car. His commander pushed back a little on the request.
Justus explained that his purpose, though personal, was
innocent enough. "It's just a lot easier to get answers
wearing a uniform and a badge. I'm not going to do anything
inappropriate with the information. Scouts honor!"

Everyone in the police station, cop or civilian, knew that
Sergeant Justus Brown was a straight arrow. He didn't just
have a line in the sand between right and wrong – he had a
trench. Justus respected his trench and he never crossed it.

The unit commander gave him his blessing but added,
"Good luck, Justus. I hope you find what you're looking for.
But if anything goes wrong, you go on the clock immediately
and play it by the book. Understood?"

Justus agreed. Consequently, Justus had a whole night to wander into emergency rooms, do safety checks at the shelters, and wellness visits at the nursing homes. His uniform and his badge wouldn't get him access to patient records, but it would get him into common areas to look around. Because he knew exactly who he was looking for, he wouldn't need to see names or charts. He'd just need to see her face.

Devera stood at the photocopier with a bouquet of flowers.

"You still taking photocopier pictures of rosebuds?" Justus asked as he passed the dispatch office. "Honestly, I've never seen such a thing, but they sure come out pretty."

"Well, I have to do something to pass the time in here. Some nights get so tedious I could cry," she responded without looking up from her work. "I'm making a collection of greeting cards to sell at the Monday market when it opens back up in spring. Besides it's a great excuse to buy myself some flowers."

"Well, you'll have to show your pictures to me when I get back. I could be late but I doubt it." Justus kept walking for the door.

Devera called after him, "But you're not really working, right Sarge? I'm not to send any calls your way, is that right?"

"Not unless the town explodes. Even if it does, I suspect I'll figure that out on my own." The two co-workers chuckled and Justus scurried out the door with a wave.

The shelter staff treated him just the way he thought they might. No entry without a warrant. Some of the other officers got angry because the shelter denied them access, but Justus understood. Better to have petty trouble makers off the streets and in the shelters. Scaring people away from the few folks in town who genuinely wanted to help them wouldn't do any good for anybody. Besides, Justus could get everything he needed by standing around back and talking to the shelter guests who came outside for a smoke break.

None of the smokers had seen an older woman who claimed to be a princess. One cheerful chatterbox described every mature person she'd seen at the shelter over the past three months. None of them fit Priscilla's description. Another quieter fellow chewed the end of a plastic tipped cigar. He sat on the edge of the picnic table. He set the sergeant straight, "We all know who Priscilla is. And she ain't been here. She ain't been here in years, I bet. Since before she took up living in the park. She in some kind of trouble? Never did know her to hurt nobody. She'd get her social security check and she'd get us hoagie coupons from the sandwich shop on the pike. She was always real nice. I sure hope she ain't in any trouble."

"I hope she's not in trouble too," said the sergeant. "Truth is, we just don't know. Nobody's seen her in months."

Justus sat down across from the man and asked, "So tell me more about the sandwiches. She'd buy them for you – so you all knew when she got her social security checks, huh? Did she ever buy a sandwich for the wrong guy, ya think?"

"Aw, no. Nothing like that. Nobody would have knocked old Priscilla over for her check. I thought that was half the reason she bought the sandwiches in the first place. An old lady like her sleeping alone in a park. She needed allies. You know what I mean? For the cost of 20 sandwiches – what's that? A hundred bucks? She had every one of us watching her back. Oh sure, she did it to be nice too. But there weren't nothing about the princess that was stupid. She know'd what she was doing."

Justus thanked the crowd of folks. Before he left, he asked the man with all the helpful information if he needed a light for his cigar. "Nah," the man said, "I don't smoke. I just come out here for the company. You have a good night, sir. Drop back by and let me know if you find the princess. And if she's okay. I'll be worrying now."

Justus agreed. He gave the assembled group some of his business cards, so they could do the same.

The walk through at the Bethlehem Mission took less than ten minutes. A mission is a sort of a shelter that requires certain behaviors, dress codes and prayer from the people they help. The folks who ran the mission loved the police. They opened the living space, bedrooms and even the bathrooms to the authorities any time they asked. Giving open access to the police sent a clear message to the people in residence. Rules must be obeyed. Lawbreakers would not be tolerated. Not surprisingly, no Priscilla.

It had been a long time since Justus had done a wellness check at the hospitals and nursing homes. The emergency rooms were all quiet except for a few folks banged up in a car crash out route 581. Justus climbed in his squad car, reached overhead and flicked on the dome light. He rummaged around thinking, All this coming up emptyhanded is making me hungry. Where'd I leave that PopTart? He munched away, spewing crumbs as he always did while he chewed.

When he got to the nursing homes Justus told the overnight staff he needed to do a spot safety check. He'd asked to check the rooms for emergency exit plans. He thought his lame excuse worked because overnight staff didn't know that codes enforcement did their own policing.

While walking through a darkened room at Mayapple Nursing Care and Rehabilitation Center, Justus met an overnight charge nurse dressed like a fairy. Her name tag read "Ginger" but her outfit said Tinker Bell. "How can I help you, officer?" She asked with a smile.

Justus, flustered and wanting to laugh, stuck to his story. He told the woman that he needed to get inside each room, "immediately." Ginger stood back on one leg and crossed her arms. When she did so, Justus saw that she was clutching a magic wand. Her outfit was playful. Her body language was "game over."

"Why don't you come back tomorrow when Bill from physical plant is here." Ginger suggested, "He'll help you out. No offense, fella, but as you can see, I'm a pretty big fan of costumes. I could have worn my police uniform instead of the fairy suit tonight if I'd known you were coming."

Ginger's accusation hit the sergeant like a ton of bricks. "You, you, you think I am pretending," he stammered.

"Look at it from my point of view. Cops don't just show up in the middle of the night without a good reason. Room checks just aren't a good enough reason. For all I know this could be a prank. Although you look a little too old for such nonsense."

"Nonsense," Justus muttered under his breath. "You accuse me of nonsense and you're wandering around like the tooth fairy."

"Hah!" Ginger laughed loudly then quieted herself. "I'd go broke being a tooth fairy around here. Half my patients take their teeth out each night! That's a good one. Ha Ha. You made me laugh. I like laughing. Why don't you tell me why you're really here? Maybe I'll help you. Otherwise, you're going to need to leave before I sprinkle you with my fairy dust and you'll be dropping colored sprinkles at work for the next two weeks. Then we'll see who gets called Tinker Bell by his buddies at work."

Justus weighed his options in his head. If he told her the truth, she might take pity on him and let him see Priscilla. Then again, she might not. There were strict rules against telling patient secrets. Maybe she'd trust him, because she knew his uniform was the real thing.

"Ok, Fairy Ginger, I'm looking for the princess of the park!" He blurted out.

Ginger threw her arms up in the air, "Why didn't you say so. You want to find Priscilla?"

Relief washed over the sergeants face. He threw his arms around Ginger and lifted her in the air, spun her around and put her back down.

"Easy, boy. Easy. You're squashing my wings. Try that again and you'll get more than fairy dust dropped on your hair." Ginger brought her wand down gently on his head with a smile. "I'm glad you're happy she's okay. And I'm happy to see you. We've been wondering for the longest time if she had any people. We were told she didn't have an identification with her when the ambulance crew responded to the park. They said she was dressed strangely and unconscious when they found her."

Justus put his hand up to speak.

"Go ahead, you can ask questions. You don't have to raise your hand."

"I'm just wondering," Justus asked, grinning from ear to ear, "If they told you to your face that she was dressed weird."

"I don't always dress up like this, smarty pants," Ginger

99

replied. "Sometimes I wear my boring nurse clothes. Anyway, let me finish. Your friend had a stroke. It looked mild according to all the tests we gave her. But she hasn't come around. She can eat, drink and dress herself, but she doesn't seem to even know her name."

"If she doesn't know her name, how do you know who she is?" the sergeant asked.

"Well, you know we're a city facility. We aren't a private hospital. So the grounds crew that maintains our yard and gardens is the same group of guys that look after the park. She was outside in a wheelchair one day when these guys were working. They told us who she was. I've seen some of the flyers up around town asking for information about her. I hoped the Parks and Rec guys would call. I would, but you know I can't."

The sergeant felt a lump rising in his throat. His face grew hot as he tried to choke back his tears. Justus started to speak, then stopped himself. He tried a second time, "I'm so grateful Ginger, Tooth Fairy, Tinker Bell. Whoever you are. I'm so grateful to you. Would it be possible to see her?"

Ginger walked two feet to the nurses' counter and grabbed Justus a tissue. "Here. Some big tough guy. I can't let you see her tonight. Everyone on this floor's finally asleep. But if you come back in the day you can ask to visit. We just call her Priscilla Doe – princess of the park was too long for the forms."

Justus hugged the little sprite, thanked her again and left.

CHAPTER 14

Visiting the Princess

Justus pulled open the front door to the Mayapple Nursing Care and Rehabilitation Center, "After you, Jillian." The sergeant motioned to his young companion to go ahead of him into the building. He turned and waved to Vivian and Edgar who decided to wait in the van.

Staying in the car had been Vivian's idea. She told the sergeant that too many people visiting at one time couldn't help and it might hurt. "Besides," Vivian elaborated, "When I meet Priscilla, I want her to feel comfortable meeting me, too."

Off to the left of the reception desk was a small waiting room. A few residents gathered there with friends or family. In the seat farthest away from the door sat Ginger. She sprang to her feet when she saw the sergeant walk into the foyer.

Justus looked at the overnight nurse and smiled.

Ginger looked him over and said, "Almost didn't recognize you without your uniform." She chuckled. "Who's your friend?"

Justus feigned shock, "I could say the same to you!

What happened to your fairy duds?"

Jillian extended her hand and introduced herself, "Hi, I'm Jillian. I'm Priscilla's friend. The chief here thought she might see me and regain some function. I'm happy to be here if it could help her remember things better."

Ginger leaned over and shook Jillian's extended hand. "Wow, kids get smarter all the time. I'm very pleased to meet you, little darlin' – come on back with me. I'll take you two to her room." Ginger turned and walked backwards a few steps so she could make eye contact with the receptionist. "These are Priscilla's people. I told you about them. I'm gonna take them back to her room. No need to sign them in."

Ginger spun back around and explained herself, "If we sign you in, we might have to answer questions about how you came to know she was here. I hung around this morning to escort you down to her room myself. I'll be hog-tied before I let someone stand in the way of Priscilla getting her life back because of a rule that was never meant to apply to her in the first place."

"Hog-tied?" Jillian asked.

"It's an old saying, darlin' – don't really know where it comes from – but it fits the bill. They'd have to tie me up to keep me helping that sweet old gal."

"Fits the bill?" Jillian smiled. "Actually, you don't have to explain it to me. I understand. But you do sound a lot like Priscilla. She was always teaching us those fun little idioms."

"Idioms!" Ginger exclaimed. "Holy Moses, where'd you get such a smart little kid, Sarge?"

The sergeant grinned when Jillian answered, "Oh, we met in the park."

A few steps later Ginger, Justus and Jillian stood outside a closed door. "I'm gonna knock, and then I'll just go in and make sure she's respectable. When the coast is clear, I'll come back to get you." Ginger disappeared inside the room.

Jillian looked up at her companion, "You didn't tell her that you haven't seen Priscilla in years, did you?"

Justus shoved his hands in his jacket pockets and looked at his feet. "I didn't tell her anything. She assumed I'd seen her recently, I guess. I didn't tell her anything but that I was trying to find the princess of the park."

"I can't wait to see her, but I'm scared too," Jillian confided. "I'm afraid of what she'll look like. And I'm afraid it'll hurt my feelings if she doesn't remember me."

Just then the door opened into the room. Jillian and Justus walked inside and looked over by the window. There sat Priscilla, in a hospital gown and robe, staring out at the snow.

Justus froze by the door. He didn't move. Jillian rolled herself further into the room. Ginger called out, "Priscilla, some folks are here to see you. You want to turn around and say 'hi'?"

Justus thought Priscilla just sat there.

Jillian thought she saw the slightest movement in Priscilla's shoulders.

"C'mon in, you two." Ginger took Justus by the hand and pulled him into the room. They walked right past Jillian and stood next to Priscilla. "This nice fella came for a visit. Now visit."

Priscilla had to be able to see Justus Brown out of the corner of her eye. But she didn't acknowledge him. She didn't respond to Ginger, either. She just stared out the window.

"See what I mean. She seems fine, but she isn't. She just stares and stares and stares. Even though her CAT scan shows very little damage. One of the psych docs thinks she's got unresolved trauma." Ginger reached over and hugged Priscilla's motionless shoulders. "Poor darlin'."

"Maybe we should talk about this outside," Justus offered. "Maybe we shouldn't say this stuff in front of her."

"Very well," Ginger said. "Let's go."

"Wait," Jillian interrupted. "Why don't you two go out and let me sit here for a few minutes? Would you please? I understand she doesn't know I'm here. But I do. I miss her so bad. I'd just like to sit with her for a few minutes. If you two don't mind?"

Ginger grabbed a box of tissues off the nightstand and handed it to the little girl in the wheelchair. "Ok, but you look like you could use these. We'll go out and see if we can find the Sarge here a doctor to explain things better. I'll be back for you in five minutes."

The two left and shut the door tightly behind them. Jillian wheeled herself up next to Priscilla's chair and reached over to take her hand. Jillian hung her head and started to cry.

Suddenly, Priscilla squeezed Jillian's hand. Jillian jerked her head up and looked at her friend. Priscilla was beaming. She had a smile from one ear to the other.

"Wha, wha, wha…" Jilllian tried to ask a question but no words came.

"Quick, we only have five minutes." Priscilla whispered and threw her arms around her young friend. "How is everyone? How are you? Are all my lords and ladies doing okay? How's the big boy? The protector of the realm…"

Jillian found her words. "Oh my goodness, I'm so glad you're okay. Is this a miracle? I never believed in miracles. But this must be a miracle." Jillian took a breath and continued, "To answer your question, the lords and ladies and protectors and family members are all heartbroken and sick worried about you. When the sergeant said he found you everyone wanted to rush over here, but we were afraid too many people might be a shock to you. What happened?"

"We don't have time," Priscilla answered. "When they come back in here, you need to be weeping into your hankies and I'm going to be back in Never Never Land."

"Why?" Jillian asked just as they heard a knock at the door.

Priscilla turned her head and looked back out of the window. Her entire expression went blank. Jillian buried her face in her hands. She was grateful for the tissues. She hid her

106

happiness in tissues filled with old tears.

Sergeant Brown spoke, "We better get back out to the car, Jillian. Your parents have waited for us quite a while." He turned to Ginger, "May we come back again?"

"We wish you would. Bring the whole posse in to see her." Ginger elaborated, "Not all at once, of course. But one or two at a time might bring her around after a while."

Ginger approached the back of Jillian's wheelchair, "Can I give you a hand, darlin'?" she asked.

Jillian replied, "Nope, been in this chair my whole life. I can get back down the corridor. Give me a second and I'll be right there."

Justus and Ginger went out into the hallway. Priscilla slowly turned her head to Jillian and gave her a big wink with her left eye. Jillian reached over to hug Priscilla who remained motionless even though her insides were screaming to hug back.

Jillian whispered, "I'll come back soon without the sergeant. I'll bring my parents. I promise you can trust them. They want to help you anyway you are willing to be helped."

Priscilla winked again. Jillian turned her chair and rolled out into the corridor to join the others.

CHAPTER 15

The Bethlehem Mission

M iss Stacie finished processing the paperwork, exited the building and walked across the parking lot. The Kritzells sat in Martha's back seat playing *I Spy*.

Stacie walked up to the passenger side. The glass on the windows was fogged by warm breath that had frozen to the glass. She rubbed her bare palm on the window until the ice cleared and peered inside. It was Beth's turn at the game, "I spy with my little eye... STACIE," She shouted.

"Well, that ruins the game if you're going to shout out your own answer," her dad teased.

"No," Beth giggled. "She's right there."

"Hey guys," Miss Stacie said as she opened the passenger side door. You're all checked in."

"Pop the trunk, will ya, Dad?" Jeff requested. "I need my duffle bag."

"Nope, sorry. No luggage," Stacie interjected. "Just one small sack with a few personal items. You don't get to bring anything else inside."

"Seriously?" Beth asked. "Why not?"

Stacie frowned, "Bedbugs."

"Ewww," the kids sang out together. "There are bedbugs in there?"

"Nope, not yet, anyway. And that's the way they want to keep it. You can't even bring clothes inside. When you leave at 6:30 tomorrow morning, you can drive somewhere and get dressed."

"This turkey don't fly, Dad. We aren't staying here. Take us back to the motel." Jeff commanded. On a normal day, any one of them saying, "This turkey don't fly" would have caused peals of laughter. But nothing about this move felt funny.

Miss Stacie pulled the passenger side door open and sat on the front seat facing backward. She looked at the children and said, "Don't get me wrong. I know this is the pits. If there were any other way to get you guys moved up the housing list, I would have done it by now. But you have to be homeless."

"The school says we are." Beth stated plainly.

"The school has a different definition," Stacey repeated herself for the 4000th time. Not to these children she hadn't. She'd only told these kids five or six times. But in the course of her five years working for the continuum of care, she'd said it over and over and over again.

Ken searched for a silver lining so that he could use it to cajole the twins into cheerfully giving this new situation a try. But he couldn't find one. There was no cause and effect to offer them. He couldn't tell them that after they stayed at the Mission for a certain number of days, they would get a home. No, living in a homeless shelter gave no guarantee of housing. Hoping they'd get chosen from the housing list was all a gamble. One they might never win.

The car got deathly quiet. They could all hear and see their own breath. Finally, Ken found his voice, "C'mon. Grab your toiletry bags and let's go inside. We can try one night. Maybe it won't be so bad. Then we can try another night. And another. And before you know it, we'll have a place of our own."

The little family climbed through their sadness and exited the car. As Stacie walked back across the parking lot, she turned to them and spoke, "Two good things about Sunday mornings. It's a fast registration because everyone is in the Sunday service and there's a great meal right after that." She looked at her watch, "Right about now!" She smiled, "Let's go eat."

The kids quickened their pace as they headed for the door. Two months of canned chili and ramen noodles made their stomachs growl for a real meal.

When they walked in, Ken was handed a long list of rules. The older lady working the front desk welcomed them to the Mission. "Hi, I'm Miss Gina. Happy to have you folks.

Mister," she stared at Ken. "Here are the rules. I suggest you read them front and back. There ain't no second chances here." The old lady's eyes narrowed. She had a job to do.

Threatening Ken didn't make her happy, but she wouldn't tell him twice. If he made one misstep, he'd get his family thrown out of the facility.

She smiled over the reception desk at the children. "You keep right next to your daddy at all times. If we find you in a different room or away from him for any reason, you'll be asked to leave. It won't be just one of you leaving. You'll all be leaving."

Beth felt a stinging in her eyes.

Jeff felt angry.

Ken put his arm around both kids and assured the woman, "Thank you, Miss Gina. Don't you worry. We'll stay together."

The old lady showed them their locker. It was two feet tall, eight inches wide and ten inches deep. "You put your belongings in here. Remember the number and don't go in anyone else's locker. You can't have locks, so don't put anything in the locker you don't want to lose. And if we catch any one of you in someone else's locker, you'll be asked to leave."

"And we'll all be leaving," whispered Beth.

"That's right," agreed the old lady. "You wouldn't want to get your brother or your father thrown out because you were wondering what someone else had in their locker, would you?"

Ken opened the locker and told the kids to put their toiletry bags inside.

"Not so fast," the old lady said. "I need to search those bags first. No contraband allowed. Read your list of rules. It's on there."

Beth was fighting her tears and losing the battle.

Jeff leaned into his sister and whispered, "They'll never know that your toothpaste tube is a bomb." Beth laughed. She surprised herself when she did. She thought she was too sad to smile.

"Okay, that's the last wisecrack I want to hear from either of you," the old lady said. Ken asked himself how such a nice-looking old lady could be so mean to two little kids without a home. He looked over at Stacie. Stacie shrugged and looked away.

Once the Kritzells closed their locker they were escorted to the lunch room. When the door opened the most wonderful smells ever created wound themselves around the little family and climbed up their noses. "Can you smell that, Dad?" Jeff asked, almost forgetting how angry he had been.

"Yeah," answered Ken. "Let's grab some seats."

The room filled up quickly after Stacie and the Kritzells sat down. "Got here just in time," Ken sighed.

"Church just let out," Stacie informed him.

One by one everyone in the room walked through the buffet line. What a feast! Mashed potatoes, coleslaw, chicken, gravy, green beans, apples, oranges and several different kinds of pie. Across one wall a banner read, *Don't take more than you can eat. Waste is a sin.*

The Kritzells got back to their seats. Beth and Jeff sat down, put their napkins on their laps and started eating. Stacie tapped Ken on the shoulder. He and the twins were the only ones sitting down. The twins were the only ones eating. "Stand up," she whispered to them, "You can't eat yet. You need to stand for the blessing."

Ken motioned to his kids that they should stand. Beth and Jeff did as they were told. But it was too late. With a loud cracking sound, a wooden pointer – the kind teachers use to point at lessons on a white board – smashed down on the table between Beth and Jeff. *WHAP!*

The sound was so startling that Beth burst into tears. Jeff whipped around, "Hey, what was that for?" He asked. Before Ken could interfere, the old woman barked at his children. "You must not eat until you give thanks to the Lord. You must talk to God before you share his gifts."

Ken started to explain that they just didn't know. They didn't understand. The old woman turned her sneering face toward him. "You shouldn't need me to tell your children to talk to God before you share his gifts. Don't you do that with them when you're not here?"

"Well, no Miss Gina. We don't." Ken spoke honestly despite his suspicion that it would get him and his children thrown out of the lunch room.

The old woman addressed the rest of the people in the room. "Be seated." The crowd did as they were told. "You all see what we have here?" she asked. "A man who did not teach his children to speak to God, and now he finds himself

114

homeless. Is there any surprise?" None of the other residents in the room looked at the woman. They all stared down at their hands. Stacie stood glaring at Miss Gina. *Every person in this room, praying or not, needs a home*, Stacie thought. *Blaming Ken for his homelessness is as illogical as it is cruel.* But, she couldn't say any of that. She needed the Mission to certify the Kritzells' homelessness.

"You and your children will talk to God when we talk to God or you will not eat here and you certainly will not

stay here," the old lady's voice was shaking. She felt very powerful and using that power felt great. She leaned down to look into Jeff's eyes. He could feel her hot breath in his face. Beth started crying again. Ken stood up and walked around the old woman to hug his daughter.

The old woman felt triumphant. She believed that one day the Kritzells would thank her for reminding them that God provides when they obey His rules. She continued staring into Jeff's small but defiant face. She asked him,

"Tell me boy, when was the last time you spoke to God?"

Jeff recoiled away from her face. She asked him again, louder, "When was the last time you spoke to God?"

Jeff heard his sister crying. He heard his father try to calm her so they could stay and give Stacie the evidence she needed to qualify them for help. He felt his own neck and face get hot. Finally Jeff spoke with a courage he didn't know he had, "I haven't talked to God since he killed my mother."

The whole room gasped. The woman stood up and grabbed her pointer in both hands. Then she turned to Ken. Ken stared blankly at her. He moved in between Jeff, Beth and the old woman and said weakly, "Sixteen months ago my wife, my beautiful Edna, died of aneurysm in her brain. It was sudden. I guess that's all the good you can say about it. She didn't suffer. But the kids and I have been suffering ever since. We didn't lose our home right away. But it didn't take too awfully long either. We've been struggling to survive. We were told by this nice woman here that you might help us." He looked over at Stacie. Tears ran down her cheeks too. "Sorry, Miss Stacie, I can't imagine how many of these hard-luck stories you hear."

Ken spoke to Beth and Jeff. "Grab your paper plates, kids. You better take that food with you. Wasting is a sin. The sign says so."

The twins stood up and held their plates in front of them. Ken turned around and helped them carry their lunch out of the meeting room. He stopped at the locker and grabbed their things. Then Ken and his children walked out of the mission and straight to Martha the Volkswagen.

"Climb inside, kids," Ken told them. He closed the door after them and walked around to the driver's side. "I don't think we'll wait for Miss Stacie. She's probably apologizing for the way we acted. Let's just head back to the motel for a while."

They drove in silence for a few minutes. Then Beth spoke, "Thanks for not making us stay there, Dad." She turned to look at her brother. "Mom would've been proud of you, Jeff." Jeff smiled a sad smile at his sister. Beth spoke again, "Dad, you want a drumstick? I have two."

Ken looked in the rearview mirror. He couldn't imagine loving his kids more. He just wished he had a way to get them a home.

CHAPTER 16

The Dinner Party

Vivian and Edgar cooked all day in preparation for what Jillian called the event of the year. The dinner was pot luck. The guests would bring side dishes, with the Hoover family supplying the entrees. Edgar brought extra folding tables and chairs out of the basement. Jillian dressed every setting with placemats, napkins and flatware. She put a small glass bowl with fresh flowers on each table. She'd picked out a bouquet when she and her mom shopped for groceries for the event. What started out as a simple mid-winter scheme to bring the posse back together, ended up a celebration. When Sergeant Justus Brown announced that he'd found Priscilla at the Mayapple, a party just created itself. Besides, Priscilla's friends needed a plan.

Jillian smiled to herself while she detailed each of the place settings and made sure everyone could reach salt, pepper and other condiments. Vivian walked through the dining room to see if Jillian needed anything else. People would be arriving soon and the plan was to sit and chat about Priscilla – not to fuss over the meal. If everything was ready when the guests arrived, none of the Hoovers would have to budge from the dinner until coffee and clearing time.

"You almost done here?" Vivian asked. "Folks should be arriving soon. Did you say someone got a hold of Beth and Jeff and their dad?" She asked and added, "I sure hope they come."

"Me too, Mom," Jillian responded. "Maggie went down to the secretary's office at school and gave your note to Mrs. Patterson. Mrs. P said she'd make sure the twins received it."

"Good!" Vivian twirled Jillian around and looked into her eyes. "What about you? You ready to spill the beans about Priscilla?"

"Oh boy, am I!" Jillian beamed back at her mom.

Jillian had been waiting to tell the others since she and Justus visited Priscilla. When she left Mayapple, Jillian climbed in the van with her parents and told them all about Priscilla pretending she couldn't communicate. The Hoover family discussed it. They agreed that no one else should know Priscilla's secret until everyone knew about it. They'd already planned to have a dinner party. That seemed like the logical time to share the news. Originally, the guest list would have included the sergeant. They changed that plan so the posse could speak openly and discuss how to handle the news.

"Hey, our first guests are driving up, I think." Edgar announced as he headed for the front entryway. He pulled the door open just as the twins raised their hands to knock. Usually unwilling to rush into new places, Jeff and Beth screamed out Jillian's name and ran for her. Squealing, happy sounds created quite a din; almost too loud for Edgar and Ken to hear each other. Edgar took Ken's coat and introduced himself, "Hey Ken, I'm Edgar and this is my wife, Vivian. We're glad to meet you. We've heard so much about the twins. It's sad we all lost touch with you folks when Priscilla disappeared."

Ken smiled, "Well, looks like that's been repaired now! Priscilla strikes again. She's brought the posse back together." He turned to Vivian, "You're the one who named them the posse, right? I must say, it sure fits."

Everyone else arrived, one after another, until the home was full of happiness and conversation.

"Well, c'mon everybody. Grab a plate and start eating. We've got a lot to talk about." Vivian put her arm through Ken's and added, "Won't you go first, Ken? Please get us started."

There were two buffet tables. One at regular height for the grownups and one lower one, so that Jillian could fill her own plate from her wheelchair without help. The other kids used Jillian's table too.

Beth looked over at her dad, "Sure is a lot nicer than the last buffet we went to, right?"

Ken winked and nodded.

Jillian called out to their assembled guests, "I put name cards at all the seats. Kids are all together at the big table and grownups are divided up around the card tables."

Tomas and Hugo's grandmother leaned over and kissed Jillian on the top of the head, "My goodness, you thought of everything, didn't you?"

"Thank you, Bela. I'm very excited that you're here. I've missed Tomas and Hugo a lot," Jillian replied.

Shewan and Gabriel put water pitchers on each table, the only thing a little too heavy for Jillian to manage herself. Everyone sat down at their assigned seats.

The room quieted down considerably except for the occasional compliment on the good cooking and other murmurs of delight.

122

Jillian took her spoon and clinked it against the side of her glass. She pulled a folded piece of paper out of her pocket and began to read, "Hello assembled lords and ladies, noble peasants that we are. I call this court to order." Hushed chuckles and louder giggles could be heard as she read, "As many of you forthwith already know, Priscilla, our princess, has been found."

The room erupted with applause.

Jillian tapped her spoon against her glass and the room hushed again. Parents smiled at the happy children.

"And while we were informed by the court constable that she is dungeoned in a home for elders who have lost their faculties…" Groans and moans of displeasure interrupted her speech. Again clinking on her glass, Jillian continued, "But I am here to tell you that Priscilla is as cogent as she has ever been."

Her words were met with gasps of dismay.

Hugo spoke, "I don't mean to interrupt M'lady, but what does cogent mean? Does that mean she ain't brain damaged?"

"Yes, Hugo. 'Tis true. She squeezed my hand when I held hers. Then she smiled and we talked." Jillian cheeks flushed with joy. "She bade me keep her secret. Which I have done and I now charge you to do as well." Jillian looked over at Hugo and then around the room at the others. "Not just you, Protector of the Realm. All of you."

Tomas let out a shriek and smashed both hands down on the table at either side of his plate. Everyone turned to stare at him. He blurted out, "This is the best news I've ever heard. I thought when Bela got off the phone with Gabriel, after Justus said he'd found her, that that was the best news. But this is so much better than that. I'm just so happy."

Hugo hugged his brother's shoulders and across the room, Bela cried tears of joy, "Look at me crying." She announced, "I'm so happy. I don't know Priscilla yet, but I'm so happy for my grandsons. For all of you."

"Wait a minute," Maggie shouted. "What's she doing in that dementia ward if she's fine?"

The room went silent.

"I think I can guess." Ken cleared his throat and went on, "Justus said Priscilla had a mild stroke the week before Halloween. We all know that fits the timeline. He said she was unconscious for more than two weeks. Does anyone else remember that big snowstorm the second week of November?"

Everyone nodded.

"Well, if Priscilla woke in a hospital bed – weak from not eating for two weeks and even a little stiff down one side of her body – what do you think would have happened to her in the park? In the freezing cold? In the snow?" Ken asked.

Beth started to laugh. Then Jeff laughed with her. The rest of the room looked a little surprised to hear the children laughing. Edgar said, "No offense kids, but this doesn't sound very funny at all."

Ken started chuckling along with his kids. "Well it does to us," he replied. Then Beth shouted out, "Don't you get it? She's faking. She's faking so they don't put her outside."

Tomas started laughing next, "She outsmarted them! You'd have to get up pretty early in the morning to outsmart Priscilla! Remember she used to tell us that when we tried to squirm out of doing our homework or if we dodged a question when she was teaching us things in the park? She'd say,

'You've got to get up pretty early in the morning to outsmart the Princess of the Park.'"

Hugo giggled, "Well, I'll be pickled. She's tricked them into giving her three hots and a cot."

"What?" Shewan asked. "Three hots and a what?" Shewan had gotten used to the news that Priscilla really existed. But that evening she found herself surrounded by nine-year-old kids who spoke like gangsters from the old black and white movies.

"Three hots and a cot," Hugo repeated. "You know, three meals and a bed. Priscilla told Vinny that's all the Bethlehem Mission was good for when he asked her about going to live there."

"They aren't even good for that," Jeff said under his breath.

Magdalena spoke up, "Well, I'm overjoyed. I'm overjoyed we found her and I'm overjoyed she's safe. But I'm kind of sad that she didn't call one of us to come help her."

Gabriel hugged his daughter.

Ken spoke again, "That's hardly a job for children. Caring for an elderly stroke victim. On top of that, she didn't trust us either. Not us parents, I mean. She told me so herself. Besides, Priscilla didn't want to be a burden when she was healthy. Let alone sick."

Mumbled agreements went around the room.

"So what do we do now?" Vivian asked.

Ken replied, "Way I see it, we got three options." Ken put one finger in the air. "We leave her be and she'll get out on her own." His second finger went up, "We figure out if there's a way to get her a place to live that she'll find acceptable. But from what I understand that's a lot easier said than done when someone's got a small fixed income." Ken put his hand down and lowered his voice. "Or we tell Justus. See if he'll help."

"That's what Vinny said we should do," Gabriel interjected. "Vinny couldn't be here tonight but he told me that he wanted us to remember his promise to the sergeant. He told Justus we'd give him information if he helped us find her."

The occupants of the room mumbled some more.

"I don't think so," Jillian piped in to the conversation. "She could have shown herself to Justus when we were in the room together. But she didn't. I don't think she wants him to know."

Maggie whined, "How much longer is this stupid winter going to last, anyway? If she's better and the weather would just improve, she could go home. To the park."

With no clear answers Shewan, Gabriel, Vivian and Edgar started clearing the dishes. Bela and Ken stood to help. "That kitchen gets crowded if too many people help. You two stay here with the kids and brainstorm. We'll be back with pie and hot cocoa."

Bela smiled at Ken. He returned her gaze and saw true kindness in her eyes. *She knows*, Ken thought. *She sees that we're in the same boat as Priscilla, I can tell by the way she's looking at us.* Ken broke her stare and looked away.

A few minutes later everyone had their dessert. No closer to a decision, the discussion went round and round until

Gabriel's phone rang. He pulled it from his pocket and looked at the screen. "It's Justus," he announced to the group.

"Answer it, Dad," Maggie commanded.

Gabriel touched the telephone icon and said, "Hello."

"Put it on speaker," Shewan whispered.

"Okay, Hun. Let me move away from these dishes," Gabriel agreed as he made space to set the phone down.

"Justus, I'm sitting here with Shewan and Maggie. They want me to put it on speaker." Gabriel mentioned off handedly as he pressed the correct icon.

"May as well," the room heard Justus respond. "They're going to learn about it soon enough."

Frightened looks shot around the room.

"Looks like they're kicking Priscilla out of Mayapple in the morning." The sergeant announced. His voice sounded sad.

The room erupted with protest. Maggie put her finger to her lips to hush them.

"What? How can they? Why?" Gabriel asked.

"One of the administrators for the nursing home decided her diagnosis didn't match the amount she was costing them. They think she's faking. Either way, they say they can't do anything else for her." Justus sniffed hard, then blew his nose.

Shewan spoke then, "Sergeant, this is Shewan, Gabriel's wife. She doesn't have any clothes. She needs a coat and warm boots. Vinny told us they threw all her things away when the ambulance took her."

"Well, it's not a good situation even if she did have clothes. Or nice weather, for that matter. It's a darn shame. Anyway, thought you'd like to know. You have a good night. I need to call the others." Justus sniffed again.

"I can tell the others." Gabriel assured the sergeant. "And Justus, we're lucky you found her when you did, or she might have disappeared for good with this discharge."

Justus sighed heavily, "No saying she won't anyway."

129

Gabriel disconnected the call. The room went completely silent.

Bela clapped her hands, cutting the silence in half, "Leave this to the old lady in the room." She pushed her chair back and stood. "Grab your things, Hugo and Tomas. Thanks for the lovely meal, Hoover family. But we're going shopping. The ValueMart is open until eleven tonight. Make a list, Tomas. We need a coat, hats, boots, gloves, blankets."

The whole room jumped into action. "Wait," Maggie yelled, "We're coming with... Can we, Shewan? Can we, Dad?"

Gabriel smiled. "Looks like we're all going."

Ken chimed in, "Then let's go straight to that Mayapple place and see her. We can bring her the new warm clothes and tell her we support her decision no matter what she decides to do."

"Just leave the dishes," Vivian hollered over the chatter. "Edgar and I will get them when we get home."

CHAPTER 17

Breaking the News

Gabriel and the others called the sergeant from the café located in the entry way of the ValueMart. They'd finished their shopping and wanted to take the clothes and other necessities to Priscilla, so she'd have them before her discharge.

Gabriel searched his contacts for the sergeant's number, tapped his name, then pressed the speaker icon and put the phone in the center of the table where he and the others had gathered. The phone call went better than expected.

"Hello Gabriel," Justus answered.

"Hey there. I'm here with the whole posse. Well, except Vinny. He had a gig tonight. You got a minute to talk."

"Wow, the whole posse. That's great. Hey, gang!"

The men, women and kids all said hello.

"Justus," Gabriel took the conversation back, "We want to see Priscilla tonight. Before they put her out. We have some clothes and some other things she'll need."

"Well, I don't see what good that will do. She's basically unconscious with her eyes open."

Gabriel looked around the table at each of his companions, "Well, actually, no she's not."

Gabriel explained what Jillian experienced during her visit. He apologized for not telling Justus earlier. "We just felt the posse should meet and discuss how to proceed. We did that tonight and at Vinny's urging, we decided to trust you."

There was silence on the other end of the line.

"Justus, are you there?" Edgar asked.

"I'm here. That you, Edgar?"

"Yes." Edgar added, "We can trust you, can't we Justus?"

The sergeant let out an enormous sigh. "I should be used to her lying by now. I haven't seen her in such a long while, I guess I'm out of practice."

The posse protested all at once. No one could be understood.

The sergeant continued, "Don't get me wrong. I understand why she lied. If she told them she was fine, she'd be out in the cold in her fragile condition. I just wish she'd trusted me as much as she did a nine-year-old."

Ken commented, "You're going to be a much happier man and a far more effective police officer when you stop taking the actions of a desperate woman so personally. Maybe you need to spend a little less time judging and a little more time helping."

Beth hugged her dad's waist.

"Will you get us in to see her, Justus?" Shewan brought the discussion back to the task at hand. "It's important to us that we get these things to her."

Justus replied, his voice barely above a whisper, "Let me call Tinker Bell, the night nurse."

"Ginger?" Jillian asked. "Why do you call her Tinker Bell?"

"Long story," Justus replied. "I'm going to tell her the whole truth. She won't care because the discharge has already been signed. But it will motivate her to let you bring in the things Priscilla needs to survive."

The posse mumbled thanks to the sergeant. "I suggest you just send in the kids and only one adult, though. Ken, you go. She talked to you before this all went down, right."

Ken nodded, "Yeah, I met her at the park before she had the stroke."

"Good. I'll tell Tinker Bell you're coming with the posse to see Priscilla. Maybe she can move the princess to a common area. I know it's late but Ginger's a character. I think she'll be into this whole caper."

The group agreed and started saying their goodbyes.

"One last thing," the sergeant spoke over the others. "Ken, see if she'll agree to let me pick her up in the morning. It's a long shot. But tell her about the little lecture you gave me. Tell her I'm trying to understand. Maybe she'll trust you. Otherwise, can one of you pick her up and bring her to the park? I have a plan."

133

134

CHAPTER 18

Posse's Delivery Service

Five cars parked with their engines running in front of
Mayapple Nursing Care Facility and Rehabilitation
Center. Reflective emblems on the side of a two-tone vehicle
told the others that Justus Brown was among them. Shewan
looked over at Gabriel, "I feel bad for the sergeant. Seems he
can't get the old lady to believe in him."

Maggie piped up, "That seems to be the biggest lesson for
all of us. Trust. Why do you think it's so hard to believe in
others, Shewan? I'm not picking on you, Mom. But you said
you'd been giving it some thought."

Shewan looked into the back seat and smiled at her
daughter. "I have." She answered. "In my case I think when
you told me about Priscilla the Princess of the Park, I heard
a truth that scared me a little. So I'd rather believe it wasn't
true. Lonely little old ladies don't live in parks and pretend
that life is better than it is. Or they shouldn't have to, at least."

"When you put it that way, it is a pretty scary thought,"
Gabriel added. "But pretty much every level of suspicion is

caused by fear. I think it takes a lot of courage to trust."

"So that means when I didn't believe Maggie, it was because I didn't have the courage to face the truth she was telling me?" Shewan asked.

At first, no one responded. Then Maggie replied, "So maybe Priscilla doesn't have the courage to hear some truths from the sergeant?"

"Can't say as I blame her," Gabriel agreed. "Even without whatever their backstory is, he's the law and he could make her life difficult. I'm sure of it."

"Well," Maggie said as she popped open the car door, "I hope we were right to trust him. I'm going to get into the car with Jillian until it's time to go inside, okay?"

Her parents nodded yes.

Maggie jumped out of the vehicle and closed the door behind her.

"What do you suppose is so special about Ken?" Shewan asked her husband as she watched their daughter climb into the Hoover family vehicle.

"You mean because he understands Priscilla so much better than the rest of us do?" Gabriel asked.

"Yeah, I guess that's it. He and his kids. Why do you think they're so in tune with her fears? Not just her fears though, her needs too. It's like he's the Priscilla whisperer."

Gabriel smiled. "Priscilla whisperer," he repeated. He sighed and continued, "You don't want to know what I think."

Shewan grabbed his hand. "No, I do. I really do. I don't want to be clueless anymore. What is it?"

Gabriel's face flushed and he wrung his hands while he answered her, "Well, I think it's because they have the same big problem that Priscilla has. I don't think that nice hard-working man and those two lovable kids have a home."

Once inside the van, Edgar and Vivian explained to Maggie that Jillian wouldn't be going inside to see Priscilla with the rest of them. "Jillian got to see her once already. She's decided to wait out here with us. You go in with the twins, their dad, Tomas and his brother Hugo.

"Are you sure you don't want to come in, Jillian?" Maggie asked her friend.

Jillian took Maggie's hand and assured her, "It'll be crowded as it is. My chair takes up too much space. Besides, you all need a chance to see her like I did."

"Okay, I'll tell her you're out here, though. I'll tell her you said, 'Hello.' Vivian, can I go get in the car with Bela and the boys?"

"Makes sense to me, you'll be going inside with them, anyway," Vivian answered.

Maggie hugged her friend and hopped out of the car.

Maggie opened the door next to Tomas and asked him to shove over to the other side of the back seat. He did. Tomas, Hugo and Bela greeted Maggie.

"Hey, Tomas. Hey, Hugo. Good evening, Bela. Thank you for having the great idea to go shopping for Priscilla. Now

137

we're going to get to see her!"

Bela smiled. "I'm glad to help. Just you remember this. If I'm ever in the hospital don't you dare let them release me in just a hospital gown!"

The kids all spoke at once promising they would never let such an awful thing happen.

Bela spoke again, "You're making me realize something. You young people befriended this woman and because of you, she's not alone. She has you and all the people that love you. And from the looks of all these cars in the parking lot, that's quite a lot."

Tomas looked down, "Priscilla taught us to be open to new friends. When she disappeared, we learned to rely on our old friends. In this case, our parents and grandparents."

"That's a very wise observation, Tomas. Remember when you and Hugo were fighting a few months back. I told you that you needed to be good to each other because some families don't have anyone to rely on when times are tough?" Bela asked.

"I do." Hugo answered. "That's probably why Tomas told you the truth. I had him all worried cause I stopped eating."

The kids nodded.

"Life would be different for Priscilla right now if she had family she could trust. For now she just has us." Bela added.

"Trust takes courage. That's what my dad says," Maggie informed the others.

Bela nodded, "I think he's right. Priscilla just doesn't have the courage to trust her family, I guess."

Ken looked into the rearview mirror at the children he admired. "You two are amazing. Have I told you that before?"

Beth and Jeff nodded. "Yes, Dad. You always praise us."

"Well, you're praiseworthy. You've lived through a lot and you've still got the energy to worry about someone else."

"Don't get me wrong, Dad," Jeff remarked. "I'm pretty

tired. But the thought of seeing Priscilla again gave me a second wind."

"Yeah. We aren't doing anything for anyone but ourselves." Beth looked at her dad's reflection in the mirror. "We miss her."

"Well, shall we get this show on the road?" Ken asked. "Nobody can visit without us. I'm the only grownup going into the center. I think they're waiting for us to make the first move."

The kids unbuckled their seatbelts. "Just one thing, Dad." Jeff spoke barely above a whisper. "What if Priscilla is a little confused and accidentally says something about us looking for a home?"

"Well," Ken took in a big breath and let it back out again. "Which is more important. Getting in there to see Priscilla or staying in hiding to keep our secret safe?"

After a brief silence Beth popped open her car door and shouted to her father and brother, "Let's get going. We don't want to sit in this parking lot all night."

CHAPTER 19

Truth Time

Ken marched down the hall at the nursing care facility. The posse trailed behind him, one after another like the little ducks in Robert McClosky's book, *Make Way for Ducklings*. Just as he approached the nurses' station, he stopped and turned. None of the children expected his quick stop. From back to front, each child crashed into the one in front of them. Ken and the posse all dissolved into giggles.

From behind Ken a voice spoke, "Shhhhh. No laughing. This is a very serious place." Ken turned around and the children peered around from behind him to see who was talking. The giggles started again.

"What is that, Mr. Kritzell?" Maggie asked. "Is, is… is she a carrot?"

Ginger the night nurse stood facing Ken. "You must be Ken." Ginger pointed past him. "I see you brought a set of accordioned accomplices."

"And you're Ginger, I presume? I heard gingers were sometimes called carrot tops, but I must say you are the first genuine carrot top I've ever seen."

Maggie added, "She's a whole carrot, really."

Ginger stood in front of her late-night guests dressed head-to-toe in a carrot costume. She had orange leggings and wore an orange turtleneck. Her arms stuck out from a carrot-colored vest with big patchwork pockets on the front. She had an orange stocking cap over her head with a hole for her face to peek through. From the top of the cap stood two feet of reshaped coat hangers. She'd covered the wire with green yarn and used it to fasten paper leaves. Her nametag, which was pinned to the vest, read Nurse Carrot. Looking completely out of place, she'd hung a stethoscope around her neck.

The children kept right on giggling. Beth raised her hand.

"I'm a nurse not a school teacher, little girl. You don't have to raise your hand," Nurse Carrot told Beth.

"Oh, sorry." Beth laughed again. "You're the one Justus calls Tinker Bell. But you're not a fairy. You're a vegetable."

"Yeah, that's me," Ginger admitted. "I work with a lot of old lonely people and I discovered a long time ago – when

142

it's just me and them in the middle of the night – it's awfully nice to see them smile. So I play dress up." Ginger's eyes were bright and her voice gentle, "Trust me. When you see a five-and-a-half foot carrot coming for you, it's easy to forget whatever else might be bothering you."

Ginger looked at the group of kids from front of the line all the way to the back of the line. "You've come to bring things to Priscilla, have you?" Each child held up a ValueMart bag to show her that they did. "That makes me happy." Ginger poked her thumb at her carrot self, "You think I'm a kidder. Priscilla wins the prize for that. She's pretended she couldn't speak or understand for almost four months now. That's hard work. She's a clever little actress."

Hugo spoke out, "Hey lady, no offense but we're really kinda anxious to see her."

"I bet you are." Ginger walked over and took Hugo by the hand, "C'mon, big boy. I'll take you to see her."

Hugo felt strange walking down the hallway holding the hand of a stranger dressed like a carrot. He decided to tell Ginger how he felt, "You know, before I met Priscilla, I'd have pulled away from you and called you a freak or something. Priscilla taught me to have more confidence. You know, not to get embarrassed by silly things. It's made me a happier guy."

Ginger stopped and turned to Hugo. "That's the best gift anyone can give you. Confidence. I used to be afraid of what people thought of me, too."

"You? Seriously? You're making that up." Hugo stared in disbelief.

"Carrot's honor," Ginger replied and continued down the hall to Priscilla's room.

Ginger knocked gently on the closed door. From inside the children heard a familiar voice, "Come in."

Nurse Carrot pushed the door open and the children rushed inside the room. Ken went last. Before he walked in, he stopped and asked Ginger, "You coming too?"

Ginger replied, "Nah, you don't need a nurse. Or a carrot. I'll be back in 20 minutes to throw you all out of the place. Enjoy your visit."

Ken smiled at his new friend and walked inside. At the far end of the room sat Priscilla. She had a blanket across her lap. One by one the children bent over and hugged her. Tears rolled down every cheek. After the posse finished greeting their princess, the children sat on the floor around her chair.

Priscilla looked up at Ken who stood silently inside the doorway. Priscilla held out her hand and Ken walked over, knelt on one knee and kissed her knuckles. The children squealed with joy. "Oh, I wish Jillian was here to see that!" Maggie exclaimed.

"Where is Jillian?" Priscilla asked. Maggie explained that she stayed out so the others could get a chance to have their first visit with her.

The children took turns telling Priscilla how happy it made them to see her again. No one asked her why she didn't tell them where she was. No one scolded her for protecting her privacy. They just gave voice to how much they loved and missed her.

This is why I love these children so much. They love me unconditionally. But I really owe them more than this. Priscilla thought.

"I want to thank you lords and ladies for searching for me. I'm sorry that I worried you so much. I had a stroke, they say. Then I woke up here. It was too cold to go back outside." Priscilla tried to explain.

Hugo cleared his throat.

"Yes, Protector of the Realm." Priscilla nodded at the big boy.

"None of that matters, Your Highness." Hugo grinned. The younger children chuckled. "We learned so much when we had you to ourselves in the park. We learned even more when we lost you, Princess…" Hugo paused for a moment to think. "Hey, we don't even know your last name."

Priscilla looked down at her hands. After a few minutes of silence, she spoke, "I want you all to tell me what it's been like for you the past few months. I want to hear about your feelings. After, I'd be mighty grateful if you'd forgive me. But we'll have to do all that another time. And, I promise, I will tell you more about me, as well. Good friends deserve a certain amount of security in their friendship. I realize now, looking at you all sitting here, that I've had you to lean on all along. However, I didn't give you what you needed from me. I will meet you all in the park on Tuesday for our tea party and we can share information then. Okay?"

Tomas spoke up, "But it's so cold in the park, Your Highness. You can't really mean to go back there."

"I do. Now off you go." Priscilla stood and said, "Goodbye, git."

"Not so fast, Princess." Ken motioned for her to sit back in her chair. "We suspected you might insist on going home to the park. We brought things to make that stay a little more comfortable."

Maggie shouted with excitement, "Look, Your Highness, we brought you a subzero sleeping bag."

Hugo added, "And this tent sets itself up in fifteen seconds. You can put it up at night and close it to tuck under your throne in the morning."

One at a time, the children gave her their bags. They brought warm clothes. Long underwear. Mittens. A hat. A scarf. Several pairs of warm socks. Some warmers to put inside her gloves and shoes. She opened all the packages. She thanked the children over and over again.

Maggie handed over the last bag. Inside was a crystal tiara. Priscilla hugged Maggie close so Maggie could place the crown on Priscilla's head. "Princess, this crown is from my mom. For a long time, she didn't quite believe there was a princess of the park. She wanted you to have this, so you'd know she believes in you now."

"I'm honored," Priscilla looked regal indeed.

Ken walked up and handed Priscilla an envelope. The princess pushed it back to him and said, "You're the last person who should be giving things away."

"It's not from me," Ken insisted. "There's some folding money in there from these kids' parents. And some gift cards for the coffee shop on the square. They're from Pastor Matthew, the parking lot minister. I told him about you a long time ago. He gave them to me to give to you, back then. I've just been holding them, waiting until I could do so."

Just then the shadow of a large carrot overtook the doorway.

"That Ginger!" Priscilla put her hands beside her cheeks and whispered to the children, "She's such a marvelous character, am I right?"

Everyone agreed.

Ginger waved the children out of Priscilla's room. "Time to go."

Ken lingered, "One last thing, M'lady."

Priscilla looked up at Ken from under her eyebrows.

"Yes?" She inquired.

"Justus." Ken watched for a reaction when he mentioned the sergeant's name. Priscilla obliged. She sighed heavily, squinted her eyes and whispered, "What about him?"

"He wants to pick you up tomorrow when they discharge you."

"No."

"That's it? No? He's outside right now. He stayed away because I told him he didn't understand what you're going through." Ken protested.

"That's an understatement." Priscilla acknowledged.

"I don't know what your special relationship is with that particular policeman. None of my business anyway." Priscilla nodded. Ken continued, "At any rate, he promised he would stop judging you. I don't know how easy that will be for him. But he promised to try."

Priscilla relaxed her face a little. She exhaled. "You're some kind of boyscout or something, aren't you, Ken?"

Ken laughed, "No. Not exactly. But as you pointed out before – you and I share the same truth. That's got to count for something."

"I imagine all the parents are outside, aren't they?" Priscilla asked.

Ken nodded.

"Which one of them should come get me tomorrow? Which one will ask the fewest questions? You can't do it. From what I can see, you still haven't saved up enough for a place so you need to work." The princess straightened the tiara on her head. "Which one will take me to the park and leave me there?"

"Edgar." He answered.

"Jillian's dad?" she asked. "Perfect. Please tell him they are discharging me at 10 a.m."

"He'll be here." Ken assured her. "And Justus? If he can't pick you up, he wants to meet you at the park."

Priscilla waved Ken away. "You better get going. The kids are waiting down the hall with a human vegetable. As for Justus, it's a free world. I don't control who goes to the park."

CHAPTER 20

The Snow Fort

Edgar drove Priscilla to the edge of the park. He walked around the passenger side of the car to open her door. Edgar had planned to carry her new sleeping bag and other items to her park bench. There was no need. Vinny stood on the sidewalk waiting and ready to help. Gabriel called the musician early in the morning and told him when the princess would return. Priscilla climbed out of the car and into a warm hug from her favorite minstrel.

"Let me get that for you, Princess." Vinny took the bags and added, "Thank you, Edgar. I've got her from here."

The Princess of the Park walked slowly back to her old home on the bench. She and Vinny spoke for a while. Before he left, the minstrel wrapped her in the foil blanket Tomas had picked out for her. Tomas said that it would keep her warm even if the temperatures dropped far below freezing.

Priscilla's heart filled with joy. She loved her old surroundings. Even under a foot of snow the park was beautiful. She felt safe in the park. Her friends knew they could find her there, again. *Besides*, Priscilla thought to herself, *in a few weeks, it'll start getting warmer*.

Out of the corner of her eye, the princess saw a man in a dark blue police uniform walking up to her. She straightened the tiara on her head and prepared to play twenty questions.

"Hello, Princess," the officer said.

"Hello, Sergeant."

"You sure had some of us pretty worried. I'm glad you're safe and sound. Do you feel okay?" Justus asked.

Here we go. Already with the questions. Priscilla thought. Instead she said, "Now you see for yourself that I'm fine. Don't you have more important things to do?"

"I guess," the policeman kicked at the snow with his boot. He shifted his gaze and looked into her eyes, "I just want to help, you know."

"I know," Priscilla responded with a voice just above a whisper. Then louder she said, "But you can't help. I'm not going wherever it is you want to take me. You're wasting your time. I'm sure there are others who need you more than I do."

"You mean like Ken and the twins?"

Justus shocked Priscilla with his response. It had been a long time since anyone said anything that surprised her.

"What do you know about them?" Priscilla scowled. "Don't you dare give them a hard time."

"Calm down. I like Ken. He's got a lot on his hands raising two kids the way he is." Justus kept kicking at the snow.

"I swear, Justus L. Brown, if you make trouble for that little family. You'll be sorry. I promise you."

Justus continued, "I first noticed them last summer. Sleeping in their car. Going to the parking lot ministry for shower tokens to use at the truck stop. He's a good dad. Still

153

awful tough on those kids, though."

"It ain't a crime to raise kids while homeless," Priscilla snarled and bared her teeth.

"Calm down. I know that. I was just asking if you thought they needed help more than you do." Justus continued. "Actually, Ken's told me to back off on judging you. It's comforting, I guess, to see you're both protecting each other."

"Well, why don't you do what he told you to do and get lost?" The princess looked old and tired, but her cheeks flushed with anger.

"I have a present for you. If you hear me out, you'll see that I've changed." The sergeant extended his hand to take Priscilla's so he could help her to her feet.

"If I come with you this one time, will you promise to leave me, Ken and the kids alone for good?" Priscilla asked. She didn't have the patience for the sergeant's games. She needed a place to lie down but it wouldn't be dark for at least five hours. So she may as well go along with his scheme.

Priscilla took the sergeant's hand and stood on her wobbly feet. She turned to pick up her belongings and saw that Vinny had returned. "It's okay, Princess. I'll stay with your things," he said.

Slowly Priscilla and Justus walked to the far edge of the park. At the corner stood the old courthouse. Hundreds of years before it had been part of a wilderness fort. Priscilla knew the sergeant couldn't arrest her at that courthouse. It had long before been converted to a museum.

"We're almost there," Justus offered. "We just need to walk around to the alley on the side of the building. Have you ever been back here, Princess?"

Priscilla's curiosity had replaced her resentment. "No, Justus." She answered. "Well, maybe. But not for a long time."

They got to the other side and saw a newly built stone wall wrapped around an old staircase that once led to the underground entrance for the fort. When the county decommissioned the courthouse, the commissioners had a public restroom installed where the access to the fort had been. Years went by and the community stopped providing public accommodations, so they built the wall around the stairs, added a gate and locked it.

"I got here early this morning and piled all that snow against the old restroom wall. I figure, as long as it's cold and snowy, no one will even take a second look at this little snow fort of mine." Justus explained.

Confused, Priscilla looked up at the sergeant.

"Here's the key, Princess. It's just a bathroom. It's nothing special. But it's warm. You can let yourself in at night, or whenever you want to warm up. Make sure you keep the door locked. I'd tell you not to bring other people down in there with you, because they might talk and get us both in trouble. But I know you're too smart to do something that reckless." Justus reached his hand out and rested it on Priscilla's shoulder.

"Ken told me to help you, if I could do it without judging you. Truth is, I'd rather just take you to my house."

Priscilla rocked her head back and forth. Going to the sergeant's house was not an option.

"Yeah, I knew you wouldn't want that. But I can't leave you out in the cold. I realize that you think freezing to death on your terms is better than being warm on mine. So I came up with this idea."

The princess cleared her throat. She put her arm high up in the air and then brought it down in a sweeping motion all the way to the ground. She stood back up from her deep bow and said, "Thank you so much, Sir Justus, Knight of the Park. Your chivalry is appreciated. To repay you for your gallant generosity, I, Priscilla the Princess of the Park, promise not to freeze to death this winter."

The sergeant smiled. "Sir Justus. I like that, I guess. Let me go get your things and we can put them down in the restroom." They started walking toward the bench. Sir Justus smiled and added, "Vinny's the only other person who knows. We trust each other. I sense you trust him too."

"I do." Priscilla responded. Then she stopped walking. She called to the sergeant, "Sir Justus, thank you. You're probably putting your job on the line. I appreciate this more than I can say."

A twig snapped and snow fell out of the tree above them. "That might be the sound of my heart breaking," Justus answered. The sergeant looked at the old woman he loved dearly and added, "I am brokenhearted, you know. But I'll survive. It took me ten years to find you, Mom. I'm not going to let you freeze."

THE
Charles Bruce
F O U N D A T I O N
HELPING WRITERS ARTISTS AND MUSICIANS

The Charles Bruce Foundation works to provide creative outlets for Writers, Artists and Musicians (WAM!). Publishing the *Priscilla* series of books as a collaborative effort between Pat LaMarche and Bonnie Tweedy Shaw allowed the Charles Bruce Foundation to raise matching funds to support Bonnie's burgeoning career as an illustrator. Funds raised through private donation were augmented by the Pennsylvania Council on the Arts.

Consequently, Bonnie Tweedy Shaw received state arts funding support through a grant from the Pennsylvania Council on the Arts, a state agency funded by the Commonwealth of Pennsylvania and the National Endowment for the Arts, a federal agency.

All proceeds from sales of the *Priscilla* series benefit the needs of others. Bulk orders are available by contacting admin@charlesbrucefoundation.org.

pennsylvania
COUNCIL ON THE ARTS

Bonnie Tweedy Shaw's dad was a minister, so she moved around quite a bit. Born in Ohio, she spent her early years there, then moved to Florida before her family settled in Pennsylvania. Bonnie had seven brothers and sisters. Her big family loved camping. They'd camp for a entire month every year. They had a boys' tent, a girls' tent and their parents slept in a pop-up camper. Bonnie's oldest brother got a tiny tent all by himself! Growing up this way made Bonnie certain of one thing – life would've been very difficult if her family had lost their home and camping was their way of life.

Bonnie's love affair with art began as soon as her hand could hold a crayon. She went to Shippensburg University and received her Bachelor's Degree in art. She shifted focus for grad school, studying GeoEnvironmental Studies. In her spare time she taught undergraduates as a grad assistant to the Art Department. Today, Bonnie's still teaching. Her art classes are popular throughout central Pennsylvania. Bonnie also sculpts and paints magnificently.

When Bonnie's not creating art, home with her husband, Peter, playing with Chumley their cat or Dewey their dog, she can be found at the library. She adores working in the Youth Services department, where she talks to young patrons about their favorite books. Bonnie's first published work, *If You Should Meet an Elephant*, is available through the Charles Bruce Foundation and wherever fine books are sold.

Pat LaMarche, born in Providence, Rhode Island, graduated Boston College and went to grad school at the University of Amsterdam. Pat has two kids and a step kid – Rebecca, John and Eden. She adores them (and their partners – Tim and Kaede). Pat's also got a couple of spectacular grandchildren, Ronan and Maggie. Though Pat lived most of her adult life in Maine, she now resides with her husband, Chad, in Carlisle, Pennsylvania. For more than a decade, Pat has worked sheltering and advocating for people experiencing homelessness.

Pat crisscrossed the United States nearly a dozen times, interviewing the nation's most economically challenged families and individuals. She's witnessed hundreds of different programs to mitigate their suffering. Too many of those attempts never addressed the fundamental cause of homelessness, resulting in failure. Pat's documented their stories in countless news articles and commentary.

Having written about homelessness, poverty and health care since the last century, her other titles include, *Left Out In America: the State of Homelessness in the United States*, *Daddy, What's the Middle Class?*, *Magic Diary*, and *The Special Present*. *Left Out in America – Again*, a fifteen year anniversary edition of her original book on homelessness is due out in the fall of 2020.

Other Charles Bruce Foundation publications

Priscilla the Princess of the Park
Pat LaMarche
Bonnie Tweedy Shaw

Daddy, What's the Middle Class?
Pat LaMarche

Dismazed and Driven
Diane Nilan

My Cat is a Hat
Phyllis J. Orenyo
Chad Bruce

The Train Whistle and the Lily Pond
Arlyn Pettingell

The Secret Ingredient
Marianne Romagnoli
Nancy Stamm

Practically Perfect Pepperoni Pizza
Marianne Romagnoli
Chad Bruce

The Boy with the Patch
Matthew C. Donnell
Fran Piper

If You Should Meet an Elephant
Ashley E. Kauffman
Bonnie Tweedy Shaw